# FREDERICKSBURG AND CHANCELLORSVILLE

GREAT CAMPAIGNS OF THE CIVIL WAR

SERIES EDITORS

Anne J. Bailey
*Georgia College &*
*State University*

Brooks D. Simpson
*Arizona State University*

DANIEL E. SUTHERLAND

---

# Fredericksburg and Chancellorsville

*The Dare Mark Campaign*

---

University of Nebraska Press
Lincoln and London

© 1998 by
the University of
Nebraska Press
All rights reserved
Manufactured in the
United States of America
⊗ The paper in this book
meets the minimum requirements
of American National Standard
for Information Sciences—
Permanence of Paper for
Printed Library Materials,
ANSI Z39.48-1984.
Library of Congress
Cataloging-in-Publication Data
Sutherland, Daniel E.
Fredericksburg and Chancellorsville :
the Dare Mark campaign / Daniel E. Sutherland.
p.    cm.—(Great campaigns of the Civil War)
Includes bibliographical references
(p.    ) and index.
ISBN 0-8032-4253-0 (alk. paper)
1. Fredericksburg (Va.), Battle of, 1862.
2. Chancellorsville (Va.), Battle of, 1863.
I. Title.   II. Series.
E474.85.S88   1999
973.7′33—dc21
98-5506
CIP

For Grady McWhiney, again

# Contents

# Illustrations

# Maps

# Series Editors' Introduction

Americans remain fascinated by the Civil War. Movies, television, and video—even computer software—have augmented the ever-expanding list of books on the war. Although it stands to reason that a large portion of recent work concentrates on military aspects of the conflict, historians have expanded our scope of inquiry to include civilians, especially women; the destruction of slavery and the evolving understanding of what freedom meant to millions of former slaves; and an even greater emphasis on the experiences of the common soldier on both sides. Other studies have demonstrated the interrelationships of war, politics, and policy and how civilians' concerns back home influenced both soldiers and politicians. Although one cannot fully comprehend this central event in American history without understanding that military operations were fundamental in determining the course and outcome of the war, it is time for students of battles and campaigns to incorporate nonmilitary themes in their accounts. The most pressing challenge facing Civil War scholarship today is the integration of various perspectives and emphases into a new narrative that explains not only what happened, why, and how, but also why it mattered.

The series Great Campaigns of the Civil War offers readers concise syntheses of the major campaigns of the war, reflecting the findings of recent scholarship. The series points to new ways of viewing military campaigns by looking beyond the battlefield and the headquarters tent to the wider political and social context within which these campaigns unfolded; it also shows how campaigns and battles left their imprint on many Americans, from presidents and generals down to privates and civilians. The ends and means of waging war reflect larger political objectives and priorities as well as social values. Historians may continue to debate among themselves as to which of these campaigns constituted true turning points, but each of the campaigns treated in this series contributed to shaping the course of the conflict, opening opportunities, and eliminating alternatives.

In the aftermath of the Antietam campaign, Robert E. Lee and the Army of Northern Virginia returned to the Old Dominion, determined to thwart any new Yankee offensives toward Richmond. The river network formed by the Rapidan and Rappahannock Rivers and the rugged, wooded terrain south of those rivers proved ideal terrain for the task of checking the invader. In December 1862 the Confederates bloodied the Army of the Potomac when it attempted to smash through at Fredericksburg; less than five months later they triumphed again at Chancellorsville in what many historians consider Lee's battlefield masterpiece. Yet both victories proved costly. Unsatisfied by his failure to deal Ambrose Burnside a more telling blow at Fredericksburg, Lee lost much when he drove Joseph Hooker back across the rivers the following May, including the services of corps commander Thomas J. Jackson, who was mortally wounded by his own men; the Virginian's thoughts turned again to an invasion northward across the Potomac in his quest to achieve decision on the battlefield. Daniel Sutherland's account of these campaigns gives due attention to the generals, but what distinguishes his examination of these operations is his willingness to give the civilians who called this region home and the soldiers who fought and died to control it their due. In so doing, he reminds us that for all the glory won in those battles, there was a price to pay in human life and suffering; many of those who survived these struggles would be present the next time a Yankee hero crossed the rivers to tangle with Marse Robert.

# Acknowledgments

The most satisfying part of completing a manuscript is to recognize all the people who contributed to its making. On the research trail, I was aided immeasurably by the staffs of the Center for American History, Austin, Texas; Fredericksburg and Spotsylvania National Military Park (FSNMP), Fredericksburg; Georgia Department of History and Archives, Atlanta; Manuscript Division of the Library of Congress; Troup County Archives, LaGrange, Georgia; U.S. Army Military History Institute (USAMHI), Carlisle , Pennsylvania; and the Virginia Historical Society, Richmond. I am particularly grateful to Richard J. Sommers at the USAMHI for sharing with me both his encyclopedic knowledge of the war and his manuscript collections; John J. Hennessy and Noel G. Harrison at FSNMP for providing insights into the campaign and tips on the most fruitful research paths to explore; and Robert E. Krick, superintendent of FSNMP, for allowing me to invade his sanctuary.

The Virginia Historical Society deserves thanks on two additional scores. First, I very much appreciate the Society's financial support in the form of a Mellon Foundation research grant. Second, and equally important, I benefited immensely on my trips to Richmond from discussions with the Society's staff, especially E. Lee Shepard, Frances S. Pollard, and Nelson D. Lankford.

Critical readings of a very unfinished draft of the manuscript vastly improved it. For this I give thanks to George C. Rable, who read the chapters on Fredericksburg, and Donald Pfanz, Brooks D. Simpson, and Gary W. Gallagher, who read the entire manuscript. Their probing questions helped me to clarify my ideas, focus my conclusions, and avoid innumerable errors. Don Pfanz was also a most gracious host at FSNMP. Whatever mistakes these gentlemen missed were quickly spotted by my copyeditor for the University of Nebraska Press, Trudie Calvert. I appreciate her diligence and sharp eye.

I also want to acknowledge the generosity of Thomas H. Flinn of Austin, Texas, who provided me with copies of family correspondence, and the financial support given my research by Fulbright College, the University of Arkansas.

Finally, I wish to thank two people who transcend all categories of support and all bounds of generosity: Grady McWhiney and Anne J. Bailey. Grady has been an ever-present influence as teacher and friend for nearly thirty years. This is the second book that I have dedicated to him, but it would require several more to do him justice. Anne has worn two hats on this project. As wife and friend, she has given me her usual encouragement and advice; as series editor, she has reminded me to an uncommon degree about deadlines and manuscript length. She performed both roles flawlessly.

# FREDERICKSBURG AND CHANCELLORSVILLE

# Introduction

A Confederate soldier called the Rappahannock River the "Dare Mark," and it is an apt description. By the summer of 1862, the Rappahannock seemed to be the major natural obstacle between the Union army and victory in the eastern theater of the Civil War. If the United States was to win the conflict, decided the Union high command, a Federal army had to penetrate and establish itself south of that major waterway. The Confederate capital of Richmond, a principal target of the army for much of the war, lay south of the river. Many of the food resources and railroads of northern Virginia, all vital to Rebel success, also rested securely behind that barrier. Most important, the Army of Northern Virginia, when not threatening the peace above the Potomac, resided below the Rappahannock. This army— Gen. Robert E. Lee's army—dared the Yankees to cross its river.

The task did not look difficult at first. Union cavalry patrols could ford the Rappahannock and conduct reconnaissance with some ease above Fredericksburg, and Federal gunboats plied the lower, more navigable reaches of the river. Union commanders believed there must be a vulnerable spot, an open road to central Virginia, somewhere between those two points and along forty miles of twisting, winding river. Gen. John Pope used the upper fords and the Orange and Alexandria Railroad to plant his Army of Virginia south of the river in July 1862. He remained less than two months before Lee dislodged him and then routed his army at Second Manassas. Gen. George B. McClellan seemed prepared to try his hand in November 1862, but President Abraham Lincoln removed him from command before he could launch his campaign. The Union army would not succeed in its quest until a year later, in November 1863, when, almost by default, and as a consequence of an unexpected engagement at Rappahannock Station, Gen. George G. Meade staked his claim below the Rappahannock.

But the most concerted and grandest Federal challenge to the river came between December 1862 and May 1863. In traditional terms, those five months encompass two separate campaigns: Fredericksburg and Chancellorsville. They were waged in different seasons and, on the Union side, by two different commanders. Yet the two operations were conducted in the same location, and important parts of both battles were fought on identical ground. The second battle raged even as the North debated why the first had been lost, and when the second battle was also lost, there followed the inevitable comparisons to the first. Most telling, the two operations had but a single object, and so, viewed against the backdrop of larger Federal and Confederate strategic goals, they may be seen as a single, extended campaign: the Dare Mark campaign.

The Confederates, led by Lee, won the campaign and maintained the integrity of the Rappahannock line. It was the most stunning Confederate military achievement in the eastern theater, perhaps in the entire war. The campaign showed Lee at his most versatile and audacious. He made a strong defensive stand at Fredericksburg and a defiantly aggressive series of offensive movements at Chancellorsville. Fredericksburg was the only battle in which Lee inflicted higher casualties, both absolute and proportional, than he received. Chancellorsville is widely regarded as the Virginian's tactical masterpiece. Even so, Lee's triumph, his last significant one, was bittersweet. Not only did he lose his right arm with the death of Gen. Thomas J. Jackson, but he and his army grew overconfident. The Army of Northern Virginia became convinced of its own invincibility, and in that spirit, and partly for that reason, the Rebels marched north to Pennsylvania in June 1863.

The campaign marked a new departure for Union strategy in the East. By December 1862, Abraham Lincoln and Gen. Henry W. Halleck had abandoned the idea of winning the war by capturing Richmond. Instead, they sought first to defeat Lee's army. Both Gen. Ambrose E. Burnside and Gen. Joseph Hooker had a difficult time grasping this new strategic goal, and each man devised a different plan to achieve it. When Burnside reluctantly succeeded the popular McClellan as commander of the army, he proceeded to fight a winter campaign, again reluctantly. He hoped originally to slip across the Rappahannock unchallenged and establish himself between Lee and Richmond. He would thus gain the tactical option of either turning on Lee or forcing the Rebels to attack him. Hooker, in contrast, was eager to fight

Lee in the spring of 1863. He devised a complex and brilliantly conceived turning movement that would allow him to crush the Army of Northern Virginia between two forces. Neither Burnside nor Hooker realized his strategic vision. The Federals lost both battles, and with them the campaign. Yet the Army of the Potomac gained strength, experience, and confidence in the campaign. A new leader, Meade, emerged from defeat to claim victory in Pennsylvania and, eventually, on the Dare Mark.

Wars, campaigns, and battles never end. They are refought time and again, first by their participants and later by historians, in countless arguments about why one side triumphed and the other lost, sometimes even over who won. We know who won on the Rappahannock in 1862–63, but it remains to explain the political and military decisions, North and South, that determined why and how those battles were waged. It remains also to explain how those decisions affected the soldiers and civilians who endured the battles and how those soldiers and civilians, in turn, responded to the rigors and trials of war. Parts of the story have been told many times, but always separately. This, then, is an old story told anew.

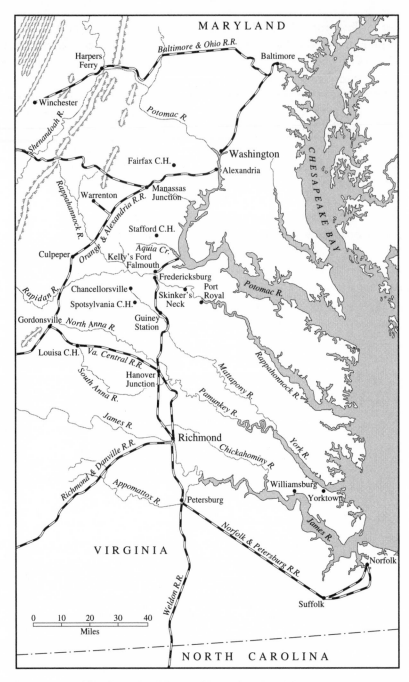

The Campaign Theater, November 1862–May 1863

# CHAPTER ONE

# Of Generals and Politicians

It began in November, and it began in confusion. The skies over northern Virginia cascaded snow all day on Friday, November 7, 1862. As he sat at his headquarters in Culpeper, Gen. Robert E. Lee was well satisfied with the performance of his soldiers at Antietam two months earlier. The Army of Northern Virginia had returned home as a result of that Maryland battle, but Lee and his men considered their departure a withdrawal, not a retreat. The men, he said, had needed a period of "repose" after several months of arduous campaigning. Yet, despite his army's undeniable successes since June—the Seven Days, Cedar Mountain, Second Manassas, if not Antietam—Lee sensed they must soon prove their mettle again. Gen. George B. McClellan's Army of the Potomac had finally roused itself and, with blue-clad cavalry already prowling below the Rappahannock River, had pressed as far as Warrenton and Waterloo. Lee had hoped to spend a peaceful winter in Culpeper. He hated the thought of campaigning in such weather with "insufficient clothing, blankets and shoes" for his men. Yet McClellan, quite contrary to his nature, suddenly seemed determined to wage war.[1]

This need for a winter campaign was all the fault of President Abraham Lincoln. And what Lee did not know on November 7—and would not know for another three days—was that Lincoln had already ordered Gen. Ambrose E. Burnside to replace McClellan as commander of the Union army. The president could suffer McClellan no longer. There was too much at stake, and McClellan had disappointed Lincoln once too often, both as commanding general of the Union armies and as leader of the Army of the Potomac.

In hindsight, McClellan's ouster had been in the cards since his failure on the Peninsula the previous summer. First stymied in his drive on Richmond by Gen. Joseph E. Johnston in late May and early June, McClellan had done little since then to earn his sobriquet as the "Young Napoleon." Lincoln wanted to replace McClellan that summer, but he had no one better. Gen. John Pope, whom McClellan detested, might have been a candidate, but when Gen. Thomas J. "Stonewall" Jackson beat him at Cedar Mountain on August 9 and Lee bloodied him at Second Manassas a fortnight later, the president shipped Pope off to fight Indians in Minnesota. McClellan remained because he had an undisputed knack for training an army and building its confidence, and he enjoyed enormous popularity among his men.

McClellan had an opportunity to regain Lincoln's favor at Antietam, but he bungled it. A day of intense fighting and the sacrifice of twelve thousand Federal soldiers on September 17, 1862, could have produced the climactic battle of annihilation for which all little Napoleons yearned. Instead, Lee slipped away, bloodied, with thirteen thousand losses of his own, but as lethal as ever. Lincoln and Gen. Henry W. Halleck, general in chief of the Union armies since July 11, prodded, cajoled, and very nearly ordered McClellan to pursue Lee, but McClellan claimed to have insufficient men, insufficient horses, insufficient shoes, blankets, overcoats, insufficient everything. Not until October 26 did his army, which had grown to over one hundred thousand men, begin to lumber across the Potomac River from its Maryland camps.

For a tantalizing moment, it looked as though a genuine southward thrust was in the offing. Lincoln expressed his excitement on October 27. "I am much pleased with the movement of the army," he informed his commander. "What do you know of the enemy?" By November 7, McClellan knew much, for his army covered a front that stretched from the Orange and Alexandria Railroad on its left flank to the Shenandoah Valley on the right, a distance of some forty miles. It seemed a sound position. He had placed himself between the halves of Lee's divided army, with Gen. James Longstreet in Culpeper and Stonewall Jackson in the Valley. McClellan's cavalry, commanded by Gen. Alfred Pleasonton, had already engaged the Rebels in more than a dozen skirmishes at Snicker's Gap, Upperville, Ashby's Gap, Warrenton, and elsewhere.[2]

But the old McClellan—indecisive, dawdling—lurked just beneath the surface. If he had a plan of action beyond crossing the Rappahannock, he never conveyed it fully to Lincoln or Halleck. He continued to excuse, justify, and complain. When Gen. James E. B. Stuart led an October raid through Maryland and Pennsylvania that netted some twelve hundred cavalry mounts, McClellan blamed his own lack of horses for his inability to halt such forays. He did not believe Lee would seriously contest a crossing, and he fully expected that the Rebel commander would risk a fight no "nearer than Richmond." He ignored Lincoln's pointed suggestion that a swift advance would place him between Lee and Richmond. "All goes well," he assured his wife, Ellen, on November 4, "except secesh who are traveling too fast to meet my views."[3]

This old, overly cautious McClellan would not do, for both the military and political dimensions of the war had changed since July. Enormous political pressure grew against Lincoln after the failed Peninsula campaign as Democrats and Republicans alike demanded a more forceful prosecution of the war. They wanted no more campaigns of feint and maneuver. It was time to end the "kid-glove warfare," time to take the war to the enemy. Lincoln had momentarily silenced his critics by appointing Halleck general in chief and allowing John Pope, commander of the newly created Army of Virginia, to initiate a more aggressive military policy against the people of north-central Virginia. Pope had failed, and Lincoln dared not allow McClellan, who had been extremely critical of the Lincoln-Pope strategy in any case, to resume his cautious ways. The president needed generals eager to advance and punish the Rebels.[4]

Lincoln had also become more comfortable directing military affairs by this time. While allowing soldiers like Halleck to formulate strategy, the president, who had been reading tactical manuals for several months past, felt free to give advice. In October, he went so far as to lecture McClellan on "the standard maxims of war," to formulate a detailed plan for the invasion of Virginia, and to tell the general what *he* would do if he commanded the army. Lincoln had his own ideas about how the war should be fought, and if McClellan or anyone else failed to share that vision or faltered in its execution, he would not retain command for long.[5]

Complicating political matters, the Radical wing of Lincoln's own party saw in his call for more forceful military action an opportunity to press its demands for black emancipation and the recruitment of black troops. Lincoln had consistently rejected these extreme measures. He had vetoed more than one military commander's efforts to place freedmen in blue uniforms, and he had undermined all congressional initiatives to broach the subject of uncompensated emancipation. Yet the new tide seemed likely to sweep over the president as Congress debated legislation that would allow freedmen to join the army and permit legal confiscation of Rebel property. On July 17, Congress passed the Confiscation Act to appropriate the property of "traitors." The law defined slaves as part of that property, or "contraband," eligible for confiscation. On the same day, Congress passed the Militia Act, which allowed "persons of African descent" to serve in the United States military. The legislature suddenly threatened to take control of the emancipation issue if the president failed to take swift, convincing action.[6]

Lincoln, seeking some way to retain public confidence and political support, understood that he could use confiscation and emancipation to fashion a tougher military policy. In September 1861, he had reprimanded Gen. John C. Frémont for attempting a policy of emancipation in Missouri. As late as May 1862, he had reproved Gen. David Hunter for following a similar course in Florida, Georgia, and South Carolina. But circumstances had changed by summer. The president now considered emancipation a legitimate tool to "subdue the enemy." Secretary of the Navy Gideon Welles reasoned correctly that "the reverses before Richmond and the formidable power and dimensions of the insurrection" had altered Lincoln's thinking. The president had even drifted closer toward accepting the most extreme of all military measures: the use of black soldiers. While still unwilling to advocate or take definite steps along such a course, Lincoln did seem "not unwilling that Commanders should, at their discretion, arm, for purely defensive purposes, slaves coming within their lines."[7]

At the same time, Lincoln told his cabinet that he would issue a proclamation of limited emancipation at an appropriate time, namely, after a Union victory. He waited nearly two months, until September 22, and McClellan's "victory" at Antietam. When, two days later, he also suspended the right of habeas corpus nationwide (extending a more limited decree of April 1861) and announced that civilians accused of "disloyal" acts would henceforth be tried in military courts, the president had taken firm control of both the military and political situations. The legislation, he knew, proclaimed a revolution in the nation's social consciousness, and the war, now to be fought in the shadow of that revolution, would be "a sterner war."[8]

Unhappily for Lincoln, the Democrats turned his revolution against him in the fall elections. As citizens from Massachusetts to Illinois selected their governors, congressmen, and state legislators, they passed judgment indirectly on the Lincoln administration's handling of the war, civil liberties, and emancipation. The voters disapproved. Democrats won the governorships of New York and New Jersey, gained thirty-five congressional seats, and piled up huge majorities in Lincoln's home state of Illinois. The results startled no one; all understood what had happened and why. Military defeats had spawned political ones. "The people," reported an Ohio newspaper, "are depressed by the interminable nature of this war, as so far conducted, and by the rapid exhaustion of the national resources without progress." Even Lincoln admitted that the "ill-success of the war had much to do" with the outcome, and he would have agreed with the judgment of New York lawyer George T. Strong: "It looks like a great, sweeping revolution of public sentiment. . . . We the people are impatient, dissatisfied, disgusted, disappointed. . . , suffering from the necessary evils of war and from irritation at our slow progress."[9]

McClellan either ignored or defied the shifting military and political rules of war. He had opposed either publicly or privately nearly every military and political initiative taken by Lincoln since July. He was horrified by the thought of waging war against civilians and told Lincoln as much. He privately criticized the Emancipation Proclamation and issued a general order to the army that, while reminding his troops of the necessity of military subordination to civilian authority, barely concealed his contempt for the president. "The remedy for political errors," he told them, "is to be found only in the action of the people at the polls." Whether Lincoln interpreted this statement as a direct challenge is unknown. We do know that the day after the polls closed, Lincoln directed Secretary of War Edwin M. Stanton to relieve McClellan of his command.[10]

McClellan's supporters did not miss the timing, and they raised a howl when the ax fell. "How can we succeed when mere trickster politicians control the movements of our generals and dictate when and how they must move?" asked a Michigan infantry lieutenant. McClellan had run afoul of Halleck, clear and simple, and his "offence was of a much older date than his removal," reasoned the Wolverine. "It is known that his removal was planned & to be carried into effect the moment the Elections were over," insisted another officer. "They did not dare to remove him before the Election."[11]

The president regretted having to dismiss McClellan. Although he considered the matter carefully and believed that not even the politically driven Army of the Potomac would mutiny as a result, public reaction—and thus public confidence—was far less predictable. Political pressure and public opinion had already forced Lincoln to remove another general from command in October. Gen. Don Carlos Buell had run afoul of some midwestern politicians by failing to invade East Tennessee before the onset of winter. Like McClellan, Buell was a known Democratic partisan and practitioner of limited warfare, and like McClellan, he seemed to have a bad case of the "slows." He certainly had not won favor with either Lincoln or Halleck by allowing Gen. Braxton Bragg to escape Kentucky after the battle of Perryville. Now the personable and politically noncontroversial Gen. William S. "Rosey" Rosecrans commanded the Army of the Ohio.[12]

Even so, the removal of McClellan would have to be softened by political discretion. Gen. Catharinus P. Buckingham went by special train through the snowstorm of November 7 to deliver the president's fateful orders. He went, however, not to McClellan's camp at Rectortown, but rather to the camp of Burnside's IX Corps, at Waterloo, eighteen miles to the north. Stanton wanted Buckingham to persuade Burnside to accept command of the army, a position he had already refused in July and September. As expected, Burnside protested the assignment, but Buckingham convinced him that McClellan was doomed in any case. If Burnside did not accept the post, the president would be forced to appoint someone else, most likely Gen. Joseph Hooker, a favorite with the public, the press, and several influential politicians. That did it. Burnside detested Hooker, whom he considered vain, arrogant, and devious. Together, Buckingham and Burnside traveled by train and on horseback to McClellan's camp. They arrived about 11 P.M. to find the commander composing a letter to his wife. McClellan suspected the purpose of the visit as soon as his visitors entered the tent, and a glance at General Order 182, which Buckingham handed to him, confirmed it. "Well, Burnside," he said brusquely, "I turn the command over to you."[13]

Meantime, Robert E. Lee had already reacted to the Federal movements with a spurt of messages on November 6 and 7 to superiors and subordinates. With the bluecoats in motion above the Rappahannock, bent, it seemed, on crossing into Culpeper County and striking his army, the general took precautions. He ordered Stonewall Jackson's corps, which had been guarding the Shenandoah Valley and threatening Federal communications, to move eastward in anticipation of rejoining the divided army. He ordered all surplus stores removed from Culpeper to Madison Court House, fourteen miles to the southwest. He requested additional shoes, clothing, and blankets for his men from Richmond, and, as McClellan had, he asked for more horses. Not even the animals rounded up by Stuart in Pennsylvania had satisfied his needs. "Our cavalry diminished by the casualties of battle and hard service," Lee informed Secretary of War George W. Randolph, "is now reduced by disease among the horses, sore tongue and soft hoof." Unlike McClellan, Lee was ready to move with or without the requested supplies and horses. Yet he knew that without sufficient cavalry he would be hard-pressed to maintain his pickets, shield his flanks, gather intelligence, and strike those people across the river.[14]

And to strike was what Lee intended. He had been patient all year, looking for opportunities to work against the enemy's flank and rear while confronting the Federals only at a time and place of his choosing. The strategy did not suit Lee's aggressive nature, but President Jefferson Davis had encouraged him to be prudent. Even so, Lee had retained the freedom to attack when he enjoyed a numerical or topographical advantage.[15]

On the morning of November 6, Lee had thought the Federal advance might be intended primarily to forage below the Rappahannock and through the counties that bordered the Blue Ridge Mountains. The size and speed of McClellan's progress soon convinced him that the Yankees had some other design. Little Mac would not throw his entire army into a foraging expedition. "He is . . . moving more rapidly than usual," Lee informed President Davis later that day, "and it looks like a real advance." He then ordered Longstreet, recently promoted to lieutenant general, to retire through Madison County and unite with Jackson, another newly minted lieutenant general. Lee would let the Federals cross the river, but his army would also be on McClellan's rear and right flank should he turn south toward Richmond. Lee knew that as the Federals advanced, McClellan's numbers and material advantages must decrease. If he remained patient and waited for the right moment, Lee could "strike a successful blow."[16]

North of the Dare Mark, most men wished Burnside well, even though he clearly lacked the flamboyance and force of personality that had enabled McClellan to inspire the army and dazzle the public. Indiana-born Burnside was, at thirty-eight years, two years older than Little Mac, but he had been the youngest available candidate to replace him. His playful nature and good-heartedness made him popular with many officers and men. His "winning smile and cordial manners bespoke a frank, sincere and honorable character," recalled one friend, and no one doubted his "sincerity and truthfulness, his unselfish generosity, and his devoted patriotism." Others, however, thought Burnside a poor judge of character, and he had no talent for delegating authority. He was not quick or clever, and, perhaps most regrettably, he really did not want to lead the army.[17]

"Burnside will try to do well, is patriotic and amiable, and, had he greater powers and grasp, would make an acceptable, if not a great, general," estimated Gideon Welles. Another cabinet member, Secretary of the Treasury Salmon P. Chase, admitted that Burnside had "some excellent qualities," but he preferred a more aggressive general, like Fighting Joe Hooker. In the army, longtime McClellan supporters reserved judgment. The army's provost marshal general, Marsena R. Patrick, reported that the men received Burnside "handsomely, but not enthusiastically. . . . All seemed to think there was one they liked much better." Many people thought the change ill-timed. "I don't care whether McClellan or Burnside commands the army, if the commander is only a capable man," concluded Capt. Robert Gould Shaw of the Second Massachusetts Infantry, "but I still believe the former is the best general we have. No one has proved himself better yet." More ominously, Col. Robert McAllister, who led the Eleventh New Jersey Infantry, concluded, "Burnside is a good man, but he is to be tried on a large scale. If he fails, the results will be disastrous." Even people who had endured enough of Little Mac concluded, "Wait and see how much better Burnside does, before 'rejoicing' over the removal of McClellan."[18]

Surely Lincoln harbored doubts, too, but he likely had a soft spot for Burnside. The general's critics, after all, sounded very much like his own. Just a year earlier, Attorney General Edward Bates had written confidentially, "The Prest. is an excellent man, and in the main wise; but he lacks *will* and *purpose*, and I greatly fear, has not *the power to command*." Burnside was just as politically conservative as McClellan, just as determined to spare Southern civilians the ravages of war, but at least he had a plan, and he seemed willing to share it with the president. The unfolding of Burnside's design in the thirty-odd days following his appointment, and Confederate responses to it, would determine where and how the battle of Fredericksburg would be fought.[19]

Diverging dramatically from McClellan's apparent intention to cross the Rappahannock and strike Longstreet's isolated corps, Burnside saw Richmond as "the great object of the campaign." He would concentrate his army around Warrenton, only a dozen miles above the river, he informed Halleck, thus giving the appearance that he intended to strike at Culpeper or Gordonsville. At the same time, he would gather enough supplies for a four- to five-day march and move quickly toward Fredericksburg, a little over thirty miles southeast of Warrenton. By crossing the river at that point, the army would have an open road to Richmond, almost fifty-five miles to the south. This plan, Burnside emphasized, would allow the army to remain between Lee and Washington DC, while taking the shortest route to the Rebel capital.[20]

It sounded plausible, but Lincoln saw flaws in the strategy. In his October 13 letter to McClellan, Lincoln had, in fact, asked for a line of advance against Richmond similar to that proposed by Burnside. He saw the same potential benefits of the Fredericksburg route: it would keep the army between Lee and Washington, and the army could be readily resupplied by wagon, water, and rail. But while Burnside saw Richmond as the great object of the campaign, Lincoln believed too much attention had been given to the capture of that city. To seize Richmond, Lincoln admitted, "would tend more to cripple the rebel cause than almost any other military event," with but one exception, and that was "the absolute breaking up" of Lee's army.[21]

Lincoln would become more convinced of this strategic principle as the war progressed, but for the moment he seemed unwilling to press the issue. Instead, he dispatched Halleck, Q.M. Gen. Montgomery C. Meigs, and military railroad superintendent Gen. Herman Haupt to discuss the options with Burnside. The trio, arriving at army headquarters on November 12, explained that the president preferred a move against Lee. They wrangled, but two days later, after Lincoln's emissaries had returned to Washington, Halleck informed Burnside, "The President has just assented to your plan. He thinks that it will succeed, if you move very rapidly; otherwise not."[22]

Ah, speed; here was another hazard. Lincoln probably approved Burnside's plan for two reasons. First, it would demonstrate his confidence in Burnside's judgment, a vote of confidence everyone agreed Burnside needed. Second, even if Burnside had selected the wrong target, he at least seemed prepared to move. Still, Burnside's success would depend on a huge logistical effort requiring precise coordination and extraordinary cooperation. He asked that at least thirty canal boats and barges loaded with commissary stores and forage be dispatched to Belle Plain in anticipation of the army's arrival at Fredericksburg. He required that stores and forage to subsist the army for thirty days be delivered to Falmouth. He wanted fresh horses and mules as well as beef cattle driven to Fredericksburg. He would also need pontoons at Fredericksburg to bridge the Rappahannock. Once across, he planned to load his wagons with at least twelve days' worth of provisions and embark on "a rapid movement" toward Richmond.[23]

Burnside assumed Meigs and Haupt would handle this logistical nightmare. Whatever other obstacles he may have faced, he never doubted that the supplies would arrive on time. He knew that the innovative and hardnosed Meigs took pride in maintaining the nation's armies "by every means" at his disposal. Haupt, too, demanded efficiency. By November 1862, the railroad chief had dealt with two other Union commanders in Virginia, Pope and McClellan, and he had always insisted on three guiding principles: railroad cars must be unloaded quickly, cars must be in constant use, and schedules must be maintained. "Will do all in my power to carry out your wishes, and keep things moving," Haupt assured Burnside on November 10. "Movement in everything and everywhere is essential."[24]

How Burnside intended to move his army and transfer such mountains of supplies without arousing Lee's suspicions is more difficult to fathom. How could the army move swiftly enough to secure the element of surprise? The Army of Northern Virginia, once reunited, would be closer to Fredericksburg than would the Union army, and Lee was already below the Rappahannock. Not only that, but Burnside would be leading a totally reorganized army. He had consolidated his six corps into three "grand divisions." Gen. Edwin V. "Bull" Sumner commanded two corps on the right wing, Gen. William B. Franklin two corps on the left, and Joe Hooker two corps in the center. Gen. Franz Sigel led the reserves. Burnside hoped this arrangement would streamline command structure and simplify movements, but it could just as easily produce confusion and hesitation once the army got under way. Still, as Burnside posed with his generals for photographs on the afternoon of Friday, November 14, all looked hopeful. The next day, Sumner's grand division set out for Falmouth, just a mile upriver from Fredericksburg.

Lee, who learned of McClellan's ouster on November 10, did not know if the change boded ill or good. "We always understood each other so well," he is reputed to have said of McClellan. "I fear they may continue to make these changes till they find some one whom I don't understand." Burnside's appointment may have, as one of Jackson's staff officers maintained, "created no apprehension" in Rebel ranks, but Lee remained uncertain of the Union general's intentions on November 15. The Union army's position allowed Burnside several options. Clearly, Longstreet's corps at Culpeper remained a tempting target; a movement toward the Shenandoah Valley by way of Front Royal and Strasburg offered another possibility. And on November 9, a Union cavalry detachment had held Fredericksburg for three hours before being run off by the town's citizens and its small Confederate cavalry garrison.[25]

"I am operating to baffle the advance of the enemy & retain him among the mts," Lee told his eldest son, George Washington Custis Lee, on November 10, "until I can get him separated that I can strike at him to advantage. His force will be thus diminished & disheartened." Two days later, he told Jackson that Burnside had as yet failed to betray what direction he might take. "Whether he will cross the Rappahannock or proceed to Fredericksburg I cannot tell. . . . General Stuart has been directed to watch the enemy closely, but you know the difficulty of determining the first movements."[26]

By November 14, Burnside's forces seemed to be shifting eastward. He had withdrawn his men from the mouth of the Valley and abandoned the upper reaches of Fauquier County, although not before the army had robbed the inhabitants of "everything within their reach and burned the stacks of wheat in the fields." With the possibility increasing that Fredericksburg might be the Union target, Lee completed destruction of the railroad spur between that town and Aquia Creek, already partially wrecked by the Union army two months earlier. He even considered, though ultimately without taking action, tearing up the railroad between Fredericksburg and Hanover Junction, below the river, and the Orange and Alexandria from the Rappahannock as far south as Gordonsville. "I am loath to add to the devastation of the country which has already occurred by the ravages of war," Lee admitted to George Randolph, "and yet think it prudent to throw every impediment to the progress of the enemy toward Richmond in his way."[27]

The movement of Sumner's wing eastward was the most worrisome sign, and it persuaded Lee on November 15 to order the Sixty-first Virginia Infantry and Norfolk Light Artillery to reinforce the small command at Fredericksburg. With winter approaching, Lee still hoped to avoid a general engagement. He was determined to outmaneuver Burnside if possible, for he feared that to attack "without too great risk and loss" would require double his strength of arms.[28]

Leaving nothing to chance, Lee continued to send a stream of requests for shoes, blankets, carbines, and cavalry horses to Richmond. Some of Lee's men had been without shoes for a month, and by mid-November, "cold and frosty" days were causing hardships. "I am Barfooted my self and no way to Git any Shooes," a member of the Fourteenth Virginia Infantry reported to his mother, "so you may know we see a hard time of it." Equipment of all sorts remained inadequate, and horses were "scarce and dear." The potential for human hardship increased when, on November 14, Secretary of War Randolph informed Lee that the army might have to operate on reduced rations during the winter. The supply of hogs was one hundred thousand less than the previous year. The corn crops in Tennessee and northwestern Georgia had been inordinately small, and "difficulties of transportation" had curtailed shipments of corn to northern Virginia from elsewhere in the South. Beef supplies would be lower, too, Randolph said, and the Virginia wheat crop was only half what it had been a year earlier.[29]

Lee already had a weary army. It had campaigned unceasingly since chasing Pope back across the Rappahannock in August. There had been Second Manassas, Antietam, and the long trek back to Virginia. Longstreet's men, assigned to Culpeper, found that Pope had swept the region clean. "Nothing to bee bought to eat," lamented one soldier, "the Yankeys having destroyed nearly every thing when they were in here Farmes layed waste and Houses made tenantless." More than that, Lee worried about the enthusiasm of his men for a fight. Christmas beckoned. Hopes for furloughs reigned supreme. Lee knew he would be asking much of his men to endure yet another campaign. "I pray God," he confided to Mary Custis Lee on November 13, "that he will confuse their [the enemy's] councils & return them to their own country." On that same day, one of Lee's men informed his wife, "You all have no idea how bad the soldiers want to visit home it is all the talk you can hear it around every fire but talk is about all no chance for Ferloughs now." A Georgian thought it just as well. "I feel sometimes that I am afraid to come [home]," he confessed to his wife, "for I know Il be worse dissatisfied when I get back here than I am now."[30]

As though these physical conditions were not test enough, Lee confronted what he regarded as a shocking decline in the moral tone of his army. Many men, with so much leisure time on their hands, engaged in conduct he deemed "wholly inconsistent with the character of a Southern soldier and subversive of good order and discipline in the army." Lee was a stickler for discipline, and the gambling and drinking that he had witnessed or heard about worried him. He responded by prohibiting furloughs for that winter. He ordered officers to drill their men regularly and to discourage "intemperate habits" through both directives and personal example. He forbade gambling in camp, and he told his men plainly that it saddened him to witness a "habit so pernicious and demoralizing" as gambling "among men engaged in a cause, of all others, demanding the highest virtue and purest morality in its supporters."[31]

Meanwhile, Burnside's plan had started to go wrong. Not anticipating— or perhaps appreciating—the slowness with which his supplies would be delivered, Burnside had set the army in motion too soon. Two difficulties immediately appeared. First, he learned just a few hours after Sumner's departure on November 15 that the pontoons necessary to cross the Rappahannock had not arrived at Washington for transfer to the front. It might be as late as November 17, he was told, before the pontoons even left Washington, the same day Sumner's troops were due to arrive at Falmouth. Believing he would still have sufficient time to outflank Lee, Burnside allowed Sumner to continue. Unfortunately, the pontoons did not leave Washington until November 19, and the army did not receive them until November 25. So much for the element of surprise.

Burnside's second, and even more serious, difficulty lay at Aquia Creek. The Union commander needed the landing and wharf, as well as the ten miles of railroad track between that point and Fredericksburg, before much of his supplies could be transported to Falmouth and Fredericksburg. Yet when Federal commissary officers reached Aquia Creek on November 19, they found both the wharf and the railroad in ruins, destroyed by Burnside himself, though on Halleck's command, in the retreat from Second Manassas. Haupt ordered immediate repairs, but the wharf was not operational until November 22, and it took another five days to complete the railroad to Fredericksburg. It could be argued that even had the army not shifted its base to Falmouth and Fredericksburg before the facilities were ready, suspicion would have been aroused by Haupt's construction activities. Still, the army's presence allowed Lee to anticipate and stymie the Federal actions that followed.[32]

The rest of the Union army followed Sumner within a matter of days. Franklin's Left Grand Division departed Warrenton for Stafford Court House on November 16 and arrived two days later. Hooker's Center Grand Division arrived at Hartwood on November 19 after a two-day march. All moved in a pouring rain, the heaviest of the season. "It rained for *five* days," complained a soggy Massachusetts soldier, "in which we suffered extremely; the third day we pitched ponchos in the rain and mud up to our ankles; wet feet, cold and wet blankets, we lay that night, the rain pouring in torrents." Fields resembled swamps. Exhausted, frustrated, and cursing soldiers "whipped sinfully" their flagging mules and horses, who strained heroically to haul artillery, limbers, and wagons. A line of dead animals marked the army's advance.[33]

Burnside rode ahead to Fredericksburg on November 19 to find Sumner entrenched on Stafford Heights, a line of bluffs rising 150 feet above the Rappahannock. The place was familiar to Burnside. He had commanded the Federal garrison from those heights in August. "The enemy do not seem to be in force on the opposite side," he informed Halleck, "but their pickets extend down to the river." Sumner, a crusty sixty-five year old who had fought Mexicans and Indians in his long army career, wanted to ford the river immediately and take the town before the Rebels arrived in strength. Burnside refused permission, partly because he wanted first to establish communications with Aquia Creek, mostly because he feared that a sudden rain would render the fords impassable and trap his infantry and artillery west of the river. Just such a thing had happened to a Confederate brigade farther upriver three months earlier.[34]

But while Sumner dealt with his commander directly, the intrigue for which the Army of the Potomac was already famous had begun. Having requested Burnside's permission to cross the Rappahannock at United States Ford, four miles above his encampment, and march directly against Richmond, Joe Hooker, without awaiting Burnside's reply, sought Stanton's blessing for the same plan. Not only that, but in his letter to the secretary of war, he presumed to make logistical arrangements to supply his division, lamented the slowness with which the army had progressed, and criticized Burnside's strategic design. "I regret that the major-general commanding did not keep up the show of an advance on the line via Gordonsville," Hooker told Stanton, "and even now I would recommend a demonstration . . . in that direction." Well aware of rumors in camp and the press that, should Burnside stumble, he would likely command the army, Hooker wished to demonstrate his military acumen for the secretary. Stanton's response is not known, but on the following day, November 20, Burnside, apparently with no knowledge of Hooker's appeal to the secretary of war, gently reminded Fighting Joe of his subordinate position. He had given the situation a good deal of thought, Burnside informed his ambitious general, and was convinced that success could be achieved only by the coordinated movement of all three grand divisions.[35]

Meantime, Burnside's men became restive. They sensed that each passing day lessened the odds of success and enhanced Lee's chances of divining their purpose. They wondered what had happened to the pontoons, why their supplies had not arrived, and when the vital railroad would be completed. "This delay is likely to be fatal to our success here," concluded one officer in his diary. He estimated that the army would not be prepared to move until at least the end of November. Unlike many men, however, he did not blame Burnside. "The weather is fine, and we are losing it all for lack of proper energy or will at Washington," he groaned; "had this [rail]road been restored and everything ready when we first arrived, we might be south of the Rappahannock . . . and ready to start for Richmond."[36]

Indeed, Burnside had done well in keeping Lee off balance. Federal activity reaffirmed Lee's belief that a crossing at Fredericksburg was in the offing, and yet just enough doubt remained for him to delay full concentration of his forces. By leaving his cavalry to threaten fords on the upper Rappahannock, and with Franz Sigel dispersing troops to Gainesville, Thoroughfare Gap, and Aldie from his main body at Centreville, Burnside controlled the situation. Lee still had to consider the possibility that Sumner's movement downriver was only a diversion to cover an advance on Gordonsville or a withdrawal toward Alexandria. Not until November 18, having digested reports from his "cavalry, individual scouts, and citizens," did

Lee decide that Fredericksburg was the Union target. Even so, two questions remained: why Fredericksburg, and where would Burnside go from there?[37]

It was a moment when the Confederacy might have exploited Federal military and political disarray, but the Davis government had its own problems. Criticism of Davis's policies of political centralization—seen most dramatically in that spring's conscription act and the suspension of habeas corpus—had been gaining strength. The voices raised against him were not so loud as those in the North that demanded Lincoln's scalp, but in mid-November, the president's military command structure faced a crisis. The crisis blew in from the West and the trans-Mississippi, where, from the fall of Forts Henry and Donelson in February to the retreat of Bragg from Kentucky in October, Davis and the Confederacy had suffered an alarming string of defeats. When the president clashed with George Randolph over who should control military policy in the West, his secretary of war resigned on November 15.

Davis replaced the stubborn but sickly Randolph with the more malleable and even sicklier James A. Seddon, a native of the Fredericksburg area, and appointed Joe Johnston overall military commander in the West. Troubled by the disorder and uncertainty that prevailed in the western part of his nation, Davis expected Johnston to restore order by coordinating the armies of Bragg in middle Tennessee, Gen. John C. Pemberton in Mississippi, and Gen. Theophilus H. Holmes in the trans-Mississippi. The president also made plans to tour the troubled region and to meet personally with his western generals. Lee, still in Culpeper, would have to look after Virginia.[38]

Lee ordered Stuart across the Rappahannock to ascertain the remaining Federal strength opposite Culpeper and to determine if there was still a threat to the Valley. He sent the rest of his supplies at Culpeper farther south and dispatched half of Longstreet's corps (the divisions of Gen. Lafayette McLaws and Gen. Robert Ransom and the cavalry brigade of Gen. William H. F. "Rooney" Lee) to Fredericksburg. On November 19, the remainder of Longstreet's corps crossed the Rapidan, and Old Pete arrived at Fredericksburg. Jackson stayed in the Valley to threaten Federal communications and guard against Federal trickery, but he stood ready to march to Longstreet's aid at a moment's notice.

Lee joined Longstreet on the hills above Fredericksburg the following day. One glance told him he did not want to fight there. The Federals had the advantage of terrain should they concentrate their artillery on the dominant northern heights. If Burnside crossed the Rappahannock, he would doubtless do so in a flanking movement. In that case, Lee preferred to fall back toward Richmond and intercept him at the North Anna River, some thirty miles south of the Dare Mark. There the terrain presented more favorable opportunities for Confederate counterattacks, and Burnside would be forced to extend his line of communications across two rivers. All would depend, Lee knew, upon "circumstances which may arise."[39]

CHAPTER TWO

# Right in the Wrong Place

Fredericksburg, home to some five thousand souls when the war commenced, had far fewer inhabitants on November 21, 1862. The town had already been visited by confiscation and martial law during a brief Union occupation the previous spring and summer. It had not suffered those indignities to the same degree as neighboring Culpeper, yet the town, as Jefferson Davis had commented on a visit that March, seemed to be "right in the wrong place." Thousands of people, black and white, had fled, secessionists moving deeper into the Confederacy and runaway blacks following the Unionists who had already gone north. Residents who remained were now trapped between two armies, and a hard, cold rain that had been sweeping across the countryside for two days did little to improve their spirits. People in many other parts of the Confederacy welcomed the foul weather and delighted at the prospects of a winter campaign. "The best thing . . . that can happen for the South," crowed a South Carolinian, "is a campaign of invasion towards Richmond. Freezing nights and boggy roads are incompatible with the safe retreat of a beaten foe. It may be a Russian campaign." But the people of Fredericksburg knew that the initial stage of any such campaign, and perhaps its conclusion, must pass over them.[1]

The shocking reality of how fierce that campaign might be came more swiftly than anyone had imagined. Bull Sumner, by direction of Burnside, sent an ultimatum to the citizens of Fredericksburg on the morning of November 21: surrender the town by 5 P.M. or be shelled at 9 the next morning. In the intervening hours, Sumner suggested, there would be ample time to evacuate noncombatants. The order seems out of character for Burnside, who was known, like McClellan, for his desire to keep civilians out of harm's way and to protect their property. But he had little choice. Shots had been fired at his soldiers from the town, and its rebellious inhabitants were furnishing provisions and clothing to Confederate armies. Sumner addressed the proclamation to Mayor Montgomery Slaughter and the town council, but when General Patrick appeared on the riverbank with a flag of truce to deliver it, he was greeted by Maj. G. Moxley Sorrel of Longstreet's staff. Sorrel carried the message directly to Lee.

Lee had Mayor Slaughter tell Sumner that the citizens' warlike behavior would cease. Lee refused to surrender the town, but he offered to evacuate all Confederate troops from Fredericksburg if the Federals would refrain from shelling noncombatants. Sumner accepted the arrangement, and in a personal conference with Slaughter at his headquarters in the two-story brick Lacy mansion, also known as Chatham, atop Stafford Heights, the general promised that he would bombard the town only in defense. Even so, Lee advised all civilians to leave Fredericksburg and made men and wagons available to those who needed assistance. Neither Lee nor his soldiers seemed to consider where these people would go.

The rain continued on November 22, as the exodus, begun the previous evening, proceeded. Several hundred people crowded onto cattle cars to escape south by rail. Some traveled as far as Richmond, which had become a haven for refugees early in the war. Many others disembarked in Caroline County, where "kind and hospitable people . . . opened their houses to them." The majority fled not by rail but by foot, on horseback, and in every description of wagon. They choked all available roads and soon flooded the countryside. Children and grandparents, loaded down with their precious few belongings, slogged through the rain and started at occasional thunder. Despite Sumner's promise, a few Federal artillery shells fell near a fleeing train, but without effect. "I was so sorry for the pore little innocent children," reported a Georgian, "and the ladies seemed to be scared out of anything like reason." To comfort them during the unexpected bombardment, the soldier told all within earshot that he had heard "bigger dogs bark than that and never had been bit yet," which caused them to laugh and "scold the Yankees" until another shell whistled overhead and they panicked once again.[2]

Homeless folk, many resigned to "living in the woods," soon overran the neighborhood. More fortunate people found sympathetic souls to take them in or received aid from the army. "Every country house for miles around is filled with these refugees," observed a soldier, "and on yesterday, cold as it was, I saw delicate women and little children away off in the woods watching their bedding and scanty store of provisions till tents could be brought out to shelter them. These are the privations and horrors of war." Many people doubtless wept and fretted at being forced to leave their homes exposed to the Federals, but most handled the situation stoically. "The citizens of this section from all accounts have suffered terribly from the presence of the Yankees in their midst," reported a Confederate officer of the refugees who arrived at his camp, some six miles from the town, "and I think are prepared to undergo any privations rather than see the enemy again among them."[3]

Relieved by the withdrawal of the innocents, Lee continued to hope that Burnside might yet decline to fight. If the armies must fight, Lee still wished to do so on the North Anna. The consequences of a battle along the Dare Mark were apparent to everyone. "We have a large army here and enemy has a large army on the other side of the Rappahannock river in full view of the town," a Confederate officer explained to his wife. "The enemy has a long run of cannon on the range of hills beyond the river that fully command the town and we have many pieces of artillery so placed on the hills this side [of] the river as to prevent the enemy from crossing it." Lee, with slightly under forty thousand men at Fredericksburg, believed he was secure for the moment, but, not wishing to take chances, he ordered Jackson's thirty-four thousand men to move east of the Blue Ridge. From there, Jackson could threaten Burnside's rear, rush to any of several strategic points by railroad, or march quickly to Fredericksburg. Jackson's availability, Lee hoped, would discourage Burnside from forcing a river crossing or undertaking operations elsewhere, say toward the James River.[4]

Burnside, it turned out, was nowhere near ready to advance. Haupt informed him on November 22 that it would take several more days to complete the railroad from Aquia Creek. Several additional days would then be needed to deliver the ten days' rations Burnside's troops must have before they could cross the river. Haupt suggested that, for the sake of speed, Burnside consider crossing farther downriver, where his supplies could be floated to him. This scheme would save time and unnecessary casualties, but it required the pontoons, and they could not possibly arrive until the following evening. Also on the twenty-second, Burnside discovered Confederate cavalry patrolling his side of the river. His last slim hopes for a lightly contested river crossing were slipping away.

The pontoons finally arrived on November 25, but Burnside had shown his exasperation the day before by ordering the arrest of Gen. Daniel P. Woodbury. The modest and studious Woodbury commanded Burnside's engineer brigade and was responsible for acquiring materials and erecting the bridges on time. Woodbury, who was not long under arrest, protested that he had not been told swift delivery of the pontoons was so critical. Even so, his men had labored heroically for nearly a week through mud and rain to reach the army. Perhaps Woodbury could have done more. One of his officers thought him "an excellent scholar [and] a fine Engineer but not a man to command men in the rough experience of actual war." But the same might have been said of Halleck, who was more to blame than Woodbury for the delay. The general in chief should have impressed upon his engineers the need to deliver and deploy the bridges rapidly.[5]

For the moment, with most noncombatants having been evacuated and the Federals apparently unable to cross the Rappahannock in the near future, the atmosphere grew relaxed on both sides of the river. Some of the town's refugees had even returned home by Thanksgiving. "I hear the soldiers also talking of the prospects and saying there will probably be no battle here," reported a resident, "as the Yankee General 'Burnside' will not risque it with the river behind him and our forces so advantageously placed." An awestruck Confederate soldier reported on November 23, "Gen'ls Lee, Longstreet, Stuart & a host of others are here and things look more warlike than I have seen them for some time." Yet he admitted that Yankee and Rebel pickets talked to each other across the river, and the army generally "seemed pretty cheerful."[6]

Frustrated officers on both sides confirmed that rival pickets refused to fire at each other—some men claimed they were ordered not to fire—and that they had become quite friendly. The soldiers exchanged newspapers, tobacco, coffee, and whatever else the other side craved, but mostly they talked, joked, and bragged. "The Yankees come down to the river opposite the town and converse freely with our soldiers and private citizens," one Rebel reported. A Union officer thought the Rebels opposite his picket post "very low-bred persons" to judge by their conversation, "for they swore and were very profane."[7]

The momentary lull and absence of danger led many Union soldiers to grumble about the want of physical comfort. Temperatures had not yet taken a decided turn toward winter, but the rain continued through November, making the air damp. While senior officers had fine stoves to ward off the chill, most privates and junior officers sat around sputtering campfires and shivered in their blankets like medieval men-at-arms. Not everyone had a blanket or enough clothing. Men complained about their diet of coffee, pork, and hard bread, too. Where were the supply trains from Washington? they asked. McClellan would not have cut them off from their depot in this way. The army observed Thanksgiving Day on November 27, but only officers and seasoned foragers could hope to dine on the turkey or ham they would have eaten at home. Soup, pork, and fried crackers were the more likely fare. "Yesterday we got three days' rations of cracker and pork, and the boys set up a howl," reported a soldier the day before Thanksgiving. "I thought there would be a mutiny," he went on, "they were yelling 'hard-tack!' even in the night."[8]

They warned friends not to believe what they read in the newspapers about the fine condition and fighting spirit of the army. "As for the weather being delightful, and stoves being in our tents, and the army being urgent to move forward, and everything being lovely, as the 'army correspondents' make it out, it is a *case lie*," insisted a New Englander. Conditions had improved somewhat by the last day of November, when the men received an issue of beans, rice, and molasses, but they continued to comment on the stark contrast between their quarters and rations and those of their officers. "This was a poor part of the country to forage in," explained one man; "the people as a general thing were poor, and then so many having passed on before us had taken with few exceptions all." One officer acknowledged, "The country around about is destitute of provisions. Our living consists of hard tack, beef & coffee." Desperate men resorted to stealing extra crackers, knowing that if caught they could lose $5 in pay and suffer the humiliation of having a placard that read "Thief" pinned to their backs.[9]

"We wander around with overcoats & gloves on or sit shivering around a smoky fire," complained an infantry captain from Michigan. "We often gaze at the rebel camps just across the river & wonder if they have as dull times as we." Soldiers could on "rare occasion" purchase potatoes at $4 a bushel or a jar of preserves for $1.50. "A more tasteless & unprofitable life," concluded the captain, "I never led." A Massachusetts sergeant missed his tobacco most of all. "It is very dear here," he complained to his wife. "Sutlers charge an exhorbitant price for everything they have. if we remain here i will get you to send me some tobaco and a few other articals i want." Men complained about their health, too, especially as December approached. And it was not just coughing and wheezing that plagued the soldiers. In November alone, the Army of the Potomac listed 39,340 men on its sick rolls. These included 852 cases of typhoid (which also produced 116 of the 365 deaths that month), 14,002 cases of diarrhea and dysentery (often brought on by eating raw salt pork), 3,207 cases of rheumatism, 777 cases of bronchitis, hundreds of cases of other respiratory ailments, and thousands of fever cases.[10]

Naturally, some of the grumbling resulted from idleness and boredom.

Officers tried to combat these maladies by keeping the men busy on picket duty, cutting and hauling wood, building roads, and constructing defensive positions. Yet, when speculating about Burnside's next move, the army's ultimate destination, and the proper strategy it should pursue to beat Bobby Lee, the men also expressed their devotion to the cause of the Union. If they grumbled or voiced frustration about the course of the war, it was because they were tired of being led by muddleheaded generals and meddling politicians. "There never was a more intelligent, self-sacrificing army in the world," insisted one Federal in early December, "but how can it hope to succeed when it is held back by an unseen agency as it were?" That "unseen agency," as every soldier knew, consisted of the politicians, civilian "croakers," and "traitors at home" who happily used the army as cannon fodder while deciding how and at what cost the war should be fought.[11]

The more convinced they became of this, the more critical they became of the nation's politicians. "The constant removal of generals, the elections in New York, Philadelphia, and Ohio, and the probable quarrels in the approaching session of congress all tend as a drawback to the doings of the army," regretted one man. "Friends at home may desire to see the army move and to hear of victories," complained a New York volunteer, "but the poor soldiers feel and know that all these glories are at their expense." Many men still bristled over the political ouster of McClellan. "I think they removed him at the wrong time just in the midst of a campaign," insisted a McClellan partisan, "thus occasioning a delay hurtful to the cause." Burnside had been forced to move the army before it was fully prepared, without adequate clothing, tents, or rations. The resulting delays had not only deprived the army of the tactical advantage of surprise, but it had also eroded the men's confidence and enthusiasm for a fight. "What a lack of interest in the cause the privates in the army have," regretted one man. "To their shame, be it said two-thirds would leave for home to-day if they were allowed."[12]

As December ushered in a taste of genuine winter weather, men convinced themselves that the threat of a campaign must surely have passed. "The desire to go into winter quarters grows stronger every day, among officers & men," admitted one officer. "Of the two alternatives, defeat or winter quarters, I think they prefer the latter." One sergeant saw "no amediate prospect of any fighting" on December 4, which was fine with him. His regiment—the Twenty-eighth Massachusetts—had constructed an "excelent camp" near Falmouth, and the thought of trying to move across an alternately frozen and muddy Virginia countryside held small appeal. On December 8, he decided, "not even the Generals themselves can tell when a battle will take place. it all depends on circumstances and there is no probability of our having a battle here at present." A Pennsylvanian prayed, "I only hope Burnside knows what is good for his army and not move this winter. I would like nothing better than to see Richmond fall but I do not think winter the time to do it."[13]

Confederate lads showed more confidence in their leaders than did the Yanks, but they, too, suffered for lack of shoes, socks, food, and shelter. "I have the worst cold and cough I ever had in my life," a Virginian informed his parents. With the snow shoe-deep and only a flimsy tent for shelter, he could not "sleep a wink." His brother did not suffer so much from the cold, but his empty belly pained him. "I buy nearly all I eat," he complained to his father, and at exceedingly high prices. Beef had become impossible to obtain, and bacon sold for a dollar a pound.[14]

A Georgian expressed dismay that his regiment's baggage remained in Richmond, particularly after a heavy snow fell on December 6. "Just think of so many thousand men camped in the naked woods without any tents and some barefooted," he explained to his wife, "some without blankets and living on a little beef and bread. Only God knows what will become of us. If this is independence I don't want it." What spare clothes the men had were with their baggage, and no one expected that to arrive any time soon. "The government is not treating us right in this matter," asserted the Georgian; "they treat the army like so many dogs." Still, like most of Lee's men, he seemed confident of success, and however angry he became with the government, he knew, ultimately, that he was fighting to safeguard his family. "They may talk of liberty and they may talk of me dying in war," he concluded, "but I want to live with my family and live in peace. . . . All I think or care about is my family. If I can just hear that they are well I am all right."[15]

The Georgian could also stand the winter weather because he believed the war would be over in six months, "some way or other." Not that he expected much to happen before spring. "I thought the other day . . . that we would have fought a battle before now," he informed his wife, "but we have not and both armies have gone to fortifying and when they commence that I never think there is going to be much fighting done." A sergeant in another Georgia regiment also doubted that the armies would fight in such weather, but more to the point, he believed Lee's soldiers could handle adversity in any form, whether frigid temperatures or hot fighting. "It is useless for a man to say what he can stand and what he cannot stand unless he tries," he wisely told his wife, "and I find as much depends upon the energy and spirit of the man as with his strength." A South Carolinian who had suffered at the onset of winter seemed well enough pleased once his regiment received tents. He had two good blankets, he reasoned, and with plenty of firewood, bread, and beef, he had "no right to complain."[16]

But others, more familiar with the reasons behind the shifting of the armies, believed a winter battle inevitable. The lull could not last. Many a man eased his fear and anxiety, endured the endless waiting, by pretending that somehow, some way, he would not fight again. His spirits were raised by believing that the politicians might decide this was all a mistake, that the armies would be sent home and be done with war. But no, that would not happen. Burnside *must* attack, given the "circumstances of his promotion." The Confederates understood as well as the Yankees that McClellan had been replaced because he had "the slows"; Lincoln wanted movement, action, an advance into Rebel territory. The Federals had tried nearly every other route to Richmond—by way of the Peninsula, Culpeper, the Valley— and now they must try Fredericksburg.[17]

Lee, too, had been convinced since November 25 that, despite all appearances, Burnside would try to cross the Rappahannock. "I think from the tone of the Northern papers, it is intended that General Burnside shall advance from Fredericksburg to Richmond," he told President Davis, and that the Federals were delaying only until they could secure their supply line from Washington. More than that, Lee continued, "should General Burnside change his base of operations, the effect produced in the United States would be equivalent to a defeat." Gen. Dorsey Pender, one of Lee's brigade commanders, still could not believe the Federals would advance, given the weather and their position. "If they were afraid to advance from Warrenton," he mused, "it would look like nonsense to attempt it here." Yet Pender confided to his wife that Lee was "anxiously waiting for a fight. He told me today that he believed he would be willing to fall back and let them cross for the sake of a fight."[18]

Northern newspapers, always a favorite source of information for Lee, had it right. Twice in late November Burnside met with Lincoln, once aboard the steamer *Baltimore* at Aquia Creek (November 26–27) and once in Washington (November 29). The president suggested that Burnside place an additional force of twenty-five thousand men downriver at Port Royal and another twenty-five thousand on the north bank of the Pamunkey River. With these two forces advancing to threaten Lee's rear, Burnside might cross successfully at Fredericksburg. If all three columns could then converge, they would have the option of marching unopposed on Richmond or turning to demolish Lee's army. Burnside and Halleck convinced Lincoln that the logistical difficulties and time required to muster such forces made the plan impractical. Lincoln relented, and he reassured Burnside that he need not strike until he was ready. But the fact that the president urged an offensive strategy implied that he wanted results, and soon. After all, McClellan could have gone into winter quarters.

Lincoln had not insisted on a specific date or place for a crossing because Burnside had clearly demonstrated his desire to push the army south of the Rappahannock at the earliest opportunity. The general told Lincoln that the army was "in good spirit, good condition, good moral [sic]" and fully prepared to "cross the river in face of the enemy and drive him away." The president was somewhat discouraged to hear his general say in late November that an assault across the river could be "risky," but he would refrain from rushing Burnside as long as his general continued to move.[19]

The president may also have begun to appreciate the difficulties faced by commanders in the field. "I certainly have been dissatisfied with the slowness of Buell and McClellan," he admitted to reformer-turned-general Carl Schurz two days before his first meeting with Burnside, "but before I relieved them I had great fears I should not find successors to them, who would do better; and I am sorry to add, that I have seen little since to relieve those fears." It had recently occurred to Lincoln that circumstances, rather than "particular generals," produced many military problems. With this step, the president was not far removed from understanding, as did his more perceptive officers, that many old rules of warfare no longer applied. The "character" of the country and the railroad, if nothing else, had altered traditional strategies and principles of war. "I believe the rules which must be observed to carry on a war in this country and at this time differ far more essentially from those which governed Napoleon's campaigns than the latter's did from those of the ancient Greeks and Romans," concluded one Union officer. "All theories seem to be upset and our generals groping in the dark . . . until some master mind can discover the principles which should regulate warfare. . . . We certainly have none such, nor do the rebels, I think, though General Lee comes near it."[20]

Perhaps Lincoln's repeated suggestions about a flanking movement finally made an impression, for in late November, Burnside announced just such a plan. He would cross at Skinker's Neck, fourteen miles downriver from Fredericksburg and a few miles above Port Royal. He hoped this movement would force the outnumbered Lee back toward Richmond. His engineers thought it a "splendid" spot for the crossing.[21]

But Lee had anticipated such a move. When Jackson's corps completed its long march to Fredericksburg on December 1 (Jackson had arrived two days earlier), Lee assigned its four divisions to several critical spots. Gen. Ambrose Powell Hill's men guarded Hamilton's Crossing, located at the southern base of forty-foot-high Prospect Hill and along the Richmond, Fredericksburg, and Potomac Railroad. Gen. William B. Taliaferro moved four miles beyond that to Guiney Station, also on the railroad, where Jackson temporarily established his headquarters. Gen. Daniel H. Hill's division marched to Port Royal, six miles downriver, where five Union gunboats had appeared several days earlier. Gen. Jubal Early, commanding Gen. Richard Ewell's division, headed for Skinker's Neck. Not only had the Confederates now blocked every point at which Burnside might challenge them, but they also held the enormous strategic and tactical advantages of interior lines. This, hoped Lee, would convince Burnside of the futility of a winter campaign, for the Confederate commander still could not conceive of an "attempt to cross the Rappahannock in front of Fredericksburg." In any case, and despite the urgings of Stonewall Jackson that he follow his initial impulse and fall back to the North Anna, Lee had decided to make his stand at Fredericksburg.[22]

Precisely when Burnside decided to challenge Lee directly remains unclear. Seemingly, his decision came in early December, when Jackson's arrival and a spell of wildly unpredictable weather—rain one day, freezing temperatures the next, with bouts of warm temperatures that melted the landscape and turned roads into quagmires—seriously limited strategic options. The fluctuating weather reminded him that time was running out for any offensive. Ironically, too, he seemed to believe that because Lee very likely did not anticipate such an audacious move, he could possibly gain the element of surprise. It is also clear that whatever patient assurances Lincoln had given him to avoid "risky" undertakings, Burnside felt unspoken pressure to strike a blow, to the point that "it became necessary . . . to cross in the face of a vigilant and formidable foe."[23]

Burnside kept his own counsel until December 9, when he met with the commanders of his grand divisions at his headquarters, located in the Alexander Phillips house, about a mile to the rear of Chatham. He had settled on a plan that combined a direct assault against Lee's center and an attack against the Confederate right flank, held by Jackson. A simultaneous diversion would also be staged at Skinker's Neck to disrupt Rebel efforts to concentrate their forces. The flanking movement probably shows the influence of Bull Sumner, Burnside's most experienced and, he believed, most reliable grand division commander. Sumner had been urging just such a flanking movement from the time he arrived at Falmouth, some three weeks earlier. Quickly finalizing plans, Burnside said he wanted to launch his attack two days hence, on Thursday, December 11. Officers and men would carry three days' cooked rations and sixty rounds of ammunition. Franklin and Hooker were less than enthusiastic about the plan, but all three generals gave verbal approval before departing to prepare their men.

Despite his clear strategic intention, Burnside's initial orders for the river crossing and his tactical plan thereafter were vague, all of which suggests he remained uncertain of how best to achieve his goal. He did understand the need for quick movement across the river and the importance of artillery support. Engineers would erect five pontoon bridges. Two "upper" bridges would lead into the upper town, at approximately the foot of Hawke Street. A third "middle" bridge, leading into the lower end of town about one-half mile downriver, would be placed below the destroyed railroad bridge. The final two "lower" bridges would be erected a mile farther downriver, near the mouth of Deep Run. The engineers would be protected during this perilous construction project by sharpshooters and artillery, the latter placed on the heights that lined the river.

The artillery positions would be critical, if not for erection of the bridges, then for the subsequent infantry crossings and advance. The engineers would be partially protected by the steep riverbank opposite them, which also made it difficult for most Confederate batteries to bear accurately on the river. Federal sharpshooters, Burnside assumed, could provide whatever additional protection the engineers might require against Rebel infantry. The advance, however, would be a different matter. Gen. Henry J. Hunt, Burnside's extremely able chief of artillery, arranged 147 of his 312 guns superbly. With his ordnance—all but 14 pieces were rifled—divided into four groups, he could cover every river crossing and most of the crucial avenues of advance from atop Stafford Heights.

A right group of 40 guns, positioned from Falmouth to just above the upper pontoon bridges, would silence Rebel guns and neutralize troops on the opposite heights. A right-center group of 38 guns, but including the 14 twelve-pound smoothbores, continued this line to near the middle bridges. They would cover the advance of Federal troops directly into town while keeping enemy troops out. A left-center group of 27 guns held the line from just below the middle bridges to above the lower bridges. They would prohibit the Rebels from occupying the plain between Hazel Run and Deep Run, thus denying the enemy a staging area for any possible flanking movement against either the middle or lower bridges. A left group of 42 guns would cover the lower bridges and protect the Federal left flank. Hunt expressed confidence that these preparations would "control the enemy's movements on the plain," "silence his batteries along the crest of the ridge," "command the town," "protect the throwing up of the bridges and the crossing of troops," and "protect the left flank of the army."[24]

The missions of the infantry divisions were less precise but required of them approximately the following. Sumner's two corps drew the most difficult—and potentially most deadly—assignment. They would drive straight into Fredericksburg across the upper and middle bridges. Hooker's men would follow them, as Sumner continued on through Fredericksburg to seize Marye's Heights, immediately behind the town. Once across, Hooker would protect Sumner's right flank and be prepared to reinforce him. Hooker should also be prepared to move in support of Franklin's grand division, which would cross by way of the lower bridges and move south along the Old Richmond Road. Thereafter—and here would arise one of the most controversial parts of Burnside's orders—Franklin's movements would be "governed by circumstances" but "with a view to taking the heights" and destroying Lee's right flank. Remarkably, Burnside delivered even these loosely constructed orders only on the morning of the attack, and in all instances he would rely for success on the initiative of Sumner, Hooker, and Franklin and their reactions to events.[25]

How the army would respond to the assault remained to be seen. Many corps, division, and brigade commanders, those men privy to Burnside's intentions, denounced the plan. So outspoken did Sumner's officers become that Burnside had to meet with them privately to ensure their "devotion." The army's engineers, upon inspecting the crossing sites opposite Fredericksburg, grew somber. "We all came to the conclusion that we might now return to our quarters and . . . execute our last Wills & Testaments," recalled one engineering officer. Still, most of the army seemed to trust the commander. Colonel McAllister, who would lead the Eleventh New Jersey Infantry in Hooker's grand division, had fretted as much as eleven days before the assault that the army would lose "an immense number of men" if it crossed at Fredericksburg. "*The time for crossing has gone by*," he emphasized. On December 9, having received his orders, McAllister could only assume that the army would move downriver to cross. "I can't think that we will move across here," he told his wife. "The loss of life would be terable. . . . This is undoubtedly only a feint." Few men saw portents of disaster or harbored doubts. "I want to let you all know at home," confided a

Massachusetts soldier on December 10, "that we start for the field with high hopes and anticipations, both for the cause and ourselves."[26]

The Rebels, for their part, remained unsuspecting. "Everything is quiet about here," a Virginian told his family on December 10; "there has been no fighting lately. . . . Our boys are getting Christmas in their bones already and are talking about having *one* big dinner." From Port Royal, a Georgian decided, "I hardly think thyel try to cross and Im sure weel not cross after them here. Gen Lee says if they will cross heel build the bridge himself for them."[27]

Important developments in foreign policy made success on the Dare Mark imperative for both armies. A crisis in British affairs, initially unknown to the Americans, had been brewing for several weeks. On October 7, William E. Gladstone, chancellor of the exchequer and foremost Liberal party advocate of British intervention in the American war, had implied in a speech at Newcastle, England, that the government of Prime Minister Henry Palmerston was on the verge of recognizing the Confederacy. A few days later, the French government of Napoleon III proposed a joint plan for intervention that included Britain, France, and Russia. The two events caused a furor in England, as Palmerston's cabinet considered more seriously than ever before the implications of meddling with the Americans.

On November 7, the same fateful day that McClellan lost his army, George C. Lewis, British secretary for war, circulated a fifteen-thousand-word memorandum to fellow cabinet members in which he clarified the exceedingly dangerous ground—both practically and legally—Britain would enter if it engaged even in a mediation of American problems. He was persuasive. Four days later, Britain informed the French that it would forgo immediate action, joint or otherwise. The cabinet had decided that economic and social issues—largely cotton and emancipation—that had earlier tempted Britain to enter the war were not compelling enough to justify the risks.

News of the secret European negotiations and Britain's decision reached America in early December, and it pleased neither the government in Washington nor the one in Richmond. The Lincoln administration expressed amazement that the European powers had discussed the possibility of intervention. Although the talks surprised few Irish Americans, who blamed England for the worldwide agitation over slavery and for seeking to divide the United States by aiding the Rebels, they prompted an official protest from Secretary of State William H. Seward. The Confederacy, for its part, was bitter over Britain's failure to act. Davis and his secretary of state, Judah P. Benjamin, had been supremely confident that England's need for cotton would compel Palmerston to intervene. But with Confederate credit rapidly dwindling in England, time was running out, and the Rebels might soon be forced to swallow their pride and resume selling the cotton they had been withholding from English manufacturers. Now, more than ever, they needed dramatic victories on the battlefield.[28]

That opportunity came at Fredericksburg. The battle began, as most accounts agree, with the dramatic firing of Confederate signal guns at about 5 A.M. on December 11. Fredericksburg's remaining civilians fled to their cellars and other safe havens; soldiers rushed to their assigned positions in dread anticipation. The predawn air was crisp; the temperature was well below freezing and a film of ice covered the Rappahannock. Despite a thick protective fog that blanketed the water, Rebel pickets had detected Woodbury's engineers several hours earlier as they made their way to the riverbank. By 5 A.M., construction crews had extended the middle bridge and one of the upper bridges more than halfway across the Dare Mark.

Gen. William Barksdale's Mississippi Brigade—some fifteen hundred men—and an attached Florida regiment watched from a strong defensive position that embraced the loopholed upper stories and cellars of buildings in Fredericksburg, connecting trenches, rifle pits, and barricades of dirt, logs, and sand-filled barrels. Now that the Federals were about to assault the town, Lee's month-old promise to Sumner to evacuate his men no longer seemed to apply. As the still shrouded forms of the pontoniers came within easy rifle range, Barksdale's men opened fire. "The bulletts of the enemy *rained* upon my bridge," swore a captain of engineers. "They went whizzing and spitting by and around me, pattering on the bridge, splashing in the water and thugging through the boats." Actually, the fog limited the effectiveness of the riflemen, and they inflicted only light casualties, but the Mississippians forced the engineers to take cover.[29]

This was a critical moment in the battle. Lee knew he could not prevent Burnside from crossing the river. Union artillery and rifles on Stafford Heights dominated the riverfront and town so completely that Lee could not position enough men in Fredericksburg or on the open plain stretching nearly a mile in front of Marye's Heights to stop him. Confederate guns on the ridge could not bombard the bridges without also hitting the town. Lee could only hope to slow the Federal crossing and retard the initial advance. That became Barksdale's mission: delay the crossing until Lee could recall Jackson's far-flung divisions and organize a defense. Union pontoniers would return to their work repeatedly during the day, but each time the Mississippians drove them back.

Following a second repulse, General Hunt provided more artillery support for the horribly exposed engineers. Seeing that the elevation of his guns on the heights could not be depressed sufficiently to concentrate on the lower side of the river, he redeployed thirty-six additional artillery pieces (twenty-four to cover the upper bridges, twelve for the middle bridges) on the riverbank to pulverize the Rebel nests. So intense was the concentrated fire that the town burst into flames in several places, and the gunners had to cease firing after an hour because the fog and smoke that had settled on the river completely obscured the town. But so well had the Mississippians entrenched and otherwise protected themselves that even this barrage could not dislodge them. Not until 12:30 P.M., as the fog finally dissipated and the temperature approached fifty degrees, did the Federals recognize the need to concentrate the full weight of their artillery on the lone brigade and the town that harbored it.

For two hours a deafening barrage rocked Fredericksburg, as every gun within range pummeled the Rebels. "'Uncle Sam's bull dogs' never barked louder and faster," decided one Federal soldier, and few on the Union side failed to be impressed with this rare event. "I have just been a looker-on in a new phase of military operations, that of shelling a city," a New York artillerist informed his family that evening. "It has been the most severe artillery fire I have seen. Judging from the fires in the city and its general appearance . . . the city must be nearly or quite ruined." A Union surgeon recalled: "The roar of the artillery was terrific, and as the winds rolled away the huge columns of smoke, we saw that the city was on fire, the flames leaping to the skies. The spectacle was one of awful grandeur. The bursting bombs, . . . the great tongues of flame from the burning buildings, . . . and the shock of the artillery which shook the earth, made up one of the most terribly magnificent of scenes."[30]

Luckily, most of the remaining residents had been evacuated by that time, although Federal gunners commented on "the most distressing sight" of women and children "running from the burning buildings." Those few who remained huddled in cellars and under stairways covered their ears against "the whizzing and moaning of shells and the crash of falling bricks and timber." One woman recalled "the shrieking of those shells, like a host of angry fiends, rushing through the air, the crashing of the balls through the roof and upper stories of the house." She would never forget the "agony and terror" of that afternoon. "I could not *pray*," she insisted, "but only *cry* for mercy." Confederate soldiers on Marye's Heights watched helplessly as old men, women, and children streamed out of "their devoted city," even though, as one Virginia artillerist reported, "It made our men very mad and indignant to see this sad and homeless procession."[31]

The Federals finally made it across in an amphibious landing, but though the landing force was large enough to wrest the town from Barksdale's men, it lacked sufficient strength to affect the outcome of the day's fighting. At about 3 P.M., beneath a canopy of artillery fire, the Seventh Michigan and Nineteenth Massachusetts infantry regiments rushed to the river and entered several pontoons being used to construct the upper bridges. They frantically paddled and poled their clumsy craft across the nearly four hundred feet of water. The Seventeenth Mississippi, taken very much by surprise, fired into them and inflicted light casualties, but after a few desperate minutes, the boats ground to a halt on the Rebel bank. Bluecoats leaped from their craft, clamored up the embankment, and tumbled into Water Street, which ran parallel to the river, at the foot of Hawke Street. In the resulting confusion and fierce fighting, some thirty Confederates were captured, and the others slowly filtered back along the streets. As Rebel resistance weakened, the Twentieth Massachusetts Infantry commandeered additional boats, paddled across, and strengthened the Union foothold. The engineers, free to complete the upper bridges in relative safety, resumed work.

But Barksdale did not intend to flee. During the bombardment, he had asked Longstreet if his men should help put out the fires. Longstreet had replied, "You have enough to do to watch the Yankees." With that in mind, and understanding the need to delay the interlopers even now, Barksdale ordered his men to keep the Yankees at bay by barricading streets and alleys that ran at right angles to the river, the routes the Federals must inevitably follow. With scores of their men crowded onto Water Street, the Federals proceeded cautiously up Hawke and Fauquier, the latter being to the left of the landing site. The Confederates, concealed in buildings and crouched behind makeshift defenses, dealt them a rude greeting. It was a confusing and terrifying fight, as rifle fire echoed through the streets. "We secreted ourselves behind houses and at street corners, and woe to the 'blue coat' who showed his face," reported a Rebel private. "We killed lots of them in the back yards and out-houses."[32]

Town streets became deadly traps for the Federals as they received a merciless fire not only from the front but from the flanks and rear. Even Union onlookers east of the river perceived the brutal nature of the combat. "We

could hear our men cheering and the Rebels swearing and the soldiers falling as they were shot by the Rebels from behind the houses and fences," testified a gunner. "We were greatly afraid that the First Regiment would be
over-powered before reinforcements could reach them." By the time his
men arrived at Main (now Caroline) Street, the second thoroughfare running parallel to the river, the landing party's commander, Col. Norman J.
Hall of the Seventh Michigan, concluded that the Rebels "could only be dislodged by desperate fighting." Moreover, he insisted, "It was impracticable
to attempt to relieve the press by throwing troops into the streets, where
they could only be shot down, unable to return the fire." Hall wanted to halt
and consolidate his position, but he soon received instructions to push
ahead.[33]

In went the Twentieth Massachusetts. Ordered by Hall to clear Fauquier, the regiment likely rushed up both that street and Hawke, but at
great cost. "Platoon after platoon was swept away," reported the horrified
colonel; the regiment lost ninety-seven killed and wounded in a distance of
fifty yards. Men were "dropping at every point," observed a private of the
regiment, "those struck in the vital parts dropping without a sound, but
those wounded otherwise would cry out with pain as they fell or limped to
the rear." A sergeant reported: "The Rebs opened on us from windows and
doors and from behind the houses. We had no choice and after loosing half
of our Co[mpany] we made a rush foer the Houses[,] broke in doors and . . .
finally drove them from town." Despite its losses, the Twentieth Massachusetts "did not falter," reported Hall, and as the winter light faded, the
New Englanders secured a position on Main Street.[34]

Yet the Federals had not so much driven out the Rebels as witnessed Barksdale's timely withdrawal. It was 6 P.M. Barksdale wanted to fight on, but
he had been ordered to retire. He had bought Lee twenty-four hours, and
neither side could inflict much more damage that day. Few civilians remained in the town, which was a shambles. Miraculously, only four people
had been killed during the bombardment. Hundreds had escaped, most of
them before the Union landings. They were now safe within Confederate
lines but with the Yankees controlling their homes. "They could not return
to the town," lamented one refugee, "and they had fled too hastily to bring
with them the comforts even the necessaries of life." As one young woman
recalled: "They would not even let my mother go back into the house to get
her purse or a single valuable. So we started just as we were."[35]

Meanwhile, downriver at the lower bridges, the Federals had committed
their gravest error of the day. Construction there had not begun until some-

time after 6:30 A.M., but two of the bridges had been completed by late morning. The Eighteenth Mississippi Infantry, positioned a few hundred yards away at Deep Run, had failed in the early morning fog to observe the pontoniers. The Rebels made a belated attempt to fire into them, but their own position was too exposed, and Federal guns on the heights drove the regiment back to prepared defenses. An additional one hundred riflemen from Hood's Texas Brigade joined them to thwart any attempted advance, but the Confederates were too few to stop a crossing. Even so, Burnside failed to seize a promising opportunity. Determined to adhere to his original plan of simultaneous advances, he did not order his men across the lower bridges until late afternoon. Had he secured a bridgehead immediately and struck at the flank of Barksdale's men in Fredericksburg, the day might have ended very differently. At the very least, such a movement would have allowed the Federals to secure the town much earlier with far fewer casualties.

So began the Battle of Fredericksburg, as Southern newspapers were quick to call it. The town had been ripped apart by the bombardment and street fighting. Few houses escaped damage from the thousands of shells and hundreds of bullets that had been fired. At least two dozen buildings still burned and smoldered by nightfall, while an equal number had been reduced to rubble. Disabled wagons, discarded military accoutrements, debris from barricades, splintered fences, and tumbled chimneys littered streets and yards.[36]

Into this eerie landscape, Burnside sent additional troops to secure his prize. The remainder of Gen. Oliver O. Howard's Second Division of the II Corps, from which the original landing parties had been drawn, joined the street fighters, and Howard himself arrived to command the occupying force. Engineers completed the second of the upper bridges while the remaining men of the grand divisions prepared to cross in force early the next day. Contrary to orders, many soldiers looted vacant houses that night, as did a few scavenging civilians, who used the calamity to rob their neighbors. Shivering Rebels above the town knew nothing of this plundering. They saw and heard nothing that night, "save when falling timbers from the burning houses would crash among the embers and send up showers of sparks."[37]

Burnside had miscalculated all around. Having shown potential as a strategist by keeping Lee guessing during the previous three weeks, he suddenly became a very unimaginative tactician. In fact, he proceeded precisely as Lee had hoped—yet dared not assume—he would. He constructed his bridges, as Jefferson Davis might have put it, right in the wrong place.

Then, once committed to the crossing, he failed to anticipate the stiff Confederate resistance at the bridgeheads. He failed to provide a sufficient concentration of firepower to force quick entry into the town. He failed to follow up the successful construction of the lower bridges. His vision of a coordinated advance prohibited a victory built on incremental steps.

Finally, even with the upper and middle bridges completed, Burnside failed to deploy a significant portion of his army that night. A Union victory could be achieved only by quick action. Burnside had lost an entire day, yet he might have redeemed the situation with a vigorous attack the next morning, as Halleck suggested that he do. Instead, he seemed content to consolidate his minor gains. Barksdale had already given Lee the freedom he needed to prepare for the next Federal move. Burnside would give his opponent yet another day.

# CHAPTER THREE

# Terrible Uproar and Destruction

"The next day was rather uneventful," recorded a Confederate artillerist of December 12. And so it was. Sumner's Right Grand Division spent the entire day moving into Fredericksburg, while Franklin's Left Grand Division crossed by way of the lower bridges and assembled on the plain below Deep Run. The Confederates watched with growing fascination and delight. Lee could not believe his apparent good fortune, for if a battle were to be fought, he could not have hoped for a more advantageous position. He held the high ground; the enemy must advance across largely open terrain to engage him; the Yankees had their backs to a formidable river. At noon, Lee and Jackson rode forward to confirm Burnside's strength and intentions. Yes, it must be true, thought Lee. His only concern now was his undermanned right wing. To remedy that, he ordered the dispersed divisions of Jackson's corps to rejoin the army.[1]

In Fredericksburg, most Federal soldiers waited tensely to advance, but not a few, given an opportunity, pillaged the town. One soldier expressed disgust as he witnessed comrades breaking into deserted houses and taking what they pleased. "Everything that they could not eat or wear," he declared, "they destroyed in pure wantonness. Beautiful pictures, books, jewelry, ladies dresses, silverware, and in fact all kinds of household furniture." "There was considerable looting," admitted Gen. Darius N. Couch, in command of the II Corps. "I placed a provost-guard at the bridges, with orders that nobody should go back with plunder. An enormous pile of booty was collected there by evening. But there came a time when we were too busy to guard it, and I suppose it was finally carried off by another set of spoilers."[2]

General Patrick, the army's provost marshal, was outraged when he arrived. The town looked dismal enough, he reported, with virtually every building battered by shells, their roofs and walls filled with holes, but far worse was the behavior of the army. "The Soldiery were sacking the town!" he exclaimed in disbelief. "Every house and Store was being gutted! Men with all sorts of utensils & furniture—all sorts of eatables & drinkables & wearables, were carried off." They prized tobacco, too, and quickly stripped shops and warehouses of that valuable commodity. Patrick tried to restore discipline, but he had arrived too late to save most shops and homes. Purely malicious behavior continued through the day, as particularly ornery men smashed piano keys with musket butts, pitched crockery out of windows, and shoveled dirt into flour barrels.[3]

The looting of Fredericksburg seemed to many people but a continuation of the new Federal approach to war. Patrick thought so, and Edmund Ruffin, the irascible Virginia secessionist, submitted, "But recently, judging by effects, it would seem as if the Yankee government & military commanders had expressly authorized & ordered that the country shall be plundered & laid waste." Yet it is hard to see the sack of Fredericksburg as part of any coherent strategy or policy. Unlike Pope's calculated attempt to exhaust Rebel resources and break civilian morale the previous summer, no specific orders sanctioned the demonstration in Fredericksburg. Burnside had been very critical of the Pope policy, although increasingly lenient rules for foraging had loosened former restraints on his soldiers. "War is awful in the extreme," a Union officer had decided in November, "but if *we* can risk *life &* *limb* do not hesitate over a few paltry *chattels* of the *enemy.*" While crossing through Virginia's Northern Neck en route to Fredericksburg, one division had "swept the country pretty clean of poultry, pigs, sheep & calves . . . beef cattle & a good number of horses and mules." After troops violated the barnyards, it was but a short step to pillaging shops and homes.[4]

Historians have speculated that the rampage originated either in frustration over past military defeats or in a hatred of Southerners, especially wealthy Southerners. The first of these explanations makes sense, but the looting in Fredericksburg was indiscriminate, and there is evidence that many soldiers in the Army of the Potomac had grown contemptuous of all Rebels, not just the wealthy. Of course, some looting and destruction of property is inescapable in war. A certain amount, though lamentable, must be expected, perhaps even tolerated. Even Confederate soldiers rummaged through abandoned Fredericksburg homes before the Yankees arrived. One Federal justified it as "decorous looting." Another said the residents had "reaped their full reward for their treason." So the episode probably resulted from a combination of factors, including both frustration and an animus toward Southerners. The Union army's original conciliatory policy toward civilians was wearing thin in many parts of the South by late 1862. The influence of McClellan and Burnside may have prohibited the Army of the Potomac from embracing a policy of "hard war," but soldiers do not loot and destroy to the degree they did in Fredericksburg unless they believe the chances of being punished are slim.[5]

Many Northern newspapers at first discounted the extent of the damage. They claimed, for instance, that the destruction and looting were far less than might be expected and that the town's churches had suffered "very little," as though the artillerists and soldiers had taken special care to spare those structures. When it became apparent that something dreadfully wrong had happened in Fredericksburg, Northern correspondents gave more realistic descriptions of the damage, but they offered no criticism. Nor did they demonstrate much compassion for the hundreds of citizens encamped behind Lee's army with only blankets, sheets, and counterpanes to shelter them. "They are now paying for their treason," judged a Philadelphia newspaper, "and if they escape from the diseases incidental to camp life, they will indeed be lucky."[6]

Burnside spent the day observing Rebel positions from Stafford Heights, talking with his generals, and formulating a plan of attack. Near evening, he descended to the town from the Phillips house for a closer look at Lee. After surveying his army's right flank and discussing possible advances with Sumner, he rode the length of his line to Franklin's headquarters at Mannsfield, the elegant house of Arthur Bernard. Bernard, who claimed to be a Unionist while objecting strenuously to the presence of Yankee soldiers on his estate, had been sent under guard to Aquia Landing. Discussions with Franklin and his two corps commanders, Gens. John F. Reynolds and William F. "Baldy" Smith, must have shown Burnside that he had already wasted his best offensive options. Yet having come this far, he believed it was politically impossible to withdraw. Practically, too, it was impossible, for to withdraw in the face of the enemy's guns at this juncture would be dangerous. He was in a fine mess. A direct assault against both flanks of Lee's army, by then six miles apart, seemed the only choice, yet it was far from a happy one. To cross the broad plain between Fredericksburg and the Rebel guns on Marye's Heights would not be easy, and here on his left, he found another open plain fraught with peril. Numerous ditches and hedges provided "good covering" to the enemy while making it "difficult" for his own men to maneuver.[7]

By the time Burnside returned to his quarters, around midnight, he had decided on a plan, one that he had committed to verbally with Franklin. He had learned from a local free black man that Lee had connected his two wings by constructing a "military road" behind his defensive line. Burnside decided to use the road to destroy Lee. He would delay his attack against the Confederate left until Franklin could "stagger the enemy" on the right and gain control of the road. Franklin could then turn and roll up Lee's flank while Sumner launched an attack against Longstreet. They would crush the Rebels with brute force. But Sumner and Franklin could not place their men in motion until Burnside conveyed specific, written orders to them, and so he would spend much of the night considering those final instructions.[8]

Soldiers on both sides seemed confident. The Federals, even those who had hoped to avoid a winter campaign, felt some relief to be in motion. They had secured the town and enjoyed the satisfaction of running off its gray-clad defenders. One more day of such punishment, they reasoned, and the Rebels would surely flee to Richmond. "I shall be glad when I hear our Artillery playing against the Rebel Capital as it did against Fredericksburgh yesterday," one soldier told his family, "and I think the time is not far off when I shall have that pleasure." Across the river, on Marye's Heights, a Rebel private recorded in his diary, "Those Yanks will have to fight tomorrow, . . . and somebody will certainly get hurt."[9]

Fog again covered the river valley at 7:30 A.M. on December 13, when Franklin and Sumner finally received their orders. Alas, Burnside's instructions were as foggy as the weather. They lacked precision, and they contradicted in some ways the verbal arrangements made with Franklin on the previous night. It has been suggested that the vagueness of these orders may be attributed to Burnside's lack of sleep and utter exhaustion by this stage of the campaign. He had, in fact, been awake most of the preceding night. But Lee was doubtless weary, too, and men who command armies of one hundred thousand troops are not permitted the luxury of getting tired. It is also a matter of perception. Burnside's orders certainly did not call for the massive assault in force that Franklin had anticipated. Rather, Burnside directed him to use "a division at least . . . to seize, if possible, the height near Captain Hamilton's." A division, at least? Not at least a corps? Franklin had a right to hesitate and to wonder what Burnside was thinking, particularly when his commander added the caution to "take care to keep it [the attacking division] well supported and its line of retreat open." Then, too, Burnside failed to suggest how Franklin's movements would complement those of Sumner or how his wing should follow up its anticipated success in turning the Rebel right.

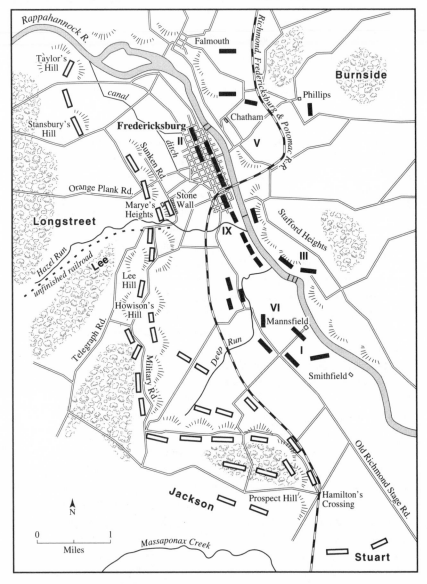

Fredericksburg, morning of December 13, 1862

Even if one ignores its lack of precision, the plan simply lacked élan; it wanted fire and the resonance of victory. It was a plan for movement, not attack. It did not inspire Franklin, who was not himself a particularly bold or imaginative officer, with confidence that Burnside had the situation well in hand. Franklin had graduated first in the West Point class of 1843, but he was more engineer than soldier. He was not likely to blunder, nor would he take chances. He needed guidance to deploy that portion of his force not involved in the initial attack, something more than to move "down the Old Richmond road," which is all the orders stipulated. He also required advice on how to attack any gaps and weak points that his anticipated success on Lee's flank would produce along the interior of the Rebel line, but Burnside said naught about that.[10]

The day began innocently enough. "Everything is quiet along our lines this morning," considered a South Carolinian. "I do not believe that we will have a general engagement today." Still, by 7:40 A.M., as men on both sides of the river drank coffee and munched crackers, Franklin ordered Gen. George G. Meade, Reynolds's most experienced division commander, to prepare to advance. Gen. John Gibbon would protect Meade's right flank, while Gen. Abner Doubleday covered his left. Indeed, events would soon dictate that Doubleday, with his own left flank anchored on the Rappahannock, necessarily protect the left of the entire army. Baldy Smith's VI Corps stood in reserve to cover the line of retreat across the critical pontoon bridges. By 9 A.M., Meade's Third Division, the smallest one in Franklin's grand division, had formed two attacking columns three hundred yards apart. With his veteran Pennsylvania Reserves ready to step forward, Meade's skirmishers engaged Rebel pickets.[11]

It was that "serious time," as one Rebel soldier called it, the prelude to battle: "The skirmish lines are popping away at each other . . . the troops moving in that silent, solemn way. . . . As time passes, suspense deepens with dread you cannot express. Is it dreading the consequences, or is it fear?" For a Texan, the fighting commenced with a punctuation mark: "The hiss and shriek of passing shot; the stunning noise of bursting shells; the deadly menace of whistling fragments, told us as they only can, that the battle was on."[12]

Lee, observing the scene atop ninety-foot Telegraph Hill, soon to be known as Lee Hill, relaxed with Longstreet and Jackson, the latter general resplendent in a new, gold-braided uniform presented to him by Jeb Stuart. Lee had remained uncertain until this moment about Burnside's intentions. It still seemed impossible to Lee that the Federals had not crossed farther downriver, around Port Royal. That is what he would have done. Not even the crossing on December 11 entirely convinced Lee that Burnside would dare throw his entire force into the jaws of the Army of Northern Virginia. Federal movements on December 12 had increased his confidence, but not until he saw the enemy massing to attack could Lee believe he had guessed right. He had offered little resistance to the December 12 crossings because he wanted Burnside on his side of the river. He wanted the Federals to attack him there. Burnside still did not realize that, unlike one of his privates. "They want us to get in," predicted the soldier. "Getting out won't be quite so smart and easy. You'll see if it will."[13]

Jackson's thirty thousand infantry, spread over nearly a mile-and-a-half front between Deep Run and Hamilton's Crossing, held Lee's right. Powell Hill's division, arranged in two lines above the railroad, formed the front ranks, but not as a solid wall. With his pickets stationed along the railroad embankment, which ran about one and a quarter miles from the river, Hill placed two brigades on either side of a six-hundred-yard stretch of marshy land, thick with undergrowth, which he deemed impenetrable. His two other brigades—Gen. Maxcy Gregg's South Carolinians and Gen. Edward L. Thomas's Georgians—sat astride the vital military road on a low, heavily forested ridge above the railroad. Thomas deployed to the left, behind the brigades of William D. Pender and James H. Lane, while Gregg sat directly above the swampy terrain eight hundred yards from Prospect Hill, which capped the ridge on his right. Generals Taliaferro and Early, the latter still commanding Ewell's division while Old Baldy recovered from the loss of a leg at Second Manassas, formed behind Hill. Taliaferro's division defended the left, Early's men the right. D. H. Hill, Jackson's brother-in-law, formed a reserve behind Early. Jackson had created a formidable defense nearly a mile deep.[14]

And that was not all, for Jackson also had thirty-five guns, commanded by his chief of artillery, Col. Stapleton Crutchfield. Crutchfield divided the guns—all light artillery—into three groups. The largest group—fourteen guns—looked down from Prospect Hill. Nine guns sat on Powell Hill's left, between his first and second lines, and twelve more guns, also on the left, sat just beyond the railroad tracks in advance of Hill's lines. Jackson also had at his disposal the guns of Stuart's horse artillery, perched on his right flank. Neither the infantry nor the batteries were well entrenched, partly because of the frozen earth and partly for a lack of entrenching tools.

Confederate artillery gained from being flexible, too. Lee had reorganized his "long arm" the previous fall, and Fredericksburg would be the first test of the new system. Following Antietam, Lee had committed himself to a "battalion system" to provide more flexibility in placing his artillery. Although his batteries remained assigned to divisions—essentially as artillery brigades—he ignored those division assignments at Fredericksburg in order to place the guns to best tactical advantage, "systematically massed for battle," as one artillerist put it. Thus Jackson's batteries could be divided into three groups. In addition, the batteries would be directed by "chiefs of artillery"—Gen. William N. Pendleton, assisted by Crutchfield—rather than by the infantry commanders.[15]

Lee's seven thousand cavalrymen, led by the flamboyant Stuart, were also prepared to play an active role in the contest, far more active than the Union cavalry could hope to play. Stuart had placed two brigades between Hamilton's Crossing and Massaponax Creek, a plain nearly a mile and a half wide, to shield Jackson's right flank. Their presence occupied Doubleday's attention throughout the day and thus tied down a sizable chunk of the Union attacking force. In contrast, Burnside failed to use his cavalry in any effective manner. At no time after his arrival at Fredericksburg did the Federal commander instruct his horsemen to mount a reconnaissance on the Rebel side of the river, and they engaged in no combat. This failure was not Burnside's alone, for Federal cavalry doctrine lacked the sophistication of Confederate doctrine at this stage of the war. The consequence, however, was to limit further Burnside's tactical options.[16]

Stuart's horse artillery, led by Alabama-born and West Point–trained Maj. John Pelham, drew first blood. As Meade's Pennsylvanians paused in their advance at the Old Richmond Road, waiting for their own artillery to be positioned, Pelham received permission to rush forward a twelve-pounder Napoleon. He placed it near the junction of the Richmond Road and the road leading up from Hamilton's Crossing, a mere four hundred yards from the unsuspecting infantrymen's left flank. At about 10 A.M., with the morning fog and uneven terrain masking his gunners, Pelham delivered two rounds into the Union lines before the startled Yankees could respond. Meade's men hugged the ground as round after round came whistling into their ranks. A second gun, a rifled Blakley, was sent forward to assist Pelham, but it was hit almost immediately as five Federal batteries responded to the threat. Overwhelmed by the weight of the Federal fire, Pelham's men slowly fell back, but they had stopped the advance of forty-five hundred infantrymen for perhaps a half hour. In a dispatch the next day, Lee immortalized the Alabamian as "the gallant Pelham."[17]

Seeing the contest begin in earnest, Reynolds ordered Meade to resume the attack. His objective was the crest of the ridge behind the marshy ground left uncovered by Powell Hill. A Federal artillery bombardment accompanied the advance, but Jackson forbade his gunners to reply. Consequently, the Federals fired blindly into Rebel positions, inflicting some casualties but, because Confederate gunners refused to betray themselves, unable to focus on the artillery. For all that, the Union advance was an impressive spectacle. "I could see fully half the whole Yankee army, reserves and all," reported a duly impressed South Carolinian. "It was a grand sight seeing them come in position."[18]

The Union cannonading stopped abruptly after about thirty minutes; shortly after that, as Meade's line came to within eight hundred yards of Confederate gunners on the ridge, Rebel batteries blazed away. They knew the range precisely, for during the previous day of preparation—the day Burnside failed to attack—the artillerists had measured the ground in their front and selected convenient landmarks by which to judge distances. At the same time, Pelham's fifteen guns opened from the Confederate right to create a lethal crossfire. Momentarily stunned, Meade's men retreated but did not break. "They advanced bravely," acknowledged a member of the Richmond Howitzers. Yet "from the time they first advanced we could see their wounded & stragglers falling back till they reached the river. Everything was in full view of us . . . and the scene was terribly exciting."[19]

Union gunners resumed firing, and the resulting artillery duel literally shook the ground. The well-positioned Rebel gunners poured a "paralyzing enfilading fire into the huddled ranks of Union infantry," although the heavier Federal guns, with their longer range, pummeled the Confederates. One Rebel gunner called it "the hottest fight I have ever heard of." The Confederates got the worst of it. One gun after another was knocked out of action—eleven in all—so that a steady line of replacements flowed from their artillery park behind Forest Hill, the home of Jane Hamilton and her sisters. Several times during the fight, shells landed directly on ammunition chests to produce impressive explosions and fireballs. So many artillery animals fell on Prospect Hill that it became known as "Dead Horse Hill."[20]

At about 1 P.M., with a lull in the cannonading, Meade resumed his advance. He had been moving among his regiments, talking to scared, mud-encrusted men and trying to maintain their spirits all through the nerve-wracking duel. Now the blue lines surged forward in what one Pennsylvanian called "the most gallant charge of the war." Rebel infantry held their fire as the Federals navigated the deceivingly difficult "open" fields, which were, in fact, bisected by no fewer than three deep ditches. The Yankees had hoped to halt and rest, hidden from enemy fire, at the railroad grade. Unknown to them, the Confederates had already deployed behind this natural breastwork. As the Federals came within range, the Rebels—mostly Georgians and Tennesseans—cut down the Bucktails "like hay before the mower's blast."[21]

Gen. C. Feger Jackson's brigade received the brunt of the fire, and Jackson himself was quickly felled when a bullet shattered his skull. The brigades of Col. William Sinclair and Col. Albert L. Magilton, on Jackson's right, were luckier. Having slammed into the railroad in front of the boggy woods that divided Hill's line, they encountered less resistance from Rebel skirmishers, although the fire on their flanks remained intense. They plunged into the woods, only to become further scattered and disorganized by the undergrowth. Some regiments veered to the right, others to the left. Both brigade commanders were soon downed, Sinclair with a mangled left foot, Magilton trapped beneath his dying horse. Their men continued to slog forward through mud and muck, for the suddenly balmy day, with the temperature approaching sixty degrees, had turned the woods into a swamp. Still the Federals pushed on until two of Sinclair's regiments, the First and Sixth Pennsylvania Reserves, reached the crest of the ridge.

Maxcy Gregg's brigade, assigned to defend the sector, never had a chance. The South Carolinians had been lying prone to endure the Federal bombardment. Their arms were stacked, and they remained blissfully unaware of the steadily approaching threat. Suddenly, the Pennsylvanians stormed out of the woods and swarmed over their right flank. The slightly deaf Gregg did not immediately appreciate the situation. Indeed, as his men hastily grabbed arms to return fire, he cursed them and ordered them to stop, certain that they must be firing into retreating Rebel skirmishers. Too late Gregg realized the truth, as a Yankee ball severed his spine and he tumbled from his saddle mortally wounded. Hand-to-hand fighting ensued until the outnumbered Carolinians were "broken, slaughtered and swept from the field." Almost by accident and certainly with a healthy measure of luck, Meade's men had taken the military road and split Lee's army. At the same time, other scattered Pennsylvania regiments turned to strike Jackson's now exposed right flank, the source of the enfilading fire that had made their advance such a perilous undertaking. As they pounced on the surprised Nineteenth Georgia and Fourteenth Tennessee, Prospect Hill seemed to be securely in Federal hands.[22]

While Meade's men enjoyed their successes and rummaged through abandoned Rebel equipment and knapsacks, John Gibbon's Second Division, advancing belatedly on Meade's right, extended the Federal break-through. Meade, Reynolds, or someone had failed to coordinate the advance of the two divisions so that while the Pennsylvanians broke toward the railroad and filtered through the woods, Gibbon's men—mostly New Yorkers and Pennsylvanians but with a few New Englanders—lagged slightly behind to exchange deadly volleys with the North Carolinians of James Lane's brigade. When the Tar Heels ran out of ammunition, Gibbon's larger force breached their line. Men grappled in "savage," primitive combat, many muskets converted to clubs. Gibbon's bluecoats, who had also charged with fixed bayonets, gobbled up two hundred prisoners while propelling the remaining Rebels backward.[23]

But then the attackers faltered. Their amazing rush had exhausted the men, badly extended their lines, and scattered their forces. A series of Confederate counterattacks would deny Reynolds his victory. Jubal Early, demonstrating a good deal of initiative, ordered his men to push Meade off the ridge. No sooner had a message from Stonewall Jackson directed Early to prepare his men to move toward Hamilton's Crossing, on the extreme right, than Old Jubal learned that "heavy columns of the enemy" had penetrated "an awful gulf" on his front. He hesitated only a moment before committing first one, then another, and finally a third of his four brigades to push back Meade and Gibbon. The fighting was intense for twenty minutes, but then the exhausted Federals slowly gave ground. When Gibbon retired with a wounded hand, his brigades lacked coordination, and these Federals, too, were soon reeling backward. Among the regiments to strike Gibbon was the Thirteenth Virginia Infantry. "We plunged through the marshes and brush-wood, for a mile," reported one elated Virginian, "and with a terrific yell . . . we fell upon the Enemy, drove them from the woods and trenches [the railroad grade] with great slaughter."[24]

David Birney's reserve division, from the Center Grand Division, now entered the fray. Birney, a son of Alabama slave owner turned abolitionist James G. Birney, had moved up from across the river nearly three hours earlier. His tardy appearance on the field caused Meade to rail and curse, but his division served to cover Meade's retreat and halt a potentially disastrous Rebel pursuit. Birney's men also endured some of the most intense fighting of the day. In a sector dubbed the "Slaughter Pen," midway between the railroad and the Old Richmond Road, they jolted the oncoming Georgians of Gen. Alexander R. Lawton's brigade, commanded by Col. Edmund N. Atkinson. Artillerists and infantry blazed away amid thick, choking gun-smoke, with "nothing . . . to be seen but smoke and dirt flying from cannon balls, ploughing up the ground . . . and dead and wounded men and horses."[25]

The rest of Franklin's grand division saw little if any combat on the day. Baldy Smith's VI Corps, the largest corps in the army, never advanced, although its skirmishers and artillerists were engaged. The same could be said of Doubleday's division. Other reserves brought from across the river or regiments on the extreme left flank of Sumner's grand division, who could see and hear the fighting, sat impatiently all day, awaiting their chance for action. "Our men were crazy," reported a member of the Second Michigan Infantry. "At every fresh outburst they would spring from the ground & rush 'en masse' to their arms which were stacked in line, stand there for a few minutes waiting for an order to advance or do something. No orders coming they would gradually fall back & lie down again."[26]

Thaddeus S. C. Lowe, the aeronaut whose observation balloon *Eagle* had gained a sensational reputation during the Peninsula campaign, served as Burnside's eyes for the fighting on the left. The heavily wooded terrain occupied by the Confederates limited Lowe's ability to report on Rebel dispositions, but he kept Burnside fairly well informed about Union movements. The general then communicated with his field commanders by means of signal flags, telegraph, and handwritten messages. Shortly after 2 P.M., Burnside sped a courier to Franklin with orders for a general advance toward his right and front. Franklin returned word that such an advance was impossible. Meade's troops by that time were falling back, and Gibbon's men were barely holding their own. Receiving this unexpected response, Burnside exclaimed in exasperation, "But he must advance," and dispatched a second courier with a more emphatic directive for Franklin "to make a vigorous attack with his whole force." Again, the grand division commander declined, claiming that he was already "engaged" with the enemy.[27]

By then, it was 2:30 P.M., and while the sounds of battle waned on the plain below Prospect Hill, they escalated upriver, at Fredericksburg. Sumner's grand division was to have held its position, which extended from Deep Run through the town of Fredericksburg, until Franklin had gained control of the military road. His initial orders, like those to Franklin, came only at 7:30 A.M., although Sumner, unlike Franklin, thought his instructions clear: when ordered forward, he was to storm Marye's Heights. But by II A.M., knowing that Franklin's men had not yet seriously engaged Jackson, Burnside felt "the importance of haste." He remained hopeful that his Left Grand Division might yet seize Prospect Hill, but he also seems to have decided that a move by Sumner could reduce the resistance against Franklin's men. At the start of the day, he had intended to use his left wing to fix the enemy and so draw reserves from the Confederate left. Now he seemingly hoped that aggressive action by his right wing might benefit the left. Abandoning—if not actally reversing—his original battle plan, Burnside ordered Sumner to attack Marye's Heights with one division "supported closely by a second." Sumner had already selected General Couch's II Corps to make the anticipated assault. Couch, from his headquarters in the Fredericksburg courthouse, chose Gen. William H. French's division to lead the attack, to be supported by the division of Gen. Winfield Scott Hancock.[28]

Once again, the Confederates found it hard to believe their good fortune. As thick blue columns funneled out of the town, while more men crossed the pontoons and drew up to bolster the point of attack, it appeared that fully half of Burnside's army was poised to strike Lee's left wing. What amazed the Rebels most was that the Yankees did not attempt to outflank Lee by crossing upriver. Rather, just as they waived the opportunity to cross below Hamilton's Crossing, the Federals seemed determined to strike at the strongest part of the Confederate line. If the Rebels could not "whip" the Yankees under these conditions, they "couln't whip anything," swore a gray-clad artillerist, "& had better give up the war. . . . From that moment," he declared, "I felt the elation of a certain & easy victory, & my only care then was to get into it somehow & help do the enemy all the harm I could."[29]

Longstreet had positioned his five divisions expertly. Gen. Richard H. Anderson's division, overlooking and extending a mile beyond the northern edge of the town, anchored the left flank on fifty-foot-high Taylor's Hill, opposite Falmouth. Gen. John Bell Hood's men held the right flank, where they merged with Jackson's left across the valley of Deep Run. Lafayette McLaws's men sat forty feet above the town on Marye's Heights and in strongly fortified positions at its base, while Gen. George E. Pickett straddled the ridge above Hood. Most of Robert Ransom Jr.'s division stood in reserve on Marye's Heights. The most notable feature of these defenses was a four-hundred-yard-long breast-high stone retaining wall that ran along Telegraph Road at the base of Marye's Heights from Hanover Street to within four hundred yards of Hazel Run.

When French's men stepped out of the shadows of Fredericksburg at about noon, they found themselves exposed on a broad, nearly unobstructed plain. The only serious obstacle was a canal drainage ditch, or millrace, that cut directly across their line of march. The ditch, running from the canal north of town to Hazel Run, was fifteen feet wide and five feet deep. Normally, it could be crossed by one of three bridges at the ends of Hanover, Prussia, and William Streets. But all three bridges had been destroyed by the Confederates so that the Federals either had to balance themselves as they advanced over planks laid at the bridge sites or wade through the canal in hip-deep icy water.

Once across, a low bluff, created by the depression through which the millrace flowed, afforded some protection. This bluff bisected the plain about three hundred yards from the edge of town. From there, the ground swept gradually upward to the base of the heights, some four hundred yards distant. One other bit of natural protection came just one hundred yards from the Rebel lines, a slight depression in the earth where a man lying prone might avoid death. A few scattered houses and fences obstructed and threatened the integrity of the Union battle line, but these were not significant either for defense or as impediments. Advancing Federals did have to pause to rip down whatever fences they encountered. Yet the critical element, as it had been throughout the campaign, would be swift movement: Union soldiers must deploy and advance before they came under Rebel fire.

But no sooner had French's men stepped forward than Longstreet's artillery began to shell the edge of town, some six to eight hundred yards away. Federal guns on Stafford Heights returned the fire, but as the infantry advanced, Yankee artillerists had to be cautious lest short rounds should strike their own men. Consequently, Rebel gunners dominated the plain from Marye's Heights. They even prevented Federal field batteries from venturing too far onto the field. On the Federal right, Confederate artillery on Stansbury's and Cemetery Hills poured death into the Union infantry, while on the left, light artillery and two huge 4,200-pound Parrott rifled guns hurled twenty-nine-pound projectiles from Howison's and Lee Hills. In the opinion of Col. Edward Porter Alexander, commanding Longstreet's reserve artillery, "A chicken could not live on that field when we open on it."[30]

The first exchange of musketry erupted when Federal sharpshooters moved forward to clear Confederate pickets from the line of advance. A few Yankee marksmen even advanced far enough to plague Rebel gunners from sniper posts in houses at the junction of Hanover Street and Telegraph Road. French's three infantry brigades, moving forward one at a time, did not encounter massed Confederate musketry until they passed over the bluff, four hundred yards from their objective. The impact, when it came, ripped open their front, and the farther they advanced, the more intense became the enfilading fire from both infantry and artillery on their flanks. Their courageous efforts carried the Federals no closer to the stone wall than the depression that stretched a hundred yards in front of it. "The shot shells and Rifle balls flew around like hail," claimed one of French's company commanders; "their was no use to dodge the little ones for you was just as likely to run your head in front of one as to get away. . . . near the front lines you could not step without stepping on the men."[31]

Hancock's division joined the assault at about 12:30 P.M. but only added to the death toll. "It seemed a terrible long distance," reported a member of the lead brigade, "as with bated breath and heads bowed down, we hurried forward, the rebel guns plowing great furrows in our ranks at every step; all we could do was close up the gaps and press forward." A heroic surge by the brigade of Col. Samuel K. Zook carried to within fifty yards of the wall, but slowly, inevitably, this high tide receded to the blessed safety of the shallow swale. There the remains of six brigades, representing six separate assault waves and stretching nearly six hundred yards across the plain, lay prone. They returned the deadly fire as best they could, but with their ranks decimated, many of their officers dead or wounded, and their units jumbled and intermingled, two Federal divisions had been neutralized.[32]

Most of the carnage was inflicted by a brigade of Georgians, led by Gen. Thomas R. R. Cobb, and a North Carolina regiment at the base of Marye's Heights. As the purpose of the Federal assault became clear, Lee, who watched the slaughter from atop Telegraph Hill, turned to Longstreet and asked if the mounting numbers of attackers might not overwhelm the defenders at the wall. Longstreet, supremely confident of his defensive preparations, replied, "If you put every man now on the other side of Potomac on the field to approach me over the same line, and give me plenty of ammunition, I will kill them all before they reach my line." Still, as a precautionary measure, Longstreet sent Gen. Joseph B. Kershaw's brigade of South Carolinians to join the Georgians. By then, three more North Carolina regiments—like the first, members of Ransom's Tar Heel division—had been thrown into the road with Cobb's brigade. The reinforcements allowed the Confederates to place their men four lines deep behind the wall so that as rapidly as one line discharged its rifles, the next line stepped forward to deliver a volley. It proved to be one of the most concentrated and continuous volumes of rifle fire witnessed during the war.[33]

Perhaps the sternest test the Confederates faced came from the Irish Brigade of Gen. Thomas F. Meagher, which followed Zook's men into the rush for the wall. All but one of Meagher's regiments having arrived on the field without their distinctive emerald-green battle flags (the flags had been shredded in previous engagements and sent home to be exchanged for new ones), he instructed his sons of Erin to declare their heritage by attaching pieces of evergreen to their caps. "We all looked gay and felt in high spirits," maintained a New York private. An observer remarked, "Every man has a sprig of green in his cap and a half-laughing, half-murderous look in his eyes." These regiments had already gained laurels in the Seven Days and at Second Manassas. Originally composed of New Yorkers, the brigade now included regiments from Massachusetts and Pennsylvania. Only the Twenty-eighth Massachusetts could be identified by its regimental banner—adorned with harp, sunburst, and shamrock—as the brigade charged up the slope.[34]

As the Irish Federals drew near the point of advance reached by Zook, one of Cobb's Celts recognized the significance of the green sprigs and supposedly called out, "Oh, God, what a pity! Here comes Meagher's fellows!" A pity, indeed, for with the cause of the Confederacy binding them more surely than ties to the old sod, the Rebels cut down nearly half of their kinsmen. "Fall back men, and every man for himself," called out a Union officer as volley after volley shredded the lines. Within minutes the battered brigade "fled in the greatest confusion." A Mississippi defender reported matter-of-factly, "We almost anihilated general Megearks Ireish Brigade." Viewed from the Federal heights across the river, where every advance could be seen as clearly as the moves on a giant chess board, it looked worse than a slaughter; it was "hopeless slaughter."[35]

Meantime, the extreme right of the Rebels' stone wall defense repulsed an assault by a portion of the IX Corps. Gen. Orlando B. Willcox held the center of the Union line stretched between Hazel Run and Deep Run. He thus formed a link between Sumner's and Franklin's grand divisions, much as Hood joined the two wings of Lee's army. Two of Willcox's divisions had been ordered to Fredericksburg as reserves, and the first one, under Gen. Samuel D. Sturgis, crossed Hazel Run just as French began his advance. At 12:30 P.M., the same time that Hancock's men moved out to support French, Sturgis sent forward two of his brigades against the Rebel right. Gen. Edward Ferrero's five regiments attacked first, followed by six more regiments under Gen. James Nagle. Both attacks sputtered to a halt two hundred yards from the wall.

At 1 P.M., after a single furious hour of combat, three Union divisions— or what remained of them—were pinned down. Perhaps understanding the futility, not to mention the danger, of retreat, General Couch ordered French and Hancock to storm the wall in one grand rush. When both generals beseeched Couch not to attempt such a tactic, he spared their men but committed a fresh division. General Howard had been protecting the northern edge of Fredericksburg and the Federal right flank when he received orders to send out his lead brigade. It was the seventh of Couch's brigades to advance that day, but nothing had changed, except, perhaps, that the volume of Confederate fire had increased. When a second of Howard's brigades reluctantly followed the first, hundreds more blue-clad bodies soon littered the ground. More than four thousand dead and wounded now covered Couch's ghastly portion of the field. Scores of wounded men, either singly or in small groups, limped back toward town. "There was no cheering on the part of the men," reported Couch, "but a stubborn determination to obey orders and do their duty." Concluded the Mexican War veteran, "I had never before seen fighting like that, nothing approaching it in terrible uproar and destruction."[36]

But Burnside would not quit. He ordered the remainder of Hooker's grand division to cross the river, and by 2 P.M., a portion of Gen. Daniel Butterfield's V Corps prepared to advance from the southern edge of town. Hooker twice asked Burnside to call off the proposed attack, once through a courier, the second time through a personal appeal. Burnside could not be dissuaded. Next, in an effort to provide Butterfield's men with close artillery support, Hooker and Couch ordered ten twelve-pounders rushed to within 150 yards of the stone wall. By 3:30 P.M., the gunners were blasting Confederate defenses with effect, but, being within easy range of the Rebel batteries, they suffered too. Gen. Charles Griffin could wait no longer. Hoping to take advantage of whatever covering fire the artillerists could provide, he signaled his division forward.

Griffin proceeded cautiously, sending out just one brigade, but toward dusk—about 4:30 P.M.—he received orders to throw his entire division into the contest. The results were predictable. The line advanced, reported a New Englander, "half crouching as it ran, and moving *sideways*, as though breasting a 'blizzard' or a wind and hail-storm." Griffin's men encountered "such a withering fire" that they, too, inevitably recoiled, broke, and fell back behind the sheltering embankment. One of the attackers had a leg ripped from his body by a round of shot. As he fell, the soldier's neck came to rest grotesquely on the shattered limb. Ignoring his condition and still possessing a wealth of gumption, he raised up on an elbow, "waved his hat and cheered for the old flag" before collapsing dead. It was a gesture symbolic of the Union army's valiant yet futile efforts on that day.[37]

Gen. Andrew A. Humphreys's division, also of the V Corps, came next. Humphreys's men, all new recruits from Pennsylvania, had never tasted battle.

As they advanced, the besieged remnants of earlier attacks yelled at them to take cover or turn back. Some well-intentioned men even tried to trip or pull the green troops to the ground. Humphreys's steadfast band pushed ahead, at some points approaching to within twenty-five yards of the wall. "With a yell we rushed up the hill," one man reported, "when whiz-z-z, whist, came shot, shell and bullets. . . . The thought of momentary death rushed upon me as the work of carnage began, and it required every exertion to hush the unbidden fears of my mind. The dead tumbled around me, and the groans of the wounded made me heartsick." Humphreys reported: "The fire of the enemy's guns musketry and artillery, furious as it was before, now became still hotter. The stone wall was a sheet of flame that enveloped the head and flanks of the column. Officers and men were falling rapidly." The Federals tried to return fire but, after a minute, slowly turned and retired.[38]

Hooker saved Butterfield's third division from being sacrificed. Gen. George Sykes's despondent troops, mostly U.S. Regulars, had advanced but a short distance from the town when Hooker took it upon himself to suspend the attack. Enraged by Burnside's stubborn refusal to stop the carnage, Fighting Joe explained curtly, "I had lost as many men as my orders required me to lose." The Regulars, who had already come under fire, had seen enough of what lay ahead to appreciate their blessing. Even the outskirts of Fredericksburg, where they had awaited their fate, was littered with abandoned knapsacks, blankets, weapons, and every kind of accoutrement, the ground "slippery with ooze, blood, and trampled earth, and sprinkled with dead, dying, and wounded men."[39]

To the left of the Regulars, Gen. George W. Getty's division of the IX Corps was not so lucky. Getty received orders to attack at about 5 P.M., when the day was turning dark. "We went double quick for about a mile," reported a New Hampshire soldier caught in the thick of things, "over fences & ditches through brooks & mud holes & about every thing else, then we charged up over a hill double quick down on the other side." Ironically, the darkness, which partially obscured Union movements, allowed the day's final assault to carry nearly to the Rebel lines. "If they had not started with a cheer I don't think that I, at least, would have known they were coming," admitted a Rebel artillerist, "for I could not see them, but only— when they began to fire—the flashes of their muskets. . . . We had almost ceased to fire for lack of a good target, when this disturbance began, & I ordered them to fire canister at the gun flashes." The Rebels prevailed. General Ransom, commanding this portion of Longstreet's defenses, reported,

"This last desperate and murderous attack met the same fate which had befallen those which preceded, and his hosts were sent, actually howling, back to their beaten comrades in the town."[40]

By then, the agonies of the wounded and dying echoed harshly across the landscape. The heartrending chorus of "groans, curses, prayers all mingled together," punctuated here and there by the "hideous, unhuman sounds" of crippled horses, could "almost deafen a person." Of the nearly thirty thousand Federals who had advanced from Fredericksburg, nearly seven thousand had fallen. Longstreet reported slightly over sixteen hundred dead or wounded, although among his dead was the stalwart Georgian Thomas Cobb. One Union surgeon insisted that the majority of wounded men in his division were carried from the battlefield within an hour of having fallen, but another doctor protested that he had been forced to abandon some of the wounded—on the slope below the stone wall—when the Rebels shot several stretcher bearers. Whatever the number remaining on the field, they left an indelible impression on survivors. "Oh how pitiful . . . to hear the wounded soldiers moan and cry for water and help," lamented a Pennsylvanian. "Several nearest us were in the last agonies of death," reported a New Englander, "exhausted, bleeding, dying by inches."[41]

Fredericksburg became a vast hospital. Virtually every unoccupied building—homes, shops, churches, and warehouses—overflowed with the dead and dying. One horrified woman whose home served the surgeons' needs reported that "every vessel in the house (even the vegetable dishes and cups) . . . [was] filled with blood and water." Large pots of gore sat on the floor, and her parlor became an operating room. Still, most surgeons could do little but wrap wounds and try to keep men warm and dry. Although supplied with ample medicine, fuel, water, and food, they attempted few amputations or major surgeries. Those who did operated in near darkness, fearful that lights would tempt Rebel gunners to inflict further damage. It was a "horrible night," confessed one doctor, with all engulfed by "groans and cries of agony." Clara Barton, who had been working among the sick men at Falmouth and the Phillips and Lacy houses for a week past, entered the town to help bathe and bandage wounds. She comforted no fewer than fifty bleeding, half-frozen men on that night.[42]

Elsewhere, irreverence intertwined incongruously with frantic efforts to save men's lives. "No one could better understand what actual war was than by traversing the alleys and byways of this almost destroyed city," decided one Federal soldier. While their comrades died by the dozens in "shell-shattered, bullet-ridden" buildings that a few days earlier might have reminded them of their own hometowns, many Union troops held "carnival." Supper fires crackled, music from fractured fiddles filled the evening air, as men danced, laughed, played cards, and swapped stories. *"All* were engaged in some kind of occupation," reported a soldier, "which . . . presented the strangest, most novel mixture of grim-visaged war and his strange satellites."[43]

No one laughed that night on the battlefield, where Union officers pulled back as many men as possible from in front of the stone wall. Sykes's division moved up to fill most of the resulting gaps. "That night was bitter cold and a fearful one for the front line hugging the hallows in the ground, and for the wounded who could not be reached," recalled General Couch. "It was a night of dreadful suffering. Many died of wounds and exposure, and as fast as men died they stiffened in the wintry air." Typical of many morbid scenes, one lieutenant approached a figure lying motionless in the dark. "I laid my hand where his breast should have been, intending to arouse him," reported the young officer, "but my *hand went through.* . . . The whole of his breast had been torn away."[44]

On the Federal left, surgeons evacuated the wounded to hospital tents— two per regiment—in addition to using Southern homes. A hint of urgency speeded the process when soldiers on both sides rushed to beat out several grass fires and rescue comrades from the smoke and flames. Although some disabled men perished "amid agonizing screams," the evacuation generally went well. The Federals were especially efficient, with each Union regiment assigned three ambulances and each ambulance assigned two stretchers. "Almost at the first [gun] fire, cooking commenced at the hospitals," reported a Yankee surgeon, "and the wounded, as quickly as brought in, were, if necessary, supplied with hot soup and coffee." Again, surgeons performed amputations and excisions only to preserve life, but even so, one chaplain reported seeing "a ghastly pile of arms and legs" outside the Bernard house. Nor did proximity to the hospitals necessarily spare a man. Late in the afternoon, Gen. George D. Bayard, commanding Franklin's cavalry brigade, had a hip smashed by an artillery shell as he stood in Bernard's yard. He died hours later.[45]

Stonewall Jackson wanted to kill more Yankees, and he finished the day with two failed attempts to mount counterattacks. As Rebels and Yankees jockeyed for more secure positions along Deep Run in late afternoon, Jackson tried to provoke the Federals into a new assault by ordering his artillery to open on the Union center. That was a mistake, as Federal guns again displayed their superior numbers and range by driving back the Rebel batteries. Next, Jackson and Stuart planned a daring night attack against the Federal left flank. A preattack artillery barrage was in full swing by 5 P.M., and it was potent. Some Federal infantry thought it the worst barrage of the day. "The cannon balls, shell, and canister was terrific," reported a Wisconsin sergeant. "Men that have been through all the battles in our regt, broke and ran. . . . It was the first time I ever heard men cry out with so much anguish and horror—horror does not express it—terror comes nearer to it." But the component parts of Jackson's command were so scattered, worn out, and disorganized that only two-thirds of his force learned of the impending attack; only half had sufficient time to prepare for battle. As the Federal guns responded once more to Jackson's batteries, Stonewall decided that an assault would be suicidal. Jubal Early recalled, "There was not a man in the force who did not breathe freer when he heard the orders countermanding the movement."[46]

As December 13 sputtered to a close, sporadic rifle and cannon fire continued, with bright bursts of flame punctuating the entire length of the battle line. "It was a magnificent sight after twilight," one Federal admitted, "if it were not for the knowledge that those lightening flashes were sending many a brave fellow to his last home. . . . The Battle is still going on in the darkness but the sounds are slowly dying away." A Michigan infantryman summarized the day's struggle: "The left was a scene of severe fighting, the right one of great slaughter."[47]

# CHAPTER FOUR

# Not a Pleasant Topic

Bickering and recriminations rocked Federal camps as December 13 drew to a close. "My God General Reynolds," exploded the excitable George Meade as his men scrambled for the safety of their lines, "did you think my division could whip Lee's entire army?" It was Second Manassas all over again, he spat, with piecemeal attacks accomplishing nothing. General Humphreys expressed equal bitterness over the way his men had been interfered with as they tried to move forward. He believed they could have carried that damned wall if their advance had not been retarded—sometimes with physical force—by other Union troops. General French cried out as he came to realize the enormous number of casualties suffered in the futile advance: "Adjutant, where is my division? Tell me where my men are. My God, I am without a command!"[1]

Burnside's men may have been whipped, and he may have been "dead with sleep," but the commanding general refused to admit defeat. Even as he assembled his commanders and listened to their gloomy reports of setbacks on every side, Burnside would not consider retreat. Instead, he announced to the startled group that he would personally lead a renewed attack the next morning at the head of his loyal IX Corps. All present argued against the brave but foolhardy plan, yet Burnside, either from obstinacy or ignorance, remained adamant.[2]

Lee returned to his headquarters shortly after dark. He had seldom experienced such elation in battle. The victory had been complete in every respect. "It is well that war is so terrible," he reportedly remarked at the height of the fighting; "we should grow too fond of it!" He had reason to be pleased, for Fredericksburg, as one of his artillerists boasted, was the "simplest and easiest won battle of the war." More than that, Lee's instincts told him that Burnside, having committed himself so far, would surely attack again the next morning. That suited him. His army held every advantage of terrain, and Lee saw no reason to assume the offense at this stage of the game. He ordered his men to form breastworks and entrench themselves in anticipation of a hard fight.[3]

The morning of December 14 began tensely along Rebel lines. Confederate soldiers on the heights could see enemy positions clearly on both sides of the river. On the Federal left, a swirl of activity around the Bernard house—still serving as Franklin's headquarters—made it seem as though the Yankees, as Lee expected, would launch another massed infantry attack. The Army of Northern Virginia waited in "fine spirits," "confident of success," yet with that unavoidable gnawing pang of uncertainty as to when and in what force the enemy would strike. "There is an awful pause to day," confessed a member of the Eighth Virginia Infantry, "its meaning we can not ascertain. The movement of the enemy seems very cautious and slow. I can not imagine their policy or design. I can not repress a considerable amount of anxiety."[4]

"Anxious" hardly describes the emotions of Federals trapped on the Fredericksburg battlefield. "This picture is one of my most distinct memories of the war," recalled a Union officer who awoke on the morning of December 14 just eighty yards from the stone wall. He and his comrades gazed almost stupidly at their carefree enemy. The Confederates were "talking, laughing, cooking, cleaning muskets, clicking locks." Suddenly, the "sharp whistle of a bullet" sounded in Federal ears, "and a rebel's face peered through the puff of smoke, as he removed the rifle from his shoulder." The warning shot sent the Federals sprawling on the ground. As the long day wore on, men continued to sit "cramped and half famished," at one hour shivering in "frozen mud, blood, and slush," at another time, wallowing "in a nice mud hole."[5]

Their predicament presented a discouraging and frustrating spectacle to the rest of the army on Stafford Heights. "What a sight!" exclaimed one officer. "To see men by the thousands lying in such a position, covered or protected by a slight rise in the ground—that rise furnishing the only barrier between themselves and death." Some men enjoyed the luxury of a bullet-riddled building or shredded fence to shield themselves, but many dared not raise their heads in daylight. Thousands of Federals lay prone through the daylight hours. Some men had as little as a foot of protective earth protruding above their heads. Particularly exposed troops used their own dead for additional cover. With so many corpses positioned so near the edge of the embankment, men did not hesitate to pile bodies like cordwood to increase the height of their barricades. "This breastwork of the dead saved our lives more than once during the day," insisted one Federal, "as they were struck several times at least, as denoted by that peculiar thud in the dead flesh."[6]

But both sides waited in vain for the battle to resume. By morning, Burnside had turned indecisive, like a man awakening from a hangover—uncertain if what he remembered of the previous day had really happened and wondering what he should do next. He had intended to attack Lee at 10 A.M., but as that hour came and went, and with even the aggressive Bull Sumner telling him that another attack would "prove disastrous to the army," Burnside hesitated. When his other general officers, including Franklin, seconded Sumner's plea, he lost his will. By 4 P.M., Burnside had decided he would reassess the situation the following day, but in truth, he had made up his mind. He rationalized that Lincoln, after all, had told him not to be hasty, not to advance until he was ready. And the president most certainly "did not want the army of the Potomac destroyed."[7]

That night, men on both sides of the battlefield shared a mystical experience when a rare aurora borealis lighted the northern heavens. As it moved from east to west, the spectacle produced a "most splendid effect," which many Rebels took to be "an omen of victory." Northern troops took no such delight in the fiery display. They thought only of the pummeling they had suffered and of the dead and wounded men still scattered across the bloody fields. That day, a brave, tenderhearted Southern soldier, Sgt. Richard Kirkland of the Second South Carolina Infantry, had risked death by repeatedly carrying water to thirst-crazed Union wounded in front of the stone wall. Federal soldiers, once they understood his intentions, fired not a shot. Still, Kirkland could not attend a fraction of the bleeding men.[8]

Burnside crossed the Rappahannock on December 15 to inspect his own and Lee's positions. He expressed dismay upon seeing that the Rebels had strengthened their earthworks. The armies also took time on this day to bury their dead. A brief truce had been called on the previous afternoon in front of Jackson's lines. In the more general armistice of December 15, some Federal corpses, many of which had already been stripped of their clothing by shivering Confederates, received rudimentary burials. So hard was the earth that the deepest graves were no more than eighteen inches deep. When burying the enemy, Rebels simply tossed the bodies in ditches and covered them with earth from the embankments. Even so, not nearly all of the twelve hundred dead could be interred in a single day. The Rebels took more care with their own men, but even at that, mass graves—long trenches about six feet wide—were the rule. "No mark of any kind to distinguish their bodies," lamented a soldier, "no requiem, no dirge, no gentle hand to touch the dead faces."[9]

In the midst of their macabre chore, hundreds of rival soldiers mingled and talked on the field of death. Officers who spotted old friends hallooed them and reminisced. "What a strange thing is war," decided one man. Strange, and gruesome, too. Not all conversations were merry. "The rebels assured our flag of truce [party] that had they chosen to destroy the town, they might have ruined our army," reported a Union captain. "And I know that they speak the truth." Clearing the field of its dead relieved both sides of a sickening sight. Swollen corpses lay in "every conceivable posture, one Rebel confirmed, here one without a head, there one without legs, yonder a head and legs without a trunk, everywhere horrible expressions, fear, rage, agony, madness, torture, lying in pools of blood, lying with heads half buried in mud, with fragments of shell sticking in oozing brains, with bullet holes all over the puffed limbs."[10]

Some Confederates wandered around like tourists to inspect the killing fields. Men who surveyed the Union right gaped at the "*breastwork*, made out of *human bodies*," that lined the ravine before the stone wall. "They had actually . . . piled them up like logs," one man marveled, "dug a trench behind & thrown the dirt upon them, & thus made a *fortification* out of *their own dead*." Death had been democratic, too, with "all ages . . . represented, from the beardless boy to the gray haired man." Notably absent, remarked one Rebel, were the remains of Yankee officers, which he believed had been removed during the fighting.[11]

Burnside dined with Sumner and Franklin at his headquarters late that afternoon. Seemingly full of surprises, Burnside used the occasion to announce that he would withdraw the rest of his army from below the Rappahannock that evening. At 7 P.M., having constructed large campfires, barricaded the streets, and mounted wooden "Quaker" guns to deceive the Rebels, Burnside's men headed back across the pontoon bridges. By 2 A.M., as a cold rain began to fall, the last of them had "floundered, plodded, limped, and dragged" themselves back to their camps. Exhausted engineers, caked with mud and expecting a Rebel fusillade at any moment, swiftly dismantled the bridges, no doubt reflecting bitterly—or perhaps thankfully—on the ease with which they managed the task. The retreat was masterful. Burnside had extracted his army from "a bad box," and the Rebels had suspected nothing. Yet, given his hopes of five days earlier,

Burnside could derive scant pleasure from the achievement. "No man can know what this has cost me!" he was heard to say. "Poor man! How I pitied him," concluded a staff officer. "General Burnside rode by us," a New Englander reported. "The stillness of death reigned over the column; not a murmur from the ranks of disapprobation; not a cheer or shout of joy of relief." The army had been drained of emotion.[12]

But if the retreat went smoothly, it was not conducted without a hint of desperation. A Michigan infantryman complained that the engineers began tearing down the bridges almost before his regiment had crossed. "The town was silent as death" by then. "A few dead still lay in the streets," reported the Wolverine, "but they had been rolled about & trampled in the mud till it was impossible to tell whether they were friend or foe. Probably very few cared. . . . We crossed at double quick & marched to our old camps." Another man conceded, "If *ever* boys were glad to get out of a scrape it was us," and years later, a Federal artillerist said it all: "Fredericksburg is not a pleasant topic to a Union soldier."[13]

The retreat also sparked a final round of "sacking and pillaging." By then, furniture, bedding, mirrors, books, china, housewares, and clothing littered the town. "All through the streets, soldiers were eating & cooking, smashing chairs for fuel & eating off china dishes," a soldier informed his wife. He and some friends had broken into one house where they secured pork, flour, fish, preserves, and canned fruit. "I got *considerably up on my bottle of wine*," too, he confessed, "& felt as good as Gen. Burnside or any other man." Having filled their bellies, these men lined their pockets by breaking into a bank and confiscating "lots of cashed drafts, checks, & some Virginia money," as well as $300 in gold.[14]

Other men sought "some memento" of their ordeal. One captain expressed disappointment when he came away with nothing better than "a commonplace edition of Byron" and a pair of children's books. "I went into nearly every house to get some nice little silver thing for mamma & Mary Welch, he told his sister, but was too late." He envied a fellow officer who "got just the thing—a little bed lamp of solid silver." A New England artillerist sent his female correspondent "a piece of patchwork . . . from the private Bureau of Miss Julia M. Allen. . . . A darkey told me here she was very pretty. . . . I also have several other articles of her wardrobe." One of those articles, a pair of pantaloons, he used as a flour sack.[15]

The sudden exodus took the Confederates by surprise. The "unusual quiet" that prevailed as yet another morning fog rolled away on December 16 inspired them to investigate. Skirmishers proceeded through the town to the banks of the river. Except for a few stragglers, who were quickly rounded up, they found no vestige of Burnside's army. Bluecoated pickets eyed the Confederates as they neared the river, but both sides seemed grateful for the expanse of chilly water. One Rebel thought the Yankees looked "a little mortified," but they fired no shots, spoke no words.[16]

Lee has been criticized for allowing Burnside to escape. Quite apart from the fact that his system of pickets was apparently so ineffective that it allowed an entire army to slip away, Lee, suggest his critics, might well have taken the offensive on December 15 after Burnside had declined to advance on the previous day. Logic dictated that the Federals were either too stunned or too disorganized to put up much of a fight. If Lee had thrown all of his infantry and artillery into the fray, he could have driven Burnside's army into the river, and the course of the war would have been altered. Even Lee later acknowledged his frustration at not being able to whip Burnside more soundly.

Yet any offensive move by Lee would have been terribly risky and probably costly. The Federal lines had been reinforced all along the river by December 15. Besides having fortified Fredericksburg, the Yankees had constructed a series of entrenchments on both sides of Hazel Run. Even had Lee been able to overrun them—a very uncertain proposition—his loss in men would have been heavy. Then there was the question of the already half-wrecked town. Some of Longstreet's artillerists had hit Fredericksburg when repulsing the Federals on December 13, but to have purposely destroyed the town for the sake of driving out the Yankees was probably more than Lee could have tolerated. The plain truth was that Lee had selected a first-rate position for defense but a poor one for offense. He knew that; so did Stonewall Jackson. That is why a position behind the North Anna had appealed to both men. There could be no counterattack in the valley of the Rappahannock.[17]

Jubilant—not to say relieved—Confederates swarmed over the abandoned battlefield in search of booty, just as the Federals had swarmed over Fredericksburg. They stripped the Federal dead that had not yet been buried. Some desperate men even dug up graves in search of clothing, and one Mississippian cut off the finger of a Yankee corpse for its ring. "These things are barbarous in themselves," admitted a Virginian, "but our soldiery has had enough to aggravate its feelings of hostility against the enemy even to barbarism." Some Southern newspapers criticized this ravaging of the dead. If the men needed outer clothing, suggested sensitive souls, they should have at least spared the Federals their underwear. Yet a lack of remorse was not uncommon among the Rebels. The shelling of Fredericksburg, the harsh occupation of other Virginia communities earlier that year, and the mere presence of the invader on their soil had hardened many men to the death they had sown. "I rode over the battle field, and enjoyed the sight of hundreds of dead Yankees," rejoiced an especially keen artillerist. "Saw much of the work I had done in the way of severed limbs, decapitated bodies, and mutilated remains of all kinds. Doing my soul good. Would that the whole Northern army were as such and I had my hand in it."[18]

As for the spoils, there were acres from which to choose. "Blankets, haver sacks, knapsacks, guns, bayonets, cartridge boxes, belts, caps, hats, and etc. lay scattered in all directions," reported a Georgian. "You may know that our brigade helped themselves to plunder. Some searched the Yanks pockets, and even stripped them to their skin." A spirited round of bartering and selling ensued, as men unable to scavenge articles they desired discovered that they had picked up something coveted by a comrade. Blankets sold for $10, overcoats for $20, revolvers for $30. A Virginian who searched the field two days later found only some underwear and an oilcloth. "All the Yankee dead," he reported, "had been stripped of every rag of their clothing and looked like hogs which had been cleaned."[19]

Another truce was called to bury more dead on December 18. The Federals collected over seven hundred corpses for interment in two common graves—long trenches, actually—and a Virginian, who paused to chat with some Yankee grave diggers, thought it "an awful sight." The staring or headless corpses had once been men full of hope and valor; they had fought nobly and, in their view, for a noble cause. Families and friends a thousand miles away would weep when they learned of their deaths, but their comrades could think only of tossing them in pits and being done with them. The putrid piles of dead did not assault one's sense of smell as fiercely as five-day-old corpses might have on a summer battlefield. Maggots and flies did not swarm in the brisk December air. Yet the human wreckage helped the Virginian to appreciate the cost of defeat. "War is surely awful," he confided to his diary that night. "I pitied these poor dead men. I could not help it. Yet these dead fellows were the *very* men, who, a few days ago, burned houses and drove old men, women and mothers with infants at the breast, and little children into a December night to die of hunger and cold." War is confusion.[20]

For wounded men and overworked surgeons, the ordeal continued, and the hospitals were nearly as grim as the field. Amputations and other surgeries not attempted earlier were performed at a rapid pace, the agonies of the wounded mercifully deadened by ample applications of chloroform. When Northern poet and sometimes nurse Walt Whitman arrived at the Federal camp in search of his brother George, a member of the Fifty-first New York Infantry, he found "a heap of feet, arms, legs, etc under a tree" at the Lacy house. Clara Barton continued to nurse and comfort men until late December, by which time she had exhausted her supplies and the last convalescent had been sent north, most of them to hospitals in Washington. "The transportation, which was partly by ambulance, partly by railroad and partly by boat, was tedious and harassing to the patients," admitted one surgeon, "although they were made as comfortable as the circumstances would permit." A final tally showed that the Federals had lost 1,284 killed, 9,600 wounded, and 1,769 missing, a total of 12,653 casualties, or 12 percent of the 106,000 engaged. Lee's army suffered 595 killed, 4,061 wounded, and 653 missing, a total of 5,309 casualties, or 7 percent of the 72,500 men who saw action.[21]

It had been an amazing battle, unlike anything seen thus far in the war. The death and terror lasted three days and extended over seven miles. It had produced some rare combat action, including the shelling of an occupied town, an amphibious river crossing under fire, street fighting, and a night assault. Defensive entrenchments were used by the Confederates in modern ways, and scores of civilians, trapped between two armies, witnessed the center of the storm.

Survivors were quick to tell friends and relatives all that had passed, although they tended to dwell on the Great Death. "I have heard of the horror of the battlefield but the reality is terrible," testified one of Humphreys's newly minted veterans. "In the action and excitement it is not realized, but the thoughts and impressions seem to be burned on my brain, the still pale faces of the dead, and the shrieks and groans of the wounded and dying. Oh! it is awful." A previously seasoned New Englander insisted, "i seen some hot work at south mountain and antietam in maryland, but they were not to be compared to this. old troops say that they never were under such a heavy fire before in any battle." A New York infantryman told his wife, "Men lay in heeps all over the battlefield, torn in every way that you can think. Oh what a cruel thing it is to see men shot down in this way." More than a few men likened the field to a "slaughter pen," with occasional references to grain hoppers. A New Jersey soldier called it "the Most Masterly pease of Bootchery that the Sun Ever Shone on."[22]

The winners found the action both awful and exhilarating. "You can't imagine what a horrible spectacle I witnessed," a Georgian told his father.

"I saw hundreds of men lying dead, shot in all parts some with their heads, hands, legs, arms, etc. shot off, and mangled in all manner and shapes." He and other Rebels, like many Yankees, used the analogy of slaughter: "The ground resembled an immense hog pen and them all killed. It put me in mind of hog killing time more than any thing else." It had been "the greatest slaughter" inflicted on the Federals thus far, judged a Virginian; and a North Carolinian chimed in, "I tell you our men did slaughter the yankeys." A Texan boasted, "The Yankees tried they [*sic*] favorite remedy for us, over whelming numbers, but they effect nothing." A Virginian marveled at the hardheadedness of the enemy. "What can possess the Yankee nation," he asked his wife. "They seem very hard to satisfy. I think they ought to be satisfied by this time that they can not subjugate us."[23]

Of course, the most honest men admitted that they could not explain what had happened or how the battle had unfolded. They told folks at home that the newspapers could relate more about the fighting than could the combatants. "We know but a little about it," a New York soldier advised his sister. "I know one[ly] the shot and shell did whistle around my head." A Georgian who could vividly describe his regiment's role in the fighting below Prospect Hill admitted to his wife, "I do not know the result of the battle of the 13th, but I think we got the best of it." A North Carolinian could only express thanks—and no little surprise—that he had done his part in the fighting. "I think after the first Rounds was fired," he ventured, "I did not mind it more than a tite Race at a corn shucking, every fellow tried to do all he could." As for the bigger picture, he confessed, "I dont hardly know myself."[24]

Many Federals believed *their* units had fought well but that other portions of the army had let them down. "Our regiment covered itself with glory," boasted one captain. "The army generally didn't fight well. The new regiments behaved shamefully, as well as many of the old ones. The whole army is demoralized." A Michigan captain insisted that his company had fought nobly, and with few exceptions "every man stood up & faced that terrific shower of shot & shell." Members of the Federal burial details even told their Confederate counterparts that some regiments "mutinied and had to be driven into the fight." General Meade confided to his wife, "My men went in *beautifully*, carried everything before them, and drove the enemy for nearly half a mile, but finding themselves unsupported . . . they were checked and finally driven back."[25]

While his soldiers wrote letters that would be read days, perhaps weeks, later, Burnside tried to limit immediate public knowledge of the disaster.

He would not permit newspaper correspondents to send telegraphic messages, and no correspondent was allowed to leave the area. Even the War Department remained uncertain of what had happened on the Rappahannock. Officials claimed that Burnside had "done well" in three days of hard fighting, but a sense of uneasiness clearly prevailed in Washington. Secretary of the Navy Gideon Welles believed something was amiss. "Adverse tidings are suppressed," he asserted, "with a deal of fuss and mystery."[26]

As the truth emerged, Abraham Lincoln expressed dismay, and Congress wanted answers. Lincoln at first refused to acknowledge the dimensions of the defeat. After slipping through Burnside's quarantine, journalist Henry Villard rushed to Washington from the battlefield to tell the president what had happened. Lincoln replied, "I hope it is not so bad as all that." Before long, everyone knew it was bad, very bad, the most "dreadful and ominous disaster" of the war. It produced "disappointment, anguish, despair and indignation" among a "shocked" Northern public. Someone had to be held accountable for this "great blunder," this "great crime." If the president would not insist on an explanation, then Congress would do so.[27]

The United States government was in turmoil in mid-December; the war for the Union had reached a point of crisis. The fall elections had revealed a lack of faith in Lincoln's administration, and the Fredericksburg defeat gave the politicians an opportunity to attack Lincoln's policies and advisers. "It really seems as though the ship of state was going to pieces in the storm," an anguished congressman declared. One general thought, "The affairs at Washington are casting a greater gloom over the country than the affairs of the army." The *Chicago Tribune* summarized the public mood: "Failure of the army, weight of taxes, depreciation of money, want of cotton . . . increasing national debt, deaths in the army, no prospect of success, the continued closure of the Mississippi . . . all combine to produce the existing state of despondency and desperation." Gen. Samuel P. Heintzelman, commanding the defenses around Washington, worried, "It will be as much as the President can do to maintain himself."[28]

The crisis took a dramatic turn during the week of December 16. In an effort to "quiet the public mind," an influential group of senators, including Benjamin Wade, Charles Sumner, James W. Grimes, and William Pitt Fessenden, met in caucus to propose substantial changes in the government. Wade said the Senate should insist that the moderate William Seward— viewed with suspicion by Radicals as an evil influence on Lincoln—resign from the cabinet and that a military dictator, "with absolute and despotic powers" and loyal to the Republican party, be named to lead the army. Much of the agitation had been inspired by Secretary of the Treasury Salmon P. Chase, who told Radical friends that Lincoln refused to consult with the cabinet on important issues and relied on the wrong people for advice. Chase hoped to emerge as the cabinet's senior member should the president give in to the senators' demands. Warned by a friend of what was afoot, Seward immediately submitted his resignation to Lincoln to spare him any embarrassment. Lincoln told no one. The senators caucused two more times, on December 17 and 18, and finally requested a meeting with the president to discuss the reorganization of his cabinet. Lincoln agreed to a meeting on the evening of December 18. "They wish to get rid of me, and I am sometimes half disposed to gratify them," Lincoln despaired to an old confidant, Orville H. Browning, a few hours before the crucial meeting. "We are now on the brink of destruction. It appears to me the Almighty is against us, and I can hardly see a ray of hope."[29]

But Lincoln survived. In the first of two meetings—perhaps the most crucial political meetings of the war—the president engaged the nine-member congressional deputation in "a pretty free and animated conversation." The first gathering lasted three hours, and the president promised to consider further the resolutions presented to him by the caucus. Lincoln met again with the committee the following evening, December 19, but this time, he also invited his cabinet—sans Seward—to participate. The meeting spilled over into the early morning hours, during which time Lincoln turned back the threat to his administration and the balance of power in the government. He did so by adroitly revealing the duplicity of Chase and by convincing the politicos not only that he had a firm hand on his administration but that he enjoyed the full support of his cabinet. Lincoln cinched his position the next day by obtaining the written resignation of his treasury secretary. Now able to rid himself of Chase should the Radicals insist that he accept Seward's resignation, the president had all but weathered the storm.[30]

A subplot unfolded on December 18, when the entire Senate directed the Joint Committee on the Conduct of the War to "inquire into the facts relating to the recent battle at Fredericksburg." On the following day, the committee's members, led by Radical Republicans including Zachariah Chandler, George W. Julian, John Covode, and Daniel Gooch, arrived at the Lacy house to interrogate Burnside, Sumner, Franklin, Hooker, Daniel Woodbury, and Herman Haupt. Wade, the committee chairman, joined them following the first caucus meeting with Lincoln. Upon the committee's return to Washington, it also took the depositions of Halleck and Meigs. Committee members, and especially those men who had been critical of Lincoln's strategy, wanted most to know why Burnside had delayed so long in attacking Lee and who had been responsible for the seemingly mindless assaults against Marye's Heights.[31]

The committee provided no summary statement of its investigation and declined to blame any one person for the defeat. Privately, committee members seemed inclined to treat Burnside charitably. They considered the general a "loyal & earnest man" who lacked confidence in himself. A committee member from Pennsylvania confided to Meade before leaving "that when he got back [to Washington] he was going [to] raise a howl, and intimated it would not be against Burnside." Yet the published testimony to the committee gave the impression of an army commander—Burnside—who had been indecisive, unimaginative, and obstinate to the point of ordering large numbers of men to certain death. "It is possible," Burnside confessed during the hearings when commenting on the assaults against Marye's Heights, "that the points of attack were wrongly ordered; if such is the case, I can only say that I did to the best of my ability."[32]

Many of the committee's questions focused on the pontoons. The river crossing, Burnside's hopes of outflanking Lee, the advance on Richmond, everything had depended on the timely delivery of those portable bridges. Why had they been delayed? Who was responsible? Should Burnside have betrayed his intention to cross at Fredericksburg before the bridges arrived? Should he have crossed the river, after receiving the bridges more than a week later than planned, against forty thousand defenders? Poor weather afforded a partial explanation for the delay. Swollen rivers and muddy roads slowed delivery of the pontoons by several crucial days. Halleck also bore responsibility for the logistical breakdown. The general in chief had given Burnside the impression at their Warrenton meeting and in their correspondence that the pontoons would arrive immediately. Yet General Woodbury, in defending himself against charges that he had caused the delay, claimed to have followed Halleck's instructions precisely and stated that neither Halleck nor anyone else had suggested to him that "the success of any movement depended in the slightest degree upon a pontoon train."[33]

Burnside, however, could not escape unscathed on this crucial issue. Halleck may have been negligent in expediting delivery of the pontoons, but when they arrived on November 25, Jackson had not yet joined Lee. Burnside had outnumbered the Rebels better than two to one. Even more to the point, Burnside should not have betrayed his intention to cross the Rappahannock at Fredericksburg before the bridges arrived. He should have delayed marching his grand divisions downriver. Montgomery Meigs, the final person to testify before the committee, literally had the last word on this subject, and he insisted that Burnside should have waited. "I think there was a mistake made in expecting pontoons . . . to be got to Falmouth while the army made two and a half days' march," stated the quartermaster general. "I do not think it practicable."[34]

Burnside did manage to salvage something of his reputation, even enhance it in the eyes of some people, by publicly accepting responsibility for the defeat. The day after testifying before the committee, Burnside traveled to Washington to meet with Lincoln. While in the capital, he heard public accusations that Lincoln and Stanton had pressured him to attack prematurely. It was not so, declared Burnside, and in a published defense of the administration, which appeared in Northern newspapers on December 23, the general nobly accepted all responsibility for the plan of battle and the decision to attack.[35]

One newspaper called Burnside's letter "Very Remarkable, Very Curious, Very Generous and Very Naive," and that seemed to sum up public opinion. A New York lawyer praised it as "a frank, honest, manly report." He continued: "We are sure now of *one* fact, and we are sure of very few. We have one man in high place who is single-minded and unselfish and sincere. His identification is great gain, even admitting his ability to be third-rate." Burnside's defense of the Lincoln administration is all the more remarkable in that he clearly *did* feel some pressure, whether direct or implied, from politicians both in and out of the army to advance against Lee. Even the Confederates recognized this fact. In a newspaper article ridiculing all those Federal generals who had been stymied in their efforts to conquer Virginia, one Rebel pundit—John Esten Cooke—concocted an imagined discussion between Lincoln and Burnside about the strategic situation on the Rappahannock. The president's persistent refrain was *"Do something!"*[36]

Defenders of the administration were quick to cite Burnside's letter and the committee's report to counter charges of political meddling and military incompetence. Salmon Chase said he was "relieved" by the letter. A New Englander stressed the nonarrival of the pontoons, caused, as he saw it, by an unfortunate clash of authority between Burnside and Halleck, as the root of all the problems. "There is no blame to be attached to the President or the Radical party, whose interest it was to have thwarted any forward movement before January 1," he reasoned. Burnside had seen a chance to surprise Lee but had miscalculated. "Nothing very wonderful in all this," he concluded. "No hidden causes at work. . . . Simple plain matter-of-fact every day life. Other people hamper and delay us until our chances of success are almost gone."[37]

Lincoln was more than willing to let Burnside shoulder responsibility. After a year of putting up with McClellan's excuses, it must have been a refreshing change for the president. More than that, the political muddle in Washington—the cabinet crisis, the congressional inquiry—made it convenient to focus attention on the army rather than on the Executive Mansion. When Lincoln did publicly acknowledge the defeat, he lauded the Army of the Potomac and very nearly blamed the disaster on natural causes. "Although you were not successful," Lincoln proclaimed to the army, "the attempt was not an error, nor the failure other than an accident. The courage . . . and consummate skill [you displayed] . . . show that you possess all the qualities of a great army, which will yet give victory to the cause of the country and of popular government." The president's optimistic assessment led one officer to comment, somewhat bitterly, "Mr. Lincoln is more flattering to this army when defeated than when victorious."[38]

Who was to blame for Fredericksburg? Contemporaries offered no consensus. "The causes . . . were freely discussed as usual by the boys, and many were the theories advanced," reported a Massachusetts soldier. Lincoln, Stanton, and Halleck did, in fact, receive much criticism. Some people labeled Stanton a "meddling murderous quack," who had "uselessly sacrificed" the nation's sons and brothers on more than one Southern battlefield. Lincoln's popularity was wearing thin, too. "A year ago we laughed at the Honest Old Abe's grotesque genial Western jocosities," acknowledged an eastern sophisticate, "but they nauseate us now." As for Halleck, one Washington socialite labeled him "chief of Imbeciles" among a set of generals that she generally classified as "the most brainless—inert set that ever the world saw." The general in chief's own testimony before the Committee on the Conduct of the War, she submitted, was "enough to hang him."[39]

Yet responsibility for martial defeats must rest ultimately with the leaders on the field, and several Union generals fell short of expectations at Fredericksburg. Hooker had been petulant throughout the campaign. He had opposed Burnside's entire plan as well as several of his commander's tactical decisions. Many of Hooker's objections were reasonable, but his delay in committing Griffin's division further crippled an already sputtering attack. Then, too, there always remains the question of motivation where Fighting Joe is concerned. Did he *want* Burnside to fail so that his own star might finally gain the ascendant?

Sumner, the most loyal of Burnside's subordinates, lacked imagination and failed to build any sustained momentum in his assault. He followed a common enough practice in sending forward his divisions one brigade at a time, and the narrow plain before Marye's Heights may have required such formations, but the distance between brigades—some two hundred yards—was too large. Neither Sumner nor Couch saw the need to propel the attack forward by reinforcing the lead brigade when it came within charging distance. Rather, each brigade was left to create its own momentum, and no one thought to repair the bridge across the canal or to build additional bridges to speed the flow of troops onto the plain.

General Franklin, known for his caution on the offensive, certainly could have moved with more dispatch and displayed more initiative. His failure to advance in force during the initial attacks against Stonewall Jackson wrecked whatever semblance of a plan Burnside had formed. Burnside may be criticized for issuing imprecise orders and for allowing an attack by a single division, but Franklin was the commander on the scene. He was the one best able to feel the pulse of battle. He should have shown more gumption and provided genuine leadership. The artillery chief of the I Corps, Col. Charles S. Wainwright, laid most of the blame on Franklin. "Perhaps Burnside did not intend originally that we should attack at all," he considered on December 18. "If so, it is singular that he should use one-half of his army to make a mere demonstration." A Massachusetts infantryman claimed that his regiment labeled Franklin the culprit, too. Franklin was a McClellan man, he reasoned, and "the old spirit of McClellanism" still infected the army. Even one of his division commanders, Abner Doubleday, charged that Franklin, with fifty-five thousand men at his disposal, did nothing but "look on and witness the failure of Meade's charge."[40]

Still, however much one sympathizes with Burnside's predicament, the commanding general's own miscalculations and lack of leadership determined the outcome of the battle. He should have been more precise in conveying his tactical plan to both Franklin and Sumner, and he never should have suggested to either one that a single division might be sufficient for any part of the job. He should have maintained demonstrations at Skinker's Neck and Port Royal far longer than he did to divert attention from his main objectives. He should have delayed his attack against Marye's Heights until he knew Franklin's grand division had secured the enemy's right flank. He should have been more careful to reach agreement with his grand division commanders over the purpose and routes of the attacks, more certain that all understood the terrain and his intentions. He should have had more confidence in himself, vacillated less, been more decisive. At the very least, even after the failures of December 11–13, he might have held on to Fredericksburg, and with additional troops under Franz Sigel, he might even have threatened to operate against Lee's flanks.

Most egregious was the slowness with which Burnside moved. He acted far too cautiously in ordering his army across the Dare Mark. He could have pushed troops over the lower bridges on December 11, and he most certainly should have occupied Fredericksburg in force that night. Even his most staunch defender calls this Burnside's "greatest lapse." Burnside justified charging directly into the town by saying, quite rightly, that Lee did not expect such a move. But he also knew such a daring maneuver had to be conducted rapidly. Burnside blamed the fog for an "unavoidable delay in building the bridges," which, in turn, allowed Lee a full day to unite his army. Yet if Burnside had placed his men in position to attack on December 12, Lee would not yet have concentrated his forces, and the Confederate right flank, at least, would have been far more vulnerable. Barksdale turned in a sterling performance, but his brigade had abandoned the town by evening. Burnside's defenders point to the difficulty of maneuvering an army at night. Yet he withdrew his army under similar conditions three days later, and to withdraw in the face of the enemy is far more perilous than to advance.[41]

And still there remain the assaults against the seemingly impregnable Confederate positions on Prospect Hill and Marye's Heights. Prospect Hill might be excused. Meade's Pennsylvania Reserves did capture the ridge, which shows that at least part of Burnside's plan, if properly conducted, might have succeeded. Even so, some Union soldiers thought "it was all useless fighting." Yes, they had briefly seized the crest, but they had not been reinforced, and "the rebels had every advantage of ground and had rifle pits and earth works all along the hills." But the blunder at Marye's Heights is much harder to dismiss, and it remains the element in the battle that makes Fredericksburg more Burnside's defeat than Lee's victory. Students of the battle have been puzzled by his repeated assaults, just, it may fairly be pointed out, as they have scratched their heads over Lee's attack on Meade's center at Gettysburg. Even to stand on Marye's Heights today and imagine the broad expanse of open terrain that led up to it from the edge of the old town staggers the observer.[42]

A daughter of Francis Preston Blair who was familiar with the area around Fredericksburg called Burnside's attacks "folly," an action none but "mad men" would have attempted. "Anybody at all acquainted with the point d'apperis," she marveled, "would see that the enemy could make themselves impregnable except by [an] army able to surround them." A

Confederate soldier concurred bluntly: "No one but an ass would have attempted to do what he did." A New York artillerist insisted: "Any man with plain farmer's common sense would have seen when the first assault was made and, indeed, before the assault was made that any attempt to break the enemy's line at that point and gain the fortified crest beyond was utterly hopeless." And a New York cavalryman summed up the tactical situation precisely: "The Rebs have too much the best of us in battle grounds they are in the woods and on a hill and are in intrenchements and we are on low ground and open field."[43]

Both soldiers and civilians continued to weigh the significance of the battle. Congressional interest remained high, even after the Committee on the Conduct of the War held its investigation. Politicians, including Vice President Hannibal Hamlin, visited the Federal encampment to view the scene of combat. Fredericksburg became "all the rage," reported one staff officer. Visitors were sobered by the hospitals filled with wounded men, the battered town, and the wreck of a battlefield. Yet most of the politicians, especially those who had been pushing Lincoln for a more forceful prosecution of the war, seemed to shrug it off. "Such is war," concluded Zachariah Chandler. "Such are the fruits of rebellion. . . . Burnside thought he could break their wing & destroy their army. He was mistaken. This is all after having tried his best." Chandler still thought Lee could be beaten and suggested on the day before Christmas that if the army attempted a flanking movement soon, it could "easily be made."[44]

CHAPTER FIVE

# Mired Hopes and Mud Marches

Christmas came just in time. Although it was an unexpectedly sad one for Northern and Southern families who had lost men along the Dare Mark, it promised hope as well and reminded Northerners, at least, that they must push on, put Fredericksburg behind them, and develop a new strategy. Glory to God and peace on earth are the eternal messages of Christmas, and some Yankees saw special significance in their meaning during this time of "trouble and disaster and impending ruin." Most hopeful, in the eyes of some people, was the president's earlier promise to announce his emancipation policy on New Year's Day and the new opportunity to recruit black men into Northern ranks. These actions could lend a new dimension to the war. They would certainly help Northerners—and Southerners, too—forget about Fredericksburg.[1]

Union soldiers attended Christmas worship services and gave thanks for having survived the battle, but few expressed real joy. Enough drunken revelers careened through company streets to keep the provost marshal busy, yet most men could not help but dwell on their personal loneliness and the bitterness of defeat. While many senior officers enjoyed as fine a Christmas dinner as they would have eaten at home, many junior officers and privates dined on coffee and hardtack or pretended that an extra ration of potatoes made for a festive supper. "We live high out here," a Massachusetts soldier reported sardonically to his sister, "raw pork and hard bread to fight on." Many men who had expected holiday packages of cakes and fruit and other treats from home saw them arrive in sorry shape or not at all. "Our Christmas passed off quietly but not as Merry as former ones," lamented one of the less fortunate men. "The regt had No boxes from friends at Home it Not being convenient to Send them to this place."[2]

Yet the ultimate concern for most Federals, muting the holidays and lending even momentary gaiety a hollow sound, was the question of what would happen next. To one soldier the army appeared "disheartened, in fact completely discouraged. I can hardly find three [men] that have confidence in any one man, unless it be the old soldiers in McClellan," he confided to his wife on Christmas eve. "I don't know how it appears to you up away out of reach of this terrible rebellion, but here at this time I must confess everything wears a dark, gloomy aspect." If not actually demoralized—and there was much debate about the mood of the army—it certainly seemed stunned, not to say embarrassed. "Though our army is not disorganized, demoralized or disheartened," insisted one stubborn Federal, "theirs is flushed and joyous—ours being quiet even to apathy. They carry with them a sort of prestige."[3]

Walt Whitman, lingering in the camps at Falmouth, saw and heard it all. A break in the weather produced "soft, brightly beautiful" days that enlivened picturesque scenes of cheerful yet purposeful activity. Railroad locomotives puffed lazily along the winding track that linked the men to their supplies at Aquia Creek, and bluecoated pickets lined the river and girdled the camps. Many men, as they lounged beside spitting campfires, complained about army life, their officers, and the politicians. Most regiments, after all, still lived in "flimsy little shelter tents," and their rations, if plentiful, consisted mostly of salt pork and hardtack. Yet the men visited by Whitman, mostly Pennsylvanians and New Yorkers, seemed content enough. "To a stranger," reasoned the poet, "the men in the ranks appear great growlers. By and by you learn this is nothing; a large proportion of men in the world, even the good fellows, would burst if they couldn't grumble."

Still, an unmistakably dark mood haunted the fringes of men's minds. It was partly the season—bleak, leafless—and partly the terrain, with the earth churned to a quagmire by tens of thousands of tramping feet and plodding hooves, farms stripped of fences, abandoned houses devoid of life. It was partly the anticipated boredom of winter camp and partly, too, a reaction to war, to the empty feeling that grips men who have witnessed senseless death. The day after Christmas, while walking through the fields of Falmouth, Whitman came upon a group of grave diggers at work. A rude thought gripped him: "Death is nothing here. As you step out in the morning from your tent to wash your face, you see before you on a stretcher a shapeless, extended object, and over it is thrown a dark gray blanket. It is the corpse of some wounded or sick soldier of the regiment who died in the hospital tent during the night; perhaps there is a row of three or four of these corpses lying covered over. No one makes an ado."[4]

Below the Rappahannock, Southerners rejoiced more genuinely. For some, the holiday provided a spark of merriment, and men who celebrated with whiskey—purchased at $20 per quart—could become "decidedly 'fussy' and . . . pugnacious." Even without stimulants, a degree of playfulness gripped many camps. Bands played, men sang and fired rifles into the sky. A group of minstrels in Hood's brigade—"make believe darkies"— staged a fine performance. Part of the Ninth Georgia Infantry held a mock battalion drill on Christmas Day, with a private, who sported "three large yellow paper stars on each side of his coat collar and riding a very small mule," serving as colonel. His men wore their uniforms inside out, substituted a blanket for the regimental flag, and otherwise made sport of army life.[5]

Yet even some Southern celebrations seemed forced. Nearly everyone confessed to being homesick. "Oh, that this war could end & allow us to return to our homes in peace," pined one Rebel who had not seen his wife and children in over a year. "Every one seems to be *Blue*," observed another fellow. "Most lonesome day I have spent since in service." A Virginian insisted, "Christmas day the poorest I have ever spent. . . . We all talk of home to day & wish to be there." Other men dwelled on the cost even of victories. They spoke in sad tones of friends and loved ones lost in the fighting and shuddered to think of the sacrifices still required of the living. It was all "very discouraging to the Soldiers," judged one man.[6]

The Confederates felt unfulfilled, too. Yes, they agreed, Lee had whipped Burnside handily. The Rebel press could not find enough superlatives to praise a victory that caused "the whole of Lincolndom [to] real like a drunken man." But why had Lee not destroyed Burnside? The Federals had suffered thousands of casualties but why not tens of thousands? Lee admitted his own disappointment and blamed it on Burnside's failure to resume the battle on December 14. "I . . . could not believe they would relinquish their purpose after all their boasting & preparations," Lee told his wife with a rare touch of disdain on December 16. "They went as they came, in the night. They suffered heavily as far as the battle went, but it did not go far enough to satisfy me." Quite simply, observed a less illustrious Virginia soldier on that same day, "Gen. Burnside . . . had given us the slip."[7]

Yet the victory also boosted morale in the Army of Northern Virginia beyond all reasonable limits. "It is no use for the nigger Government to try to take Richmond, 'that can't be did,'" decided a Louisiana soldier. "Our army can't be whipped, no matter how large a force the nigger government may send against us." An army surgeon reflected, "It does not seem possible to defeat this army now with General Lee at its head." By Christmas, even Lee seemed less glum. He marveled that despite the terrible, disproportionate losses he had inflicted on Burnside, his army had not struck with its full force and had yet to demonstrate its full potential for waging war. "I was holding back all that day," he told Mary Custis Lee of his preparations on December 14, "& husbanding our strength & ammunition for the great struggle for which I thought he was preparing. Had I devined that was to have been his only effort, he would have had more of it." There would have been the tens of thousands slain. In the end, decided Lee, "I am content."[8]

For a fortnight after the battle, camp life on both sides of the Rappahannock reverted to routine, which is to say, things became dull. Federal officers tried to keep men busy with inspections, drills, picket duty, and fatigue work when weather permitted, but the elements seldom cooperated during these winter days, and the men resented what they considered useless labor even more than the boredom. "If you had Seen the hardships that I have sense I left washington then you never would come down here for to be niggerd," complained a New Jersey soldier encamped near Aquia Creek to his brother. "We are now doing work on the dock unloading boats and loading up cars sometimes night and day." He added sarcastically, "A grate place down here it is up in the morning by 4 or 5 Oclock and eat A hard Cracker and A Strong cup of coffee and off for to work."[9]

Only an occasional turn at picket duty served to remind most men that the enemy remained as close as a mile away, and even the pickets, having "agreed not to fire on each other," soon resumed their familiar ways. A favorite Rebel jest had them telling the Yanks they would find it a hard road to Richmond, what with a "*Longstreet* to travel, two *Hills* to climb, and a *Stonewall* to get over." But the two sides also had many frank exchanges. "Most of them are bully fellows," decided a Pennsylvania cavalryman, "and are as tired of the war as we are and are anxious to have it settled." "They are the same kind of people as we are, kind & sociable," a New York infantryman decided after he had traded some coffee for tobacco with the Rebels. A Michigan sergeant maintained: "A most perfect feeling exists between the privates of the two armies. They are quite as sick of this inhuman, wholesale manslaughter as we. If a vote of those composing the rank and file of both armies could settle this, there would be no more battles." And this feeling existed despite the fact that many Confederate pickets walked their posts in blue overcoats taken from the dead at Fredericksburg.[10]

In Lee's camps, again strung as far south as Port Royal, the want of adequate shelter and sufficient food magnified the meaningless days and numbing boredom. "The day has passed without anything to disturb the monotony of camp life," conceded a Georgian from near Port Royal. "The only employment of the soldiers is making fires and warming by them." The next day, he reported, "Camp life very dull. Much complaint of ennui." Men assigned to garrison the town enjoyed the luxury of being "comfortably domiciled . . . & sheltered from the cutting blasts of the wintry winds," but their infrequent contact with civilians in the still largely deserted town reminded them of how much they missed the "pleasures of domestic life." Other men enjoyed the interlude, and if the quiet did not signal the end of the war, they hoped, at least, that the fighting was over until spring. "Everything has been quiet since the fight at Fredericksburg," verified one Rebel. "I hardly think theyl [the Federals] attempt to go this rout again this winter."[11]

Rebel warriors were also angered by the condition of the citizens of Fredericksburg and Spotsylvania County. The countryside still teemed with homeless people, a few wandering aimlessly, some seeking shelter, others cautiously returning to their homes. Many who returned, frightened or apprehensive though they may have been, had little choice, for they had fled with only the clothes they wore. Not a few found their homes and farms severely damaged. Several soldiers encamped at Hazlewood Farm lamented that its once "magnificent" and "stately" house had been "reduced to ashes by the incendiary's torch." Its "splendid yard" had been obliterated, and the entire year's wheat crop, still in shocks, stood rotting in the fields. "There has been great destruction of farms & property in this country," declared one man. "It will take a century for this country to get back to what it was before this war commenced."[12]

The most obvious symbol of war's destructive power, perhaps because it was so concentrated, was the town of Fredericksburg. Even Northern newspapers estimated the cost of the damage to be no less than $750,000. "Nearly every house in Fredericksburg was struck either by shot or shell and some of them were completely riddled," reported a shocked observer. "Quite a number were burned, and whilst the town was in possession of the Yankees well nigh every dwelling was robbed. . . . The town presents quite a scene of desolation." One resident reported, "You can form no idea of the destruction and desolation of this place—want of provisions is another serious difficulty." Another soldier estimated that there remained "but few houses worth repairing," the shelling and the Yankee soldiers having knocked "the houses and everything into pie." "Town very much shattered," agreed another man. "A monument to the barbarity of the abolitionists."[13]

The degree and type of damage varied. Some estimated their losses at but a few hundred dollars, while others, like J. G. Hurkamp, who lost $10,000 worth of tobacco and tens of thousands of dollars in all, had been hurt severely. Some people believed their houses could eventually be repaired, although they remained uninhabitable for the moment. The "confusion and dirt were appalling." Not a few people felt "utterly disheartened," unable to think, or plan, or make any rational decision about the future. "My house not even fit to live in," grieved one woman. A Federal surgeon believed, "If the rebels succeed in holding the city, it will be many years before it can be made tenantable. In fact, I think they may as well found a new city as to undertake to repair the old one." Nor did it help that a scarlet fever epidemic continued unabated through the last of the year. During November and December, thirty-one children, none of them older than eleven years, died from its effects.[14]

The sight of the torn town and tortured people inspired two immediate reactions in Rebel ranks. First, it hardened men's attitudes toward the Yankees, even to the extent of justifying the barbarities they had perpetrated on the corpses and graves of their slain foes. It certainly made the slaughter in front of the stone wall seem like just retribution. "After beholding the scene [of the ruined town] you may imagine I was not in a frame of mind to contemplate with feelings of sorrow the field on this side of the town literally covered as it was with the dead bodies of Yankee hirelings," a Virginian admitted.[15]

The second, more generous, impulse prompted Confederate soldiers and Southern civilians—mostly Virginians—to collect funds for needy townspeople and suffering rural residents. Perhaps spurred by rumors that Lee intended to destroy what remained of Fredericksburg and fall back to Hanover Junction, Rebel soldiers from privates to generals, and Virginians from Richmond to Lexington, dug deep into their pocketbooks. Within weeks, $170,000 had been raised. The army's generosity may have been inspired in part because at least a portion of the town had been destroyed by Longstreet's artillery as it tried to disrupt the deployment of Federal columns on the battlefield. "May the Lord use it for relieving the real need of many hundred sufferers," prayed the chaplain of the Second Virginia Infantry, which donated $505.05 to the cause. "Truly the town presents the horrors of war, in desolation, vacancy, poverty & ruin." Citizens of Fredericksburg began immediately to apply for some portion of the relief funds.[16]

But while soldiers prayed for a season of repose, generals knew they could not rest, not yet. On the last day of 1862, Lee praised the "fortitude, valor, and devotion" of his men, but he reminded them that the enemy, "still numerous and strong," could strike again at any moment. For his part, Burnside wanted to redeem himself. On the same day that Lee addressed his army, the weary Union commander met with President Lincoln to propose a new offensive. The atmosphere was tense. Generals Franklin and Baldy Smith, à la Hooker, had already sent the president their plan to capture Richmond, and other officers had publicly belittled Burnside. When Burnside, in response to complaints by a fretful Halleck that the army sat idle, planned a flanking movement across the river, it was scuttled by a pair of Baldy Smith's subordinates, John Newton and John Cochrane. The two politically connected generals wangled a meeting with Lincoln to inform him of Burnside's rumored operation and emphasize the lack of support for it in the army. Lincoln almost immediately countermanded the movement and told Burnside to attempt no new operation without first consulting him. Even some of Burnside's critics called the president's action "monstrous." General Heintzelman observed, "There is great disgust that the President interferes with military matters." Confused by Lincoln's interference, Burnside rushed to Washington. Thus the December 31 meeting.[17]

When the president told his general how he had learned of the plan, the stunned Burnside told Lincoln he still wished to advance, even though he knew most of his officers opposed an offensive before spring. Lincoln listened but remained cautious, and he declined to approve any plan not endorsed by Halleck and Stanton. Discouraged, Burnside met for several more days with the president, secretary of war, and general in chief, alternately pressing his demand for a new offensive and offering his resignation. Lincoln continued to withhold his support for the former but refused to accept the latter. Halleck still pushed for action, although he remained, as usual, singularly unwilling to suggest or endorse any particular plan. Only a commander in the field, Halleck insisted lamely, could judge the best course of action. When pushed for suggestions, he, too, threatened to resign. Lincoln became more than a little disillusioned with Halleck during these days. Finally, on January 5, Lincoln gave qualified approval to Burnside's plan while avoiding, as he had for the previous two months, any suggestion that he was *insisting* on an advance. "Be cautious," he warned Burnside, "and do not understand that the government, or country, is driving you."[18]

Both Burnside and Lincoln understood the benefits of action. For one thing, it might restore the army's confidence. By mid-January, many soldiers, like Burnside, sought vindication; they wanted to get on with the war and prove their mettle. They began to rationalize their defeats so that even disasters like Fredericksburg did not loom so large. "We were not defeated, but only repulsed," reasoned a Pennsylvanian some two weeks after the battle. "We will soon be on the move again, and test rebel courage at some other point. I am just as sure of success now as I was when I first enlisted." A New Jersey colonel did not believe the army was demoralized, only "tired of war," and when called upon, he said, it would "fight to the last." It behooved Burnside to nurture that spirit by gaining a victory before spring. Then, too, not a few people still hoped to see McClellan back in command. Some men wanted him to replace Halleck; more often, they longed to see McClellan return to the field. No one, friend or foe, thought Little Mac would have blundered as badly as Burnside had at Fredericksburg. "We can never win another victory till he comes back," asserted a Union captain. More pointedly, he swore to his family, "If the small fry at Washington want to hear treason talked, let them come to the army. . . . McClellan alone can save the army." Neither the president nor Burnside wished to face that prospect.[19]

It was also a good time to distract the army, keep it busy, and not let it consider its grievances, of which there were many. High on the list was the government's failure to pay its soldiers. By mid-January, the Army of the Potomac had not seen a paymaster in six months, a hardship not only for the men but, in many instances, for wives and children who depended on government wages for their support. "Men are discouraged that their families are in want," observed one officer, "and, of course, have no hart to work or fight." Burnside recognized that the delayed wages had caused "great dissatisfaction" among both his soldiers and their families as well as "much gloom and despondency throughout the entire command."[20]

Then there was the "Negro Question." People had been speculating about whether the president would enact his proclamation of emancipation as promised on January 1. The Radicals feared he would not. Once he did so, large numbers both in and out of the army spoke against it. "We thought we were fighting for the stars and stripes," spat a soldier in expressing the widespread opposition, "but we find out it is for the d—— nigger." A Pennsylvania corporal claimed, "The soldiers are a good deal dissatisfied about Lincoln and I do not believe this army will fight as well anymore as it used to do." Even a man who supported emancipation recognized the passion of the dissenters and conceded, "Some that were Republicans are now Democrats." One particularly cynical fellow who held no love for the abolitionists decided, "I care not if the Niggers eat the Whites or the Whites kill the Niggers, just so that the War be ended. But alas-a-lack-a-day, the Proclamation will not go even as far as our bullets go."[21]

The additional announcement that black regiments would be recruited also produced an initially negative response. A Massachusetts soldier believed blacks lacked the courage to fight, and should black troops fail to do their part in battle, they would "meet as hot a reception in their retreat as in their advance." He elaborated: "The feeling against niggars is intensely strong in this army as is plainly to be seen wherever and whenever they meet them. They are looked upon as the principal cause of this war," especially in Irish regiments like his own. "Negroes are not loved in our army especially by the irish," verified a non-Irishman, "and I think that a regiment of negroes unless it did all the dirty work might as well go to ———— as to be joined to the army of the Potomac." Blacks were "lazy and dont know what freedom means," he continued, "what honor would we gain by having them as allies, how it would degrade us as a nation."[22]

It is difficult to generalize about the reaction of one hundred thousand men to such emotional issues, but morale clearly was low in the Army of the Potomac between mid-December and mid-January. A New York infantryman confided to his father, "our men dont fight as well as they did when we first came out. there is not the same spirit in the men. they have ben in so many battles and seen so much hardships that they are demoralized." A New Englander chimed in: "Our soldiers are losing their patriotism, & who can blame them. they are getting sick of war, of fighting without any good result." Another man agreed unequivocally: "It is the opinion of every one out here that this war will never be settled by fighting." A Pennsylvania infantryman told his mother, "The papers say so much about the men eager for the fray, but to tell the truth, you will not come across one man in the whole army who is not heartily tired of the whole thing and would like to see it settled any way at all."[23]

The spirits of some men had sunk so low that they no longer believed they could whip the Rebels. Some Northerners even thought Southerners were better soldiers. "The rebel army was never so strong before as it is to day," stated one man even before Fredericksburg. "I do not think that we can ever conquer them." A New Yorker told his wife the army was "sick of fiting" because it thought the Rebels could "never" be defeated.[24]

Still, few Federals would admit that the Confederates were better fighters; the difference, then, must be in leadership. "I think myself ther has been to many mistakes with our offersers," volunteered one recruit. "I think if thay had been as determed as the south it wood been over before this tim." A Michigan soldier told the home folks, "I have lost all of my patriotism since I see how the thing works, and taking us across the river as they did right before such works, and not a leaf to hide us." A Pennsylvania cavalryman judged: "[The South] can and will keep up till they gain their Independence if it is twenty years to come. I think they have proven their army to be equal to ours and their Generals I believe are superior to ours except *our* Gen. McClellan."[25]

Not a few men also realized that although another attempt at a winter campaign defied logic, political and popular pressure on Burnside to close out the year with a victory was intense. The country—and thus the politicians—remained "clamorous" for an offensive, observed a disgusted Pennsylvania soldier, "and our rulers, not being able or not having the moral courage to resist the clamors of the dominant party, will of course do something to check the criticisms of the press, if nothing to suppress the rebellion." Why would not Lincoln and the civilian leaders leave the generals free to do their job, to plan strategy and win the battles? "I am tired of this way of carrying on war," complained a Michigan volunteer.[26]

The belief that public opinion and ignorant politicians were the source of its ills became a powerful force within the Army of the Potomac. Fredericksburg, they came to believe, had resulted from "the orders . . . of those high in authority who . . . insisted on an engagement at once let the cost be what it may." These men and those who egged them on cared nothing for the suffering of the soldiers or for the widows and children produced by the war. The army had "good enough" generals, one man told his mother, but "the old fogies and accursed traitors at Washington" meddled and interfered too much with them. The army was "tired and sick of being bamboozled around hither and hither according to the caprice of those in authority and gaining nothing." An infantry sergeant told his wife, "God grant that the people in the North will rise in their might, & hurl the rotten politicians in Washington to Hades, & give us a Gen. to lead us or call us home before we die of exposure or are killed in useless battles." Said another soldier, "I feel like a man in a ship with a crazy pilot and rocks ahead—gaily we sail on . . . going swiftly, going surely to the Devil." A New Englander concluded with emphasis, "There is *something wrong somewhere* at Washington I think," while a Wisconsin sergeant stated flatly, "The army has long since lost all confidence in all the officials at Washington."[27]

They also resented civilians—the "stay at home party"—who criticized the army's slow progress on the road to Richmond but contributed nothing to the cause. It was all very well for soft men to sit safe by a warm fire, play with their children, sleep with their wives, and line their pockets, but no one seemed to care about the poor soldier who ate raw pork, shivered in a single blanket, and risked his life. The resentment felt by some soldiers even spilled over against family members. A Pennsylvania soldier told his brother that he did not blame the Fredericksburg disaster on old "'Sides'" but on "you Abolishionists at home for crying out 'On to Richmond.'" The North had terribly underestimated the South's will to resist, he continued. The only way to put down the rebellion was to place all men aged eighteen to forty-five under arms "and then let them go at them and kill, kill. . . . But you Radicals stay at home and leave the Conservatives (who foresaw this) to fight it out."[28]

The most damaging effect of all this military and political chaos was that it caused men to question the value of the war, even its purpose. "Every thing looks gloomy," a Michigan soldier confessed to his sister. Another change of commanders seemed inevitable, he told her, or the army would be sent to fight in some other theater—one where it could win. The simple fact, concluded this Wolverine, was that the Rebels fought better than Union boys because they had a stronger motivation: "independence & a separate government." Why was he fighting? Neither he nor his friends knew, and certainly "the object to be attained" seemed to be "very different" from when they enlisted. "Here we are with winter on us, living in little kennels that would freeze an iceberg," charged another infantryman, "changing ground so often that we have no chance to build log huts, fighting & dying under a fool of a General, & for what? God only knows, I dont." A Pennsylvanian agreed. "One day we fight for the Restoration of the Union," he scoffed, "but the next . . . we are striving for the predominence of some Abolitionist Scheme."[29]

Adding to the nation's woes, Union military fortunes outside Virginia had not sparkled in late December and early January. True, Rosecrans had eked out a victory at Stones River on December 31–January 3, but his army had lacked the stamina to pursue the retreating Bragg. Gen. Ulysses S. Grant saw his plan to close in on Vicksburg disrupted when Gen. Nathan Bedford Forrest wrecked his supply depot at Holly Springs, Mississippi, on December 20, and Gen. William T. Sherman suffered defeat at Chickasaw Bayou on December 29. Then came reports that the ironclad *Monitor* had foundered and sunk off Cape Hatteras, North Carolina, and that Gen. John B. Magruder had recaptured Galveston, Texas, for the Rebels.

Meanwhile, Lee tried to anticipate Burnside's next move, should he make one. Lee had sent his army into winter quarters on December 20 while heavily fortifying the area around Fredericksburg. He preferred to act defensively, to "meet the blow wherever it falls," but he was willing to strike if need be. He had kept his cavalry in constant motion since December 16, probing along the Rappahannock and making occasional forays east of the river to sniff out Yankee intentions. He also constructed or strengthened artillery batteries at strategic points all along the Dare Mark. "For several days past there have been indications of some movement by the army of Burnside," Lee told Jefferson Davis on January 13, "but nothing sufficiently definite to designate it if true." Rumors ran rampant, he admitted, but he still could not judge if Burnside planned to advance, retreat, or only shift position.[30]

Burnside unveiled his plan to the army on January 16. Halleck had been no help. The general in chief had reemphasized that Lee, not Richmond, should be the focus of the offensive, but he still refused to commit himself to any specific operation. Following a petty reminder that Burnside had ignored his strategic suggestions the previous November, Halleck would say only, "It devolves on you to decide upon the time, place, and character of the crossing. . . . I can only advise that an attempt be made, and as early as possible." Burnside did get advice from Montgomery Meigs, who insisted that a successful crossing upriver would allow him to outflank Lee as Lee had outflanked John Pope at Second Manassas. Properly positioned, said Meigs, Burnside could sever Lee's communications, get between the Rebel army and Richmond, and force Lee to fight or retreat. With that scenario in mind, Burnside ordered his three grand divisions to advance toward Banks's Ford, less than five miles above Fredericksburg. The usual people—Franklin, Hooker, and their friends—still opposed the movement, but many other officers, particularly Meade and Reynolds, strongly supported it.[31]

The mood of the army was cautious as it prepared to march. Some men continued to belittle their commander and the Lincoln government. Rumors spread that the Rebels already knew the details of Burnside's offensive and had prepared to meet it. Men talked openly of refusing to fight or insisted on the impossibility of victory. Burnside's own provost marshal observed: "I believe the men are unwilling again to fight, at this point, if they can get clear of doing so. . . . There is a bad state of things all around." Yet much of the army seemed to welcome a chance for redemption, and even men who thought Burnside's plan half-baked had grown weary of the dissidents. "Burnside may be unfit to command the army; his present plan may be absurd, and failure certain," reasoned Colonel Wainwright, "but his lieutenants have no right to say so to their subordinates." Nor did all their grumbling and foreboding inhibit the combat potential of Burnside's soldiers. The Union army had shown no lack of courage at Fredericksburg, and whatever their complaints about politicians, the press, stay-at-homers, and generals, these men could hold their own on any battlefield. As Gideon Welles said of the army's supposedly low morale, "There is, I think, some truth and some exaggeration in all these reports."[32]

Not a few men wrestled with conflicting loyalties and contradictory emotions. One junior officer—a lieutenant in the Second Michigan Infantry— confided to his diary two days after the evacuation of Fredericksburg: "Yesterday was one of unmitigated rage, hate and shame. These gradually gave way to the blues but my elastic nature has lifted the load. There is no denying the defeat, but I begin to be hopeful again & never felt more like fighting till the last man falls." Yet, a month later, as the army received preparatory orders to march, he admitted: "The morale of the army is not now right for such a move. If we go the little that I can do shall be done with a will but I hope it will not be tried at present." A Michigan enlisted man, this one in the Twenty-fourth Infantry, still believed the Union cause was "just and right," but he prayed that Burnside would not cross the Rappahannock at Fredericksburg, to be "Butchered again."[33]

The Rebels watched and waited. Lee still did not know Burnside's intentions, but he betrayed no concern. His cavalry kept him well informed of Federal actions; his men closely guarded all accessible fords. "The enemy is apparently making some movement," he informed his wife, "though concealed from our view." Burnside was headed upriver, Sigel had left Stafford Court House, and there was a demonstration—a diversion Lee assumed— at Port Royal, but only Burnside mattered. Lee would have to be patient; he must wait for Burnside to make the first move. To maneuver his troops prematurely in such weather would be futile and foolish. Perhaps the rain and mud would "dampen their ardour," fancied Lee. A confident Mississippian who had fought with Barksdale in the streets of Fredericksburg summed up the attitude of Lee's privates: "They are . . . a brave people no mistake about [it]," he said of the Yankees, "but we are brave and better shooters."[34]

In the end, it did not matter, for Burnside never tried to cross the river. No sooner had his grand divisions left their camps—spread from Stafford to Falmouth to White Oak Church—than the rains came. The first day of the advance, January 20, began well enough, "a good one for marching," commented one officer, but by dusk, the army was entangled in wilderness while the temperature dropped, the wind howled, and rain fell in sheets and torrents. This "regular northeaster" continued for thirty-six hours, and the hapless Burnside found his army bogged down in a "Mud March." Men could move only by slipping and sliding in the ooze; pontoon and artillery trains became mired in "ass deep" mud. Thousands of horses and mules collapsed in harness from exhaustion. Desertions, which had already been running near 25 percent, increased sharply as hundreds of men changed direction and started home. Many men had threatened to desert even before the march began. A whiskey ration issued in one brigade to warm the men produced a donnybrook. "It would be hard to tell which was the meanest . . . time the Army of the Potomac ever had," one soldier would recall, "but for mud, rain, cold, whiskey, drowned out men, horses, mules, and abandoned wagons and batteries, for pure undulterated demoralization . . . and downright cussedness, this took the cake."[35]

Burnside ordered the men back to their camps on January 22, and the retrograde movement along laboriously constructed corduroy roads began the following day. Men who had not been discouraged at the start of the march surely were by then. They spoke of the rain as a godsend that had spared the army from another humiliating and murderous defeat. Some soldiers wondered that Burnside had shown enough sense to give up his folly. "*I imagine he heard some plain talk as he passed along the lines and took the hint,*" guessed one infantryman. Perhaps, again, it was a matter of timing. Had Burnside been a day or two quicker, had he acted with dispatch to cross the Rappahannock before the rains came, he may well have surprised Lee. The Confederate commander had been aware that Burnside was in motion, but he had no indication of where the Yankee army was headed or where it might cross the river. Lee also defended a far longer portion of the Rappahannock than he had in mid-December; swift deployment would not have been easy for him.[36]

So Lee's men remained relatively dry and at ease, but no amount of miserable weather could dampen the animosity and anger in the Army of the Potomac. Rebel pickets taunted their opponents with placards that read, "Burnside Stuck in the Mud," and they offered to trade "a lame corporal" for the Federal general. "'Tis mortifying," conceded one Yankee. The Mud March, once Burnside's hope for redemption and a tonic to restore morale, became the last straw for soldiers seemingly on the verge of mutiny. "The Army of the Potomac is no more an army," decided a New Jersey infantryman. "Its patriotism has oozed out through the pores opened by the imbecility of its leaders, and the fatigue and disappointments of a fruitless winter campaign." Burnside could not be blamed for the weather, acknowledged fair-minded men, but the mud, combined with his failure a month earlier, spelled "lack of success," and that alone, predicted the majority, must lead to his removal.[37]

Even the usually genial Burnside was fed up. He had learned that some senior officers had groused aloud to the men all through the march about the insanity of his plans and his unfitness for command. So, while the army slogged back to camp, Burnside traveled to Washington to demand that Hooker and three of his cronies be dismissed from the service and that Franklin, Baldy Smith, and three other officers be relieved of their commands. Meeting with the president, he told Lincoln plainly that he would no longer tolerate disloyal and insubordinate officers undermining his authority, turning the men against him, and complaining about government policies. Lincoln had heard enough. Burnside, like McClellan, had failed once too often. The next day, Lincoln did relieve Franklin of command, but he also conveniently accepted Burnside's long-standing request to be relieved of duty. In his place, he appointed Joe Hooker.

CHAPTER SIX

# Hurrah for Hooker

Burnside's Mud March proved to be the last straw. Fredericksburg might have been shrugged off as a tragic miscalculation, but this latest failure appeared to be sheer blundering, and it further undermined confidence in Union strategy and generalship. Soldiers were angry and, yes, demoralized, "totally demoralized," regardless of what the newspapers said. "Must the Army mutiny before they understand that they are not in 'excellent spirits?'" asked one man rhetorically. "We can fight Rebels but not mud," piped up another fellow. Another man, thoroughly disgusted by the numbing effect of the march, believed the army had hit rock bottom. "I am geting pretty near tierd of it [the war] for it is a dogs life there is lots of soldier diserting and going home and I doant blame them mutch mary I have prety near turned out to be a democrat since I came to the armey."[1]

But if, as many people claimed, the Army of the Potomac was not so much broken and demoralized as discouraged and apathetic, then perhaps a change at the top would infuse the men with renewed enthusiasm. That was Lincoln's hope when he appointed forty-eight-year-old "Fighting Joe" Hooker. Although the general cringed at mention of his moniker—the result of a newspaper compositor's error during the Seven Days' battles—he had all the right credentials. A native of Massachusetts and a West Point graduate, Hooker had won a brevet lieutenant colonelcy in the war with Mexico, only to resign from the army in 1853. He spent the next seven years farming in California and working as superintendent of military roads in Oregon before returning east to enter the war. Once the target of Hooker's critical barbs, Gen. Winfield Scott refused to give him a commission. President Lincoln, however, made him a brigadier general after being told by the audacious Hooker that he was "a damned sight better general" than any of the

Federal officers who had commanded at First Manassas. Lincoln liked
Hooker's boldness.[2]

Yet the president acquired Hooker's boldness at a price. No one would
deny that the general was a better than average soldier. He had turned in
solid performances on the Peninsula, at Second Manassas, Antietam, even
Fredericksburg. Many people in and out of the army had thought him a
likely successor to McClellan. A muscular six-footer with sandy hair and
blue-gray eyes, Hooker looked the part of the great captain. He had been
called the most handsome man in the army, and even rank-and-file soldiers
were impressed by his sturdy stature, ruddy countenance, and youthful appearance. Officers and politicians, however, thought Hooker talked too
much, too boastfully, and indiscreetly. Though not associated with any particular faction in the army, Hooker had a way of keeping the pot stirred.
And he could be annoyingly arrogant. More than a week before his appointment, Hooker bragged to some staff officers that he could have command of
the army whenever he gave the word.

Lincoln was not insensible to Hooker's weaknesses. He had been a target
of some of the general's more outrageous statements, as when Hooker insisted that the country needed a dictator to direct affairs and win the war.
But Lincoln also knew that the public adored Fighting Joe and that, in any
case, there were few other generals to whom he could turn. McClellan was
out of the question. The president briefly considered Rosecrans, but Rosy
was a western general, and Lincoln's only other attempt to put a western
general—John Pope—in command of an eastern army had been a disaster.
Reynolds and Meade were good men, but Hooker outranked them. The
president knew that Stanton and Halleck—with whom Hooker had a running feud over a decade old—would be displeased with his choice, but
Chase and the Radicals would applaud it. So he made his own decision and
braced himself for the consequences.[3]

Upon receiving word of his appointment, Hooker rushed to Washington.
The president greeted him with a sobering and astonishingly frank letter of
appointment. Lincoln praised his new champion as a "brave and skillful soldier," but he also warned the general that he disapproved of his subversive
behavior and rash statements. Hooker had injured the country in his efforts
to thwart Burnside, charged Lincoln. The president stressed his willingness
to ignore all of those recent slips, but Hooker must go out and whip the
Rebels. Legend has it that Hooker humbly accepted Lincoln's chastise-
ment, but he also sought a favor. He wanted Lincoln's assurance that as
commander of the army he would report directly to the president, not, as

normally would be required, through Halleck. Hooker feared repercussions from his feud with the general in chief, and he did not, in any case, want to be undermined by Halleck as Burnside had been. Lincoln granted his request.[4]

Hooker returned to the army elated. He had received a free hand to accomplish the same mission given to Burnside: defeat Lee. As long as he covered the approaches to Washington and Harpers Ferry, he would be left to judge "when and where" to strike the enemy. Still, Hooker knew he faced a formidable task. The spirit of his army was low, while that of the Rebels had apparently never been higher. Desertion in his army, though declining since December, stood at nearly two hundred per day. His men still did not receive adequate supplies, and most of them had not been paid for months. "It needs a strong arm to deal with this army just at present," considered a junior officer. "Some severe remedies must be applied at once or it will be decomposed."[5]

The army did, in fact, yearn for a strong commander, but not everyone thought Hooker was that man. Some soldiers shouted "Hurrah! for Hooker!" but the majority wished to reserve judgment, as they had with Burnside, until they saw how Hooker responded to the pressures of command. A few men still favored Burnside. They may have doubted Burnside's ability to lead an army, but they liked him and recognized that many of his failures had resulted from "unfortunate circumstances." On the Mud March, judged one surgeon charitably, he had been "defeated by Divine, not by human agencies." Other officers and men would not be placated until McClellan returned. One McClellanite suggested a compromise. Let Little Mac "take Military dictatorship of the whole," he proposed, and make Hooker "the fighting Gen."[6]

At best, Hooker's appointment inspired a "sardonic satisfaction . . . that any sort of change must be for the better." It was apparently easier to accept anyone in place of Burnside than it had been to accept Burnside in place of McClellan. Some men, bothered by the name "Fighting Joe," feared he would be "too rash & anxious to fight." Observed another, "As far as haste or rashness is concerned Hooker is worse than Burnside," and, indeed, it was largely because of such assumptions that Hooker so disliked his sobriquet. One officer doubted Hooker's mastery of the "higher branches" of generalship. "His bravery is unquestioned," he confessed, "but he has not so far shown himself anything of a tactician." A New Englander pessimistically predicted, "We all expect Hooker will soon make his grand failure & patiently wait for it."[7]

Some aristocrats and old army men scorned Hooker as a drunkard and womanizer. Capt. Charles F. Adams Jr., son of Lincoln's diplomatic minister to the Court of St. James, called the new commander "a man who has not the confidence of the army and who in private character is well known to be—I need not say what." As with so many of the charges leveled at the controversial general, the drunkenness and lechery could be exaggerated. A drunkard he probably was not. Rather, he seemed to have a low tolerance for alcohol so that a single glass of wine might turn his complexion florid and further loosen his naturally active tongue. As for the women, that was another matter. "I never saw him that I thought him the worse for liquor," admitted Colonel Wainwright, but the artillerist feared that Hooker may have had a genuine "failing . . . in the way of women." The oft-repeated charge that Hooker's name became a synonym for low-class prostitutes has a very murky pedigree, and yet the fact that such a notion gained wide circulation suggests his reputation.[8]

Hooker had little time to spare. The Northern public may have cheered his appointment, but it also had "great expectations" of him. Most of the army was willing to give him a chance, but he would have to capitalize on its goodwill while proving the naysayers wrong. To nearly everyone's astonishment, Hooker did just that. Over the next two months, he reorganized his army and introduced reforms that won the confidence of all but the most die-hard McClellanites. He benefited from circumstances to some degree, as when Congress approved a $100,000,000 loan to pay the army. But for the moment, Fighting Joe would become Administrative Joe. "Hooker is determined to do a great many things that are right & some probably that are wrong," concluded General Patrick. Mostly, he did the right things, and he would dazzle the army.[9]

First, Hooker appointed a general staff, and to head that staff, he enlisted Gen. Daniel Butterfield. Not everyone liked the choice. The diminutive "Little Dan," who had operated an express company before the war, carried a reputation for being imperious. He delighted in "papers and Orders," and he rubbed many officers the wrong way. Most men thought he had a meager grasp of things military, even though he had written a valuable handbook for the soldier, *Camp and Outpost Duty for Infantry*, and had fashioned a new "lights out" call, "Taps," from an old cavalry bugle call. Still, Butterfield had an undeniable knack for organization and administration, and in many ways, as he and Hooker sought to restore the army's morale and combat efficiency, the new chief of staff would serve his commander well.[10]

Next, Hooker moved to curtail desertions. About 25 percent of his men

(86,636) were missing when Hooker took over the army. The numbers were lower than when Burnside assumed command, but they had risen in January. Hooker knew that men deserted for any number of reasons: they were frightened, they found army life disagreeable, they no longer believed in the nation's cause. But he also knew that many men left camp not with the intention of deserting but because they wanted to visit their homes. After all, thought these citizen soldiers, it was winter; the army was not going to fight; why should they not be allowed to see their families? Thus Hooker, in a shrewdly calculated effort to reduce the number of unauthorized absences, if not hard-core deserters, expanded the opportunities for enlisted men to receive furloughs. Specifically, he permitted two of every one hundred men to be away from their commands for up to fifteen days. The practical benefits of his action may have been slight, but most men hailed it as an "excellent order" that would "tend greatly to make all contented and amiable." Hooker also limited the number of officers who could be away from their commands so that he appeared to be the soldier's friend, determined to treat officers and enlisted men equally.[11]

At the same time, to discourage men too restless to wait for a furlough, Hooker told the Potomac naval flotilla to be more vigilant in watching for deserters who tried to cross the river. Furthermore, having learned that many men slipped through the lines dressed in civilian clothing, he ordered that all packages sent to the army be inspected for such apparel and instructed pickets to permit no one through the lines, soldier or civilian, who did not have authorization. Indeed, he told his pickets to shoot anyone who failed to halt when challenged.

Lincoln approved of these actions and helped the general's cause in early March by pardoning all deserters who voluntarily returned to the army by April 1. Hooker, whose vigorous measures had produced a large number of prisoners, asked that the president extend his pardon to men awaiting trial or punishment because it seemed unjust to punish soldiers unlucky enough to be caught while rewarding those clever enough to have evaded apprehension. At the same time, Hooker warned that the guilty would be punished swiftly and surely. Once a sentence was imposed, he said, there would be no appeals to the president, who was notorious for commuting the death penalty. Officers applauded Hooker's sternness. "If the government had . . . punished desertion by death in the beginning," one man reasoned, "the US Army would be larger by some 70,000 men to day."[12]

Hooker next attended to the physical comfort and health of men in camp. Under the watchful eye of his medical director, Dr. Jonathan Letterman, and the United States Sanitary Commission, he had new hospitals built and old ones renovated. New regulations governing sanitation resulted in drainage ditches, rotation of camp sites, and separation of sites used for latrines and drinking water. Soldiers received a healthier diet, too, one that included desiccated mixed vegetables and potatoes once a week, fresh vegetables—onions and potatoes—twice a week, and fresh ("soft") bread four times a week. The army soon received eight hundred tons of supplies daily, and Hooker ensured their speedy delivery by having all camps not tied by railroad to the wharves at Aquia Landing connected by corduroy roads. "Within a week," confirmed a Maine volunteer, "a change was perceptible in our cuisine. Our larders began to fill and we had no occasion to patronize the sutlers."[13]

Hooker, like Napoleon, also bolstered morale symbolically. For instance, upon his return to the army, Hooker inspected the picket lines in a raging snowstorm. Five inches of snow covered the ground, with a layer of mud and water beneath that. Having experienced the biting cold for himself, the commander sent half the pickets back to camp, an act that increased his popularity a hundredfold. "This is a small & a transparent act," recognized a junior officer, but it made an immediate impression on men who had never seen an army commander stray far from his quarters in stormy weather.[14]

More was to come. Hooker invigorated a year-old order that permitted regiments and batteries to inscribe their colors with the names of battles in which they had fought. "No better incentive could be given to this army for future effort than this honorable recognition of their past services," Fighting Joe insisted. In mid-March, upon the urging of General Butterfield, Hooker assigned a system of division and corps badges, to be worn on the caps of all officers and men. Butterfield, with a flair for promoting small gestures that became military traditions, had earlier urged this same system on McClellan without success, although Gen. Philip Kearny, one of McClellan's division commanders, adopted the badges for use by his men during the Peninsula campaign. Butterfield, while commanding the Twelfth New York Militia earlier in the war, had issued identifying medals in the shape of a Maltese cross (which now became the emblem of the V Corps) to his own men. The new badges were meant to improve battlefield control and unit cohesion while reducing straggling and misconduct, but people also recognized the sense of pride such badges instilled—the "'esprit de corps' and elevation of morale," as Butterfield put it.[15]

More formally, Hooker reorganized the army in some profound ways. First, in early February, he scrapped Burnside's grand divisions and returned to a system of corps organization. This change gave Hooker less direct control over the army, and it required him to find eight, rather than three, principal field commanders, but Halleck applauded the alteration, as did most of the army. Hooker selected the reliable Reynolds for the I Corps, with the II Corps going to an ailing Couch. Gen. Daniel E. Sickles, best known for having killed his wife's lover on the streets of Washington four years earlier, received the III Corps. Meade took the V Corps, while Hooker gave Uncle John Sedgwick, a West Point classmate, command of the VI Corps. Franz Sigel would lead the XI Corps, which contained a large number of first- and second-generation Germans. Gen. Henry W. Slocum, Hooker's youngest corps commander at age thirty-six, got the XII Corps.

It was a fairly solid group. Some men, including the perceptive Meade, distrusted Sickles—a former congressman and political crony of Hooker and Butterfield—as an opportunist, notorious for using political and journalistic connections to promote his military career. And, in fact, Sickles was the only non–West Pointer Hooker entrusted with a corps. Still, one of the few people to express displeasure over the new assignments was Franz Sigel. As a former grand division commander, Sigel felt slighted about what he regarded as a demotion. Not only had he been relegated to corps commander, but he had been given the smallest of the seven corps. Denied redress by Halleck and Lincoln and in a state of deteriorating health, Sigel requested and received a leave of absence. His departure actually proved a blessing for Hooker, who had also heard complaints from Oliver Howard. Howard thought he, rather than Sickles, whom he outranked, should have the III Corps. With Sigel's departure, Howard got his corps, although, as a result, Hooker immediately heard complaints from Carl Schurz, who, as senior division commander, thought he should lead the mostly German unit.

Hooker also consolidated his cavalry into a single corps. John Pope had taken a step in this direction the previous summer when, during the Second Manassas campaign, he centralized command of the scattered cavalry regiments of each corps. It had been a popular move, and so Hooker formalized it, thus organizing Federal horsemen along the same lines as their Rebel counterparts. Gen. George Stoneman commanded the corps, which he carved into four divisions under Gens. Alfred Pleasonton, William Averell, David McM. Gregg, and John Buford. Hooker intended that his horse soldiers should play a more offensive role than they had assumed in the past, but the innovation would produce mixed results.

The artillery acquired a new look, but one opposite that given the cavalry or even the Confederate artillery. Rather than place a single artillery chief—

Henry Hunt—in control of his guns, as Burnside had done at Fredericksburg, Hooker allowed his corps commanders to decide how their guns should be used. In turn, corps commanders distributed their allotted number of batteries to their divisions. General Hunt protested vigorously that this reorganization would impede rapid and efficient tactical deployment of the artillery. Hooker, himself an artillerist, emphasized that the new system would boost morale. "In my old Brigade and Division," he insisted, "I found that my men had learned to regard their batteries with a feeling of devotion, which I considered contributed greatly to our success."[16]

The army's new commander believed that hard work kept an army in fighting trim and gave it less time to grumble, gossip, and intrigue. With that in mind, Hooker ordered frequent drills, reviews, and inspections. He created numerous construction projects, too, including fortifications, corduroy roads, and wharves, and instructed corps commanders to keep on hand no fewer than 750 shovels, 250 picks, and 500 axes for these "special purposes." To inspire his men in their work, he publicly identified regiments and batteries that had or had not reached a "proper state of discipline and efficiency." Units that pleased him received additional furloughs; slovenly or ill-disciplined units lost furloughs. To help survey and measure the efficiency of his regiments, Hooker appointed an inspector general for the army, Col. Edmund Schriver.[17]

Hooker also issued a flurry of directives to improve the army's discipline and image. In a move that must have startled his critics, he insisted that the Sabbath be strictly observed in camp. He then took steps to halt the systematic plundering and intimidation of Southern civilians. Hooker knew that many men—sometimes entire units—boasted of their depredations. A member of the 123d New York Militia, for example, claimed that his regiment stole sheep and hens "for the purpose of . . . putting down the Rebellion." The New Yorker told his brother frankly, "You may feel thankful that this War is not being carried on in your neighborhood, for the Soldiers would not think any more of taking your last sheep or Cow, and if no other wood was near to cook it with, of taking the Pickets off your front fence than they would of eating a hard Cracker." To root out this spirit, Hooker assigned safeguards to households that requested them, and he authorized requisitions only for forage and fresh beef. "Plundering and pillage will under no circumstances be permitted," he directed emphatically, and he held officers accountable for the actions of their men. If reconnaissance parties or pickets found it necessary to arrest suspicious-looking civilians, they must do so only "upon proof sufficient to warrant" their arrest.[18]

Hooker tightened security in the army, too. He started by forbidding fraternization with the Rebels, especially the exchange of newspapers. Like many generals, Hooker feared the press, both as a means of passing on useful information to the enemy and as a source of discontent among his own troops. As one soldier noted of the latter problem, "The infernal papers with their treasonable language do more to demoralize the army than anything else." In response to this threat, Hooker barred irresponsible journalists from his camps and prohibited the distribution of newspapers he considered disloyal. Thus the pro-administration *New York Times* circulated freely among his men while the "treasonable" *Herald* was banned. To limit general access to his camps, Hooker also required that all civilian purveyors, sutlers, newsboys, and news agents not formally attached to the army register with the provost marshal.[19]

Equally as important as stopping leaks in his own army was the need to gather information about Lee. Fighting Joe replaced the existing intelligence system with a new agency, which came to be known as the Bureau of Military Information. Lafayette C. Baker had directed the old spy network from Washington, while General Patrick had seen to intelligence for the Army of the Potomac. Thirty-five-year-old Col. George H. Sharpe directed the new bureau, which he patterned on the intelligence system used by George Washington during the Revolution. Rather than restrict the acquisition of information to espionage and interrogation of prisoners, as had Baker and Patrick, Sharpe, a former New York lawyer and prewar acquaintance of Dan Butterfield, created an elaborate network of "agents" to scout enemy positions and question Southern civilians extensively. Sharpe integrated this information with intelligence gathered from balloon observations, cavalry reconnaissance, Confederate newspapers, interpretation of Rebel signal flags, and other sources. "The secret service of Gen. Hooker is far superior to anything that has ever been had before," one observer concluded; "nothing transpires in the enemy's camp which he is not speedily informed of."[20]

His army responded as Hooker hoped it would. In December and January, men had spoken of conditions—the cold weather, sparse rations, skeleton quarters, and their vulnerable position in enemy territory—as their "Valley Forge," a "tale of suffering" they would one day relate to their grandchildren. But morale, comfort, and health quickly improved under Hooker's command, and with the improvements came a reevaluation of the commander. Even many officers and men who had been skeptical of Hooker grudgingly admitted the success of his reforms. Colonel Wainwright, one of those who had professed low expectations, acknowledged a fortnight later, "Hooker seems to be gaining the confidence of his generals by degrees." Wainwright, like many other officers, still complained about the load of paperwork that accompanied the changes, but he conceded that many of Hooker's orders were "good." Even so seemingly small an improvement as "soft bread" gained the unbounded gratitude of the men, who would recall many years after the war how "Old Joe" had placed the army "in the best of spirits." One officer concluded: "The army like General Hooker. They like him because he is 'fighting Joe Hooker.' They like him because of the onions and potatoes he has furnished, and . . . because . . . they expect him to lead them to victory."[21]

The reassessment came from all ranks. A Michigan colonel judged that Hooker was "fast winning the love and confidence of this army—He seems to *appreciate* the material of which his splendid army is composed." A newly promoted major declared, "General Hooker gains favor with the Army, and all about us looks better." An infantry captain thanked God for Hooker, "a thorough soldier and possessed of an indomitable *will*," who punished deserters and rewarded loyal soldiers. A Massachusetts lieutenant and staunch McClellan man praised Hooker's furlough system, especially the practice of granting additional leaves to outstanding regiments. A midwestern corporal, relieved to see the condition of the army so much improved, decided that Hooker was "the right man in the right place." A Connecticut soldier assured his mother, "He has done better by us than any one has before." A Pennsylvania private told his sister, "The army is getting confidence in Hooker, and the expression of the soldiers is quite different from what it was a few months ago."[22]

Many benefits and improvements were measurable. The number of desertions, for instance, declined dramatically, as pickets collared hundreds of men and hundreds more voluntarily returned to the army. Many soldiers learned from example not to test their new commander. "There is a man to be shot soon for desertion," a New Jersey officer matter-of-factly informed his family. "One from our regiment is to have his head shaved, the letter 'D' branded on his skin, and drummed out of camp in the presence of the whole Brigade." A Michigan brigade formed into a hollow square to witness six of its number drummed out of service. One lad, who thought the ceremony a "most revolting spectical," swore that he would rather return home in "a coffin" than be disgraced in that way.[23]

Instances of sickness and disease in the Army of the Potomac declined sharply. From November through January, 134,443 men reported sick in

135 different medical categories, and 1,590 of them died. Of course, those were only the officially listed sick; many more men suffered from colds and complained of various ailments in the winter weather. "I am nearly well of my cold," one sergeant dutifully reported to his wife. "It is a general complaint here amongst the men and some have been so bad with it that they had to go to hospital." But after January, despite continuing damp, miserable weather, the numbers of men entering the hospital or incapacitated by their afflictions declined. From February through April, only 88,384 men appeared on the sick rolls, a difference of 46,059, and only 1,068 died.[24]

Communicable diseases and sicknesses caused by unsanitary conditions fell even more dramatically. Instances of typhoid fever dropped from 3,435 cases and 595 deaths to 1,992 cases and 400 deaths. Various forms of diarrhea and dysentery fell from 46,204 cases and 326 deaths to 25,105 cases and 184 deaths. Instances of scurvy dropped from 440 to 258. A New York soldier assured his wife that his regimental camp was "a pretty one neat and clean" and that the army had plenty of large hospital tents, "with good beds, everything clean and comfortable."[25]

That Hooker took command of the army in winter gave his reforms a chance to work. The men led "a very quiet life" through most of February and March. "Drills take place when the weather will permit," commented a junior officer, "but mud and rain is generally the rule." The very fact that they would not be fighting any time soon improved the spirits of most men, and the comfort of winter huts and heated tents allowed them to endure occasional storms in relative comfort. Camp began to seem like "home" for the soldier.[26]

Growing numbers of men sought to mend their souls, too, as a battalion of agents from the United States Christian Commission and American Tract Society joined army chaplains to prepare men for death. Some chaplains, believing the agents "infringed upon their rights," resented this intrusion, but more often harmony prevailed. There was, after all, much work to do. While the chaplains preached to full houses, the commission's "missionarys" held prayer meetings and distributed religious tracts, Bibles, and hymnals. At Falmouth, where a church had been made into a barracks, commission agents transformed an abandoned tobacco warehouse into a chapel. "I think they are doing much good," decided a Pennsylvania private. "There is a great many very good men here in the army as well as some very bad ones, and I think the army is growing better, if anything." One colonel claimed that hundreds of men in his regiment sought, and received, Bibles from commission agents.[27]

Still, soldiers are notorious cynics. Some men scoffed at the short time allowed for furloughs, more an "aggravation" than a relief, they said. "I would not give five a cent to go home and be obliged to come back here again," groused a Massachusetts artillerist. "I am afraid if I got a Furlough I should never return." One infantryman told his sister that men returning from furloughs warned their friends not to go home. "They don't feel so contented since being in civilized society again," he explained. Yet this same soldier—and probably most of the army—decided, "If I thought I could get one I would risk it, I think." Other men complained about the small number of furloughs available or decided that only the "favorites" of the officers received them anyway.[28]

Even the improved diet drew sarcasm. One infantry private admitted that the quantity of food had increased, but he could not say much for the quality of the meat. "I can hardly cal it beef either," he complained, "for it is nearley al boans and what meet is on them is [so] tough that we can hardly get it." An Indiana soldier praised both quantity and quality, but the army's improved "culinary condition" also inspired a gloomy thought. "Soft bread, Potatoes, onions, Molasses, beans, beef, and butter are among the things we now eat," he conceded. "Like a herd of poor oxen they are fattening us for the slaughter."[29]

And so winter camp became "an improvised 'debating society,'" as men in pairs and groups jawed about recent changes in the army and the country and argued over the nation's future. The Conscription Act, for example, had everyone in an uproar. As Lincoln and the Congress weathered the public outcry against compulsory military service, the army also discussed its merits. Some officers and men were hostile to it. "If the north stands a draft thay are fools," pronounced a Pennsylvania sergeant. Other men doubted that conscription would make any difference or expressed disappointment that so many occupations and religious groups had been exempted. One soldier declared two such groups, Quakers and clergymen, "as full as much to blame for this war if not more so than any other class of [the] community."[30]

Most soldiers, however, thought the draft a good thing. It was high time, they said, that all able-bodied men helped squash the rebellion. A Michigan man assured his father, "We go in strong for the draft and conscripting, and if there is any resistance just let them send for the gallant Wayne Co[unty] Tigers." Soldiers expressed particular glee when they considered that conscription would draw on those people about whom they had been complaining all winter. It was time for all "cowards" who sat safely at home and filled their purses with wartime profits to demonstrate their patriotism. "And if it would be their lot to fall," decided an artillery lieutenant in mock sympathy, "their Widows and Orphans could live comfortably." An Irish immigrant serving in a Massachusetts regiment confessed, "I am glad it has passed. it will bring the people to their senses and the war will either be settled or the skulking blowers at home will have to come out and do their share of the fighting."[31]

Many men welcomed conscription if blacks were to be drafted. Congress was wrong to pass the bill, asserted a New York infantryman, but if it meant that African Americans must finally "fish or cut bait," he would cheer it. Many men remained bitter about emancipation. "When I enlisted I supposed that [it] was to fight to restore the Constitution and the laws," spat a New Englander in mid-February, "but . . . it has been all nigger nigger. as for me I did not come out here to shed my blood for the sake of raising the niggers on an equal footing with the whites." Contact with former slaves who sought refuge in Union camps confirmed the suspicions of many men that blacks were not worth fighting for—much less dying for—as seemed to be the government's new purpose. So perhaps it was time, they decided, to send blacks to the front along with white shirkers. "It is nothing but a niger war an so let the nigers fight as well as the wite," decided a Pennsylvanian. Perhaps fighting for the country would "cool them down a little."[32]

Still, if white troops could agree on the wisdom of using blacks as cannon fodder, it remained quite another thing to fight alongside them. Although Lincoln's plan for emancipation stuck in many a craw and divided the army as well as the country, most soldiers gradually—very gradually—came to accept it. But the idea of depending on blacks in battle and the inherent implications of a racial war required significantly more adjustment. "For my part," one infantryman told his wife, "I do not like to fight side by side with the niggers to kill white men. I do not think the Government gains much by employing niggers as soldiers. it will lose just as many whites." An army surgeon predicted that the presence of black troops would demoralize the army and increase racial animosity. "Place a black Regt. side by side with the 105th [Pennsylvania,]" he declared, "and this Regt., though composed almost entirely of Republicans, would charge and drive them with more delight than they would the rebels. I don't say I approve of this—but I do say it would be done."[33]

A relatively new annoyance on the home front came from an increasingly shrill Copperhead movement. Copperhead agitation reached a head in mid-January, just before Hooker took command of the army, when Clement L. Vallandigham delivered a speech in Congress that "counselled peace & sub-

mission to the rebels." Having been defeated for reelection in October, the
Ohio representative used his final days in the capital to call for European intervention and demand "practical recognition" of the Confederacy. The
"treasonous" manifesto caused a backlash against the antiwar movement.[34]

By the end of March, most of the Army of the Potomac deemed these
Peace Democrats a menace, far worse than the stay-at-homers. It was one
thing to pay lip service to the war while shirking military duty. Soldiers
could understand if not sympathize with such behavior. It was quite another
thing to embrace peace at any price. "My *first* object is to crush this infernal
Rebellion," declared an infantry captain, "the *next* to come North and bayonet such foul miscreants as Vallandigham." A noncommissioned officer
vowed that the Union would be preserved "in spite of the copperheads."
There could be no peace terms with traitors, he emphasized. The army, if
turned loose against such people, would "give them that *Peace* that Knows
no Wakening. By the Bayonet, or U.S. union Pill." A Pennsylvanian cursed
them as a bunch of "desperadoes" who had created "much dissatisfaction in
the army." If men were to be conscripted, another soldier proposed, then let
the "fault-finding" Copperheads and "sympathizers of Jeff" be the first to
go. Such low life "can't be sent too soon," he declared.[35]

Entire units drew up resolutions and signed petitions to voice their support for the war and to announce that they favored the severest measures
possible, including conscription and the arrest of all Copperheads, to ensure
victory. "The whole 24th [Michigan] . . . go in for a vigorous Warfare and
not stop till every *armed Rebel* is swept from the states," declared one man to
his family. His regiment had signed just such a resolution and had concluded its patriotic ceremony by delivering three rousing cheers for the
"gallant" Joe Hooker. "If any one ask you what the opinion of the 24th [is],"
he emphasized, "tell them it is for a vigorous Prosecution of the *war* if it
takes every man in the *north*." A New Jersey regiment passed a similar resolution "in favor of a rigorous prosecution of the war, . . . and denouncing
severely the *Copperheads* of the North."[36]

Hooker's reforms, in combination with anger at meddling politicians and
cowardly civilians, wrought a change in the army. As men became more dissatisfied with events at home and less unhappy with life in the army, a spirit
of genuine hope and enthusiasm surfaced. They began to look forward to
another crack at the Rebels. "I have made up my mind that a country that is
worth living in in time of peace is worth fighting for in time of war," confessed an infantryman. One junior officer assured a lady friend back in Indiana,
"I love peace but I love my country more. I am now wedded to war and

while God gives me strength I mean to share her fortunes until the issue comes." If men now spoke of concluding the war short of total victory, they nonetheless insisted that it be won on "*honorable* terms."[37]

In March, Hooker and his generals evaluated the progress of their men by holding a series of formal reviews. Brigade commanders reviewed regiments, corps commanders reviewed divisions, and Hooker undertook a systematic review of all corps. The men looked and felt ready to fight. "We go on Dress Parade now in a few minutes," a midwestern soldier hurriedly scribbled to his wife. "I have got to believe that we look pretty well with good clothing, shining steel, noisy Drums, and flying colors. I believe we look like respectable soldiers." A New Englander, much impressed by all the drills and reviews, decided that Hooker "intended to make an army of some force." More than that, he added, "I have some reason to hope that with fighting . . . we may accomplish something to raise the drooping spirits of an unfortunate country."[38]

Unfortunately, Congress would not let the corpse of Fredericksburg rest in peace. On the day Hooker succeeded Burnside, the Senate called for additional hearings by the Committee on the Conduct of the War. The stated purpose was to investigate charges that John Newton and John Cochrane had used political connections to scuttle Burnside's strategic plan of late December. Once convened, however, the committee strayed to new questions about the causes of the Fredericksburg defeat, particularly Franklin's alleged failure on the Federal left. All through February and March, the principal players—Burnside, Franklin, Meade, Gibbon, Birney, Reynolds—trooped to Washington to face Wade, Chandler, Gooch, and the other legislators.

By the time Meade arrived to testify, on March 16, the newspapers hummed with new allegations about Franklin. Burnside and Franklin fell out publicly in a dispute over the former's precise orders to the latter. Meade returned to Falmouth convinced that "Franklin was to be made responsible for the failure at Fredericksburg" and that the real reason for resuming the hearings was to accumulate "all the testimony they can procure to substantiate this theory." Colonel Wainwright, who was not called to testify, did not place much faith in the integrity of the committee, whatever its findings might be. "In fact, these committees of investigation seldom are really just," he observed. "They are appointed and start with a foregone conclusion on the subject in hand, . . . call their witnesses and put the questions accordingly."[39]

By the end of March, the army seemed ready once more to challenge Lee along the Dare Mark. Hooker, as yet, had no firm plan for doing so, but he received new intelligence almost daily about the size, strength, and disposition of Lee's army. More important, the Union army had responded to his leadership. "The *morale* of our army is better than it ever was," George Meade told his wife on March 30, "so you may look out for tough fighting next time." That same day, a New England infantryman confirmed the general's opinion. "The Army was never so good as at present," he told his sister. "I know not how the numbers are, but if we have any thing like Equality with the other side, nothing can stop Old Joe from levelling rebeldom."[40]

# CHAPTER SEVEN

# The Chinese Game

At another time and place, Robert E. Lee might have been more optimistic. After all, only a few weeks earlier he had directed the most lopsided Confederate victory of the war. He had enjoyed watching the enemy's frustration as it failed to cross the Dare Mark before the onset of winter. That the weather had contributed as much to Federal failure as his own carefully constructed defenses did not matter. The fighting would enter its third year before the Yankees could again challenge him. The best hope of Confederate victory was to wear down the Union army and increase war weariness in the North. Lee and his men were doing just that, and their strategy would grind ponderously on.

Yet, in late January, Lee was anything but optimistic or even content. He had been astonished on a brief trip to Richmond in mid-January to hear President Davis say that victory was within sight. Lee doubted it. He knew he must prepare his army for a spring campaign in a country with dwindling resources. At the moment, the Army of Northern Virginia was in "excellent condition, physically & morally." The "spirit of our soldiers," he informed the secretary of war, "is unabated." Lee intended to maintain that spirit and condition, but to do so, he would have to make changes and overcome substantial obstacles. In fact, he found himself in a situation similar to Hooker's during February and March. In those weeks alterations and reforms would be made in Lee's army, and while his men waited for spring, Lee would try to anticipate what Hooker might do next and again find a way to baffle Yankee designs.[1]

Lee had first to maintain the size of his army, which would, in any case, be outnumbered by the Federals. Summarizing the state of the army for Secretary of War Seddon, Lee emphasized on three separate occasions in

January the need to raise more troops. While acknowledging a growing Federal threat in North Carolina and southeastern Virginia, he also underscored the danger of dividing his own army as a way to neutralize advances elsewhere. Lee stressed the "absolute necessity" of increasing the size of all Confederate armies. "The success with which our efforts have been crowned," he reminded Seddon, "should not betray our people into the dangerous delusion that the armies now in the field are sufficient to bring this war to a successful and speedy termination."[2]

The Confederacy had conscripted men since the previous spring, but too many legal loopholes remained for those who wished to avoid service. Worse still, as one government war clerk discovered, enrolling officers, surgeons, and other officials charged with enforcing conscription had allowed thousands of able-bodied men to escape the draft "for a price." Of twenty-five thousand men drafted in East Tennessee, only six thousand actually entered the army. "The rest," charged this clerk, "were exempted, detailed, or deserted. Such is the working of the Conscription Act."[3]

Lee knew that conscription was not working. Condemning the civilian "laggards" who demanded victory at the cost of other men's lives, he betrayed a sharpness rarely seen in his official communications. The armies had been dangerously reduced by disease and battlefield casualties since the previous spring, he told Seddon, and many more men would die if the armies entered battle against vastly superior numbers. "This blood will be upon the hands of the thousands of able bodied men who remain at home in safety and ease," warned the commander eloquently, "while their fellow citizens are bravely confronting the enemy in the field, or enduring with noble fortitude the hardships and privations of the march and camp." Lee also complained about the thousands of men exempted from military service and the hundreds more already in the army who sought discharges or transfers to safer berths behind the lines. What remained clear, he told the secretary with feeling, was that the number of deaths, discharges, and reassignments in his army far exceeded the number of new recruits and conscripts he received. With an adult white male population one-third that of the North, the Confederacy needed a larger proportion of its men in military service.[4]

The government ignored Lee's warning. Not only did he receive few replacements, but strategic necessity finally compelled him to divide his army. In mid-February, he learned that Hooker had sent the IX Corps down the Potomac to Hampton Roads. It looked like a Union move in force against either Charleston or Wilmington or an attempt to occupy southeastern Virginia. Worse still, Lee foresaw a possible Federal move up the James River, which, if not blocked, would force him back toward Richmond, conceding the Rappahannock line to Hooker. To contend with any eventuality, Lee ordered James Longstreet to Richmond with two divisions, Pickett's and Hood's. Old Pete, delighted to have an independent command as head of the newly created Department of Virginia and North Carolina, established his headquarters at Petersburg, twenty miles south of Richmond. Over the next few days, he positioned his troops on the Peninsula, at Petersburg, in North Carolina, and around Suffolk, Virginia, sixteen miles west of Norfolk, to protect the approaches to the capital. The deployments were clearly necessary, but they cost Lee some sixteen thousand men.

Hooker's movement to the southeast and Lee's countermove heartened Confederates on the Rappahannock. Even though the Federals continued to mount "demonstrations" all along the river, it appeared that the "bloody fighting" would move closer to the coast and Richmond. "I am glad that we are to be left here," a Georgian informed his wife. "Wee have this country all fortified from Fredricksburg to Port Royal. I have helped to build them, and if I have to do any more fighting I would like to have some of the ditches to fight in on the Rappahannock: it is now the strongest position that our army has ever occupied." A Virginia soldier also saw promise in the movement, although for a very different reason. He hoped that the rest of the army would soon follow Longstreet and occupy a part of the state where the men could be properly fed. He was tired of Fredericksburg, he said, "where nothing can be had fit to eat at no price."[5]

The need to feed his men was perhaps the most serious problem Lee faced that winter. On the day that Hooker became his new nemesis, Lee had only a week's worth of provisions on hand. In the past, he could depend on the surrounding countryside to supply his men, but most of the communities around Fredericksburg had been picked clean by both armies. He could confiscate needed provisions from the population, Lee admitted, but that would "produce aggravation and suffering among the people" with no substantial gain for the army. The Richmond, Fredericksburg, and Potomac Railroad still delivered supplies to Hamilton's Crossing, a distance of fifty-five miles from Richmond, but it was an old, single-track road with unreliable rolling stock. Besides that, Col. Lucius B. Northrop, the Confederacy's commissary general, operated a notoriously inefficient department, and Samuel Ruth, the Pennsylvania-born superintendent of the railroad, had been suspiciously slow in dispatching just two supply trains each day to the army.[6]

Several other elements compounded the problem of provisions, as well as other supplies. First, the more troops Lee acquired—troops he badly needed—the more dire his shortages became. Not only did a larger army require more food and shoes, but every man brought into the ranks was one less person at home to raise, harvest, and deliver food, one less person to produce shoes, blankets, rifles, and other manufactured goods. The Confederate people had worked mightily to meet the demand for supplies, and their efforts reached a peak in the spring of 1863. At the same time, the strain of this effort on Confederate resources and morale also reached a breaking point. The enemy added to these woes by continuing to gobble up Rebel territory, which further restricted the amount of land and means of production available to the South. Federal gains in Virginia and Tennessee, in particular, had drastically reduced supplies of grain and livestock. And to bring the conundrum full circle, the Confederacy had lost much of that territory because it had an inadequate number of troops to defend it.

By late March, the government had reduced daily rations to eighteen ounces of flour, four ounces of bacon, and occasional issues of rice, sugar, or molasses. To obtain vegetables and prevent scurvy, the men had to forage daily for sassafras buds, wild onions, lamb's-quarter, and poke sprouts. "There is more anxiety felt on the provision subject than all others," conceded a Rebel surgeon, who appreciated better than most that reduced rations not only left soldiers undernourished but also made them more susceptible to sickness and disease. As for the men, they knew only that the army was "pretty bad off," with a diet of "old rusty bacon & musty flour & not enough of that."[7]

"The men are cheerful, and I receive but few complaints," Lee reported proudly to Seddon, but the general knew his army could not maintain its "health and vigor" under such conditions, and it most certainly could not be expected to "endure the hardships of the approaching campaign." The men did, indeed, manage to take the shortage of food in stride, as they did most of their privations. They could even joke about it to some extent, but their good humor sometimes betrayed pinched stomachs. "The Yankees say that we have a new gen'l in command of our army," a Georgian claimed, "& say his name is *General Starvation* & I think for once they are about right." It was a fair retort to Johnny Reb's taunt about the Yanks being stuck in the mud.[8]

Horses and mules have a less finely honed sense of humor than do men, but their condition was even more pitiable. Lee needed these animals to support his cavalry, transport his wagons, and haul his artillery. The army simply could not function without them. Yet if the depleted Virginia countryside could not support his soldiers, it could provide even less sustenance for the animals. This might not have mattered had the beasts been able to survive as well as the men on half rations, but they could not. Cavalry horses had to serve on picket and conduct raids. Mules had to draw the wagons that carried the supplies that fed the men who would win the war.

Lee's difficulty in finding provisions and fodder was eased by the extent of his defensive line, which stretched twenty-five miles from Banks's Ford to Port Royal. While strategic concerns forced him to scatter his army, he benefited from this lack of concentration by occupying a broader area from which to draw supplies. Longstreet's two divisions had been sent not only to defend Richmond but also to obtain provisions and forage below the James River, an area less touched by war than the Rappahannock line. Lee kept Grumble Jones in the Shenandoah Valley, both to prevent the Federals from penetrating it and to live off the Valley's relative bounty. Stuart's cavalry used Culpeper County as its base of operations, where they could also draw supplies from Greene and Madison Counties. Lee detached units to other parts of the state, too, to gather beef, sheep, hogs, and cured meat. Some of his officers believed that the only solution was to move back into Maryland or to invade Ohio or Pennsylvania as soon as possible.

This dispersal of his troops and the shortage of animals left Lee unable to contemplate large-scale offensive operations against the Yankees. With the departure of Longstreet, he had just sixty-two thousand officers and men at his command. The mud, snow, and rain forced Lee to stifle his naturally aggressive impulse, and the inactivity gnawed at him. In mid-February, he informed President Davis, "The most lamentable part of the present condition of things is the impossibility of attacking them with any prospect of advantage." The Dare Mark could not be forded, and the only useful bridge, at Rappahannock Station, was too distant—some twenty miles upriver from Fredericksburg—to be of practical use, given the "liquid state" of the roads. The high water could be seen as a blessing, however, for, as Lee informed Seddon, "The army in front of us at present is certainly very large."[9]

In addition, it was difficult to anticipate what that large army might do. Lee had a reputation for reading his opponents, but it had never been easy for him, and his most recent experience with Burnside had showed that Federal commanders could behave in the most inexplicable ways. In playful reference to Fighting Joe's nom de guerre, Lee complained to his wife that "Mr. F J Hooker" was keeping him in an unnecessary "state of expectancy." He mused to Mary in late February that Hooker "ought to have made up his mind long ago what to do." Lee's first concern had been to shore up his defenses, and so his men had spent most of January and February digging entrenchments and constructing artillery positions at strategic points along the river. He had no notion of where or when the Yankees would strike. To his daughter Agnes, Lee noted of Hooker, "He is playing the Chinese game. Trying what frightening will do. He runs out his guns, starts his wagons & troops up and down the river, & creates an excitement generally." A Confederate surgeon summed up the situation: "We are too well entrenched for them to attack us here, but it is hard to tell what these crazy, fanatical Yankees intend to do."[10]

While waiting for Hooker to make up his mind, Lee filled gaps in his command structure. Jackson and Longstreet, of course, would still lead his two corps. Most of his division commanders remained in place, too, with Anderson and McLaws continuing to lead the two divisions Longstreet had left on the Rappahannock. In Jackson's Second Corps, Jubal Early, promoted to major general in January, formally took charge of Ewell's division. At the head of Jackson's old division—now named for Isaac Trimble, who was still convalescing from a wound received at Second Manassas—stood Gen. Raleigh E. Colston, a former Virginia Military Institute professor and an old friend of Jackson. Powell Hill retained command of Jackson's third division. Most of the changes came at brigade level, where death, sickness, and resignations forced Lee to appoint seven new commanders. All of these men were generally more experienced and better known to their men than were Hooker's brigadiers.

Lee also further reorganized his artillery. Having assigned individual artillery battalions to divisions before Fredericksburg, Lee, after consulting with artillery chief Gen. William N. Pendleton, took another step toward centralization. He divided most of the battalions, with four batteries apiece, between his two corps, leaving just one battalion at the disposal of each division. Doing this required that he reduce the army's reserve from some twenty batteries to six. Lee made corresponding changes in the artillery's command structure, but consolidation constituted the significant reform. A few men worried that he had undermined the army's esprit de corps by weakening "that knowledge of and confidence in each other" that had been engendered by having infantry and artillery serve together in camp, on the march, and in battle. But Lee and Pendleton believed that consolidation would promote more efficient use of the guns and enhance the army's ability to concentrate its firepower at critical points of attack and defense. Firepower was also enhanced by exchanging most of the army's six-pounders for newly recast twelve-pounders.[11]

While the armies maneuvered, postured, and wondered what to do next, the citizens of Fredericksburg found themselves in the thick of things once again. Confederate soldiers tore up their streets and yards to construct rifle pits and trenches. They garrisoned every unoccupied residence and, sad to say, did not always serve as models of decorum and patriotism. The guardians of the South were "ruining what the Yankees left," complained one woman. "The entire destruction of Fredericksburg is highly probable," moaned another resident. "Indeed our troops are plundering and defiling every house in town," this man continued, "and yet we must be silent for fear of giving encouragement to the enemy. To the dwellers on the frontier, civil war is no pastime." The old town acquired a "ghostly" appearance as yet another exodus of frightened citizens commenced.[12]

Nor did the countryside benefit from the army's presence. Soldiers seeking warmth and comfort in abandoned houses and slave quarters seldom took care of the property. They stripped the region of fencing for twenty miles around in search of firewood and construction materials. Farmers who had stockpiled cordwood, fodder, and grain turned a handsome profit by selling their treasures to the army. Arthur Bernard, at Mannsfield, sold twelve thousand cords of wood and other supplies for $37,000. But such huge sums were a rarity, and most people felt lucky to realize any gain before their resources were confiscated or stolen.[13]

A Methodist minister who had remained in Fredericksburg to provide moral glue for the community and the army while his family sought refuge in Culpeper tried to see the bright side. "I am afraid the tragedy here is not yet ended," he reported to his wife, and yet he believed the number of Federals across the river had diminished by late February and that they might be moving their base of operations. Townsfolk spoke of having the refugees return by summer. It was true, admitted the minister sadly, that Confederate soldiers had further damaged the town in fortifying it. They had even pulled down abandoned houses and enclosures to acquire fuel. Yet he had also seen many soldiers protect the property of citizens. "Some of the *better sort* are quartered in our kitchen," he told his wife, and they seemed "to take pride in keeping out others [and] preventing depredations." Far more depressing were reports that some Fredericksburg refugees in Caroline County had been turned out of their rented quarters because they could no longer pay their bills.[14]

Meanwhile, Lee ordered a series of cavalry raids to determine the exact size of that "very large" army across the river. He had sent out raiding parties all through December and January to collect information and gather supplies, but those forays had been against Burnside, who had maintained very poor security. Hooker had thrown out a thick screen of cavalry to protect the flanks of his army, and for the most part, he stymied Lee's efforts to penetrate Federal lines. One exception came on February 25, when Gen. Fitzhugh Lee, the commander's flamboyant nephew, conducted a raid of tremendous daring. Breaking through Union outposts at Hartwood Church, five miles in the rear of Falmouth, the Rebels killed 36 and captured 150 Yankees while losing only 5 of their own men.

Even more dramatic, in concept if not in results, was a series of raids and reconnaissances led by Lt. John S. Mosby. Mosby conducted his first raid with just nine men on January 10, when he struck at pickets along the Alexandria, Loudoun, and Hampshire Railroad. Over the next two months, his detachment, which fluctuated in size from sixteen to thirty men, continued to annoy, threaten, and bewilder Hooker's army. By serving apart from Stuart's main body of cavalry, Mosby initiated a brand of warfare long familiar in the western and trans-Mississippi theaters. He drew his raiders from several sources, including volunteers from "regular" cavalry regiments, men on furlough, boys too young to enlist in regular units, even hospital convalescents. They hailed mostly from neighborhoods in Loudoun and Fauquier Counties, where they largely served. The region soon became famous as "Mosby's Confederacy."

Mosby's defining exploit came on March 8, when he slipped into the headquarters of Gen. Edwin H. Stoughton at Fairfax Court House. His special target was to have been Col. Percy Wyndham, a former British army officer who commanded a Yankee cavalry brigade and boasted the finest mustachios in the Army of the Potomac. Wyndham had called the Rebel raider a horse thief and threatened to retaliate against Confederate civilians if Mosby continued his activities. Mosby wanted to capture the pompous Englishman at Fairfax but learned upon arriving that Wyndham had left camp. Mosby settled for Stoughton, the youngest general officer in the Union army at twenty-four years, whom Mosby literally snatched from his bed and escorted back to Culpeper along with thirty-eight other men and fifty-eight horses. This exploit, added to his earlier achievements, earned Mosby promotion to captain; he would be a major by early April. More important, Mosby received permission from Lee and President Davis to organize an independent company of partisan rangers. The company soon became a battalion, the Forty-third Virginia. While Lee, the West Pointer, remained somewhat embarrassed about using partisans, he could not ignore results, and he freely praised Mosby's talent for harassing the enemy.[15]

But it was Hooker's reorganized cavalry that initiated the biggest fight of the winter. Union horsemen had been probing the Rappahannock since December, and on March 17, they provoked a telling engagement at Kelly's Ford, in Culpeper County. Still uncertain of Hooker's intentions, Lee had assigned much of his cavalry to Culpeper, where convenient fords across the Rappahannock had drawn an uncommon amount of attention from the Federals. It was from Culpeper that Fitzhugh Lee had launched his Hartwood Church raid. Hooker had been enraged by that episode. "We *ought* to be invincible, and by God, sir, we *shall* be!" he had shouted at General Averell. "You have got to stop these disgraceful cavalry 'surprises.' I'll have no more of them." And so Averell drew the assignment of crossing the Dare Mark and punishing his old West Point classmate, Fitzhugh Lee.[16]

The resulting battle of Kelly's Ford pitted 2,100 Federals against 800 Confederates. The Yankees took 56 casualties and lost 22 men captured in five hours of fighting; Lee had 99 casualties, including a mortally wounded John Pelham, and 34 men captured. The Federals scampered back across the river when they ran low on ammunition. They had gained nothing, and yet they had fought the vaunted—if heavily outnumbered—Rebel horsemen to a standstill. Averell was in such high spirits in retreat that he left a package for Fitz Lee at the river ford. With the package was a reply to a note that Lee had left for him at Hartwood Church. Lee's message had quipped, "If you won't go home, return my visit and bring me a sack of coffee." Averell now replied, "Dear Fitz: Here's your coffee. Here's your visit. How do you like it?"[17]

R. E. Lee, who had been in Richmond when news of the fight arrived, rushed back to camp and put his army on alert. For all he knew, this sudden Federal thrust was part of a broader advance. An assault against Fredericksburg might come next, or another flanking movement. Lee considered having Hood rejoin the main army, and Rebel camps all along the Rappahannock reverberated to the sound of drums beating the long roll. Nothing happened. Hooker had not intended any additional action, and the Rebels breathed a sigh of relief. Some men were convinced that premature bloodshed had been further delayed when a heavy snow fell over the next few days. "I hope that providence will stop them at every attempt they make by some means or other," a grateful infantryman told his sister.[18]

Most Confederate soldiers had given up on Providence in at least one respect, for by March, as men gossiped around evening fires and speculated about the generals' plans, they had decided that peace was a forlorn hope. The Federals would apparently not melt away, and predictions of Northern political disintegration had not been realized. A faint renewal of hope accompanied rumblings from the Midwest—center of Copperhead agitation and the railings of Vallandigham—about a separate peace, secession from the Union, and so on, but by and large such reports inspired only grist for the gossip mill. "I havent but little faith in it," declared a Georgian of such rumors. "We all think that there is a very poor chance for the war to end," echoed another soldier. "I fear that it will last two years longer," predicted one man, "until Lincoln's time is out and I think we might just as well prepare our minds to it."[19]

Still, having acknowledged that the war must continue, increasing numbers of Confederate soldiers looked to Providence to get them through the ordeal. In the battered churches of Fredericksburg, at large revival meetings, and in small rustic chapels, constructed by the men in regimental and brigade camps all along the Confederate line, hymns, prayers, and sermons, the echoes of rebirth and redemption, resonated in the winter air. "The soldiers made the old Church ring mellodious with the songs of praise to God," reported a Mississippi private. "It seemed that the Lord really was there among our Mississ troops." The enthusiasm swept up hundreds—perhaps thousands—of men in all three principal Southern Protestant denominations: Baptists, Methodists, and Presbyterians. Besides regular worship services and prayer meetings, the nondenominational Christian Soldiers Association and Soldiers Union Society sponsored gatherings. By late March, the society, with hundreds of members of all faiths, assembled every evening after roll call and three times on Sunday to pray and sing. "God is reviving his believers," a pious Alabamian assured his sister. "The Soldiers amids hardship and privations are now more zealous for the Cause of Christ Than our Christian friends at home."[20]

The men hoped that God would return the favor by displaying his zeal for their cause and shielding them on the battlefield. Religious fervor was not as widespread, and perhaps not as intense, as it would be the following winter, when Lee's army rested along the Rapidan River. Yet many men, having reflected on the precariousness of life, thought it best to guard their souls just as they protected their bodies when the bullets flew. With so many comrades already gone and a new round of bloody encounters awaiting them, they calculated the odds against survival. "Men generally listen more attentively to the preaching of the gospel than they formerly did," thought one veteran. Even soldiers who resisted the enthusiasm were often touched by the spirit. "Susan I have not been sensibly converted," confessed one man to his wife from Fredericksburg, "but I am not as wild as I was before I left home. I dont curse nor gamble nor cheat my fellow soldiers nor lust after the base women of this town of which there is a number."[21]

Lee certainly welcomed divine intervention. He estimated that the North's Conscription Act and a new national banking and currency system, both signed into law on February 25, placed 3 million men and $900 million at Lincoln's command. With those resources, the Northern president could wage war as long as he wanted and with as much ferocity as he desired. Lee despaired. "Nothing now can arrest . . . the most desolating war that was ever practiced," he confided to his son Custis Lee, "except a revolution among their people." By extension, the general reasoned, "Nothing can produce a revolution except systematic success on our part." Success, Lee hardly needed to say, would have to come on the battlefield and, more particularly, on his battlefields—the battlefields of Virginia.[22]

Yet, despite the cold, hunger, shortages of supplies, and occasional discouragement, Lee's men were as primed and ready to fight as Hooker's revitalized army. They were "finely drilled and disciplined, in good spirits and excellent health," boasted one Confederate, "their sentiments thoroughly enlisted in the cause." "We will never despair though these deprivations may last for years," insisted a particularly fervent Virginian toward the end of March, "but onward we go, with stout hearts & high spirits to drive an invading foe from the sacred soil of our sunny South." As long as the soldiers knew they were supported by the home folks, and especially the women of the Confederacy, he continued, their "zeal & patriotism" would never fail. "Who wouldn't be a Confederate soldier & contend for his rights & his home & his country," asked a cavalryman. "Hurrah for Jeff Davis & southern rights."[23]

The Army of Northern Virginia had become convinced of its invincibility, and foolishly so. This theme appears repeatedly in the letters and diaries of Confederates along the Rappahannock during the winter of 1862–63 and is akin to the irrational confidence many Union soldiers felt in George B. McClellan. "Our army seems somewhat spoilt," recognized James Longstreet. "The troops seem to think they can whip the Yankees with the greatest ease whenever they may choose to come, and wherever they come." A Virginian agreed. "The morale of the army is superb," he declared. "The idea of a defeat never occurs to them so great is their confidence in their own prowess, and skill of their generals." All successful armies must feel such confidence. Whether their triumphs are produced by skillful generals, excellent training, deficiencies in the enemy, or just plain luck—and there must always be luck—soldiers who believe they will win are better soldiers and more likely to win. Yet conviction and faith can go only so far, and undermanned, poorly equipped, and ill-fed armies cannot prevail indefinitely against superior numbers and resources.[24]

Confederate faith was fed partly by experience and the fact that Robert Edward Lee led the army. Lee also exuded confidence, which was nearly as exaggerated as that of his men. Some historians have accused Lee of taking Hooker too lightly, thereby breaking a cardinal rule of command: never underestimate the enemy. It is more likely that Lee's confidence, perhaps even his overconfidence, had been inspired by the previous performances of his army, which had never failed him and had always exceeded expectations. He was proud of his men and they of him. They could almost feel sorry for the Army of the Potomac, filled with brave men but plagued by a string of overrated commanders. "When we meet in the spring the result will be the same old tale," reasoned one Rebel. "They have never been accustomed to any thing else [but] defeat and disaster from us and they will hardly look for anything else now." Another Confederate concluded, "'The Grand Army of the Potomac' in soldiers parlance is 'played out,'" its men and officers "disaffected" by the recruitment of black troops. In contrast, "Genl Lee governs his army as the pilot does his vessel," this soldier maintained. "Hookers is like an old raft and cant be managed at all."[25]

Anger also fueled their faith. "If you could just see how the people of Northern Virginia have suffered from the hands of the Abolition Vandals you would say there is nothing to mean and base for them to do," fumed a Confederate. "They have gone systematically to work to starve us out and destroy all we have," a North Carolinian insisted, "to make the country a desert." Experience had shown him that Yankee soldiers were "unprincipled, cowardly, treacherous, sacrilegious, dishonest and not to be trusted in anything whatever." One of Stuart's staff officers, John Esten Cooke, confided to his diary: "The war grows in bitterness and looms larger and darker. So be it. I for one intend to die fighting them, if necessary. It is better than having my neck under a blackguard's heel."[26]

Some men claimed the remedy was to "play at the same game" as the Yankees by invading their territory. Lee occasionally mentioned the possibility of a second Maryland raid to acquire food and horses while, at the same time, removing the war from Virginia. One of his soldiers believed Lee should brush Hooker aside and move into Ohio and Pennsylvania to strike at Rosecrans's rear. Then, he predicted, with Rebel "feet upon their necks & our bayonets at their throats," the midwestern states would sue for peace. "Our people have suffered from the depredations of the Yankees," an officer told his wife, "but if we ever get into their own country they will find out what it is to have an invading army amongst them." Many officers—though not Lee—he insisted, would not try to curb their men, and even chaplains told them "they must spoil and kill" if given the opportunity.[27]

Folks at home also realized that the war must go on. The early months of 1863 were a bright, hopeful time for the Confederate nation. Although political sniping and criticism of the president had grown during the first two years of the war, most Southerners still expressed confidence in their political and military leaders. Compared to the political turmoil in the North, Confederates resided in near bliss. Still, the Davis government was wrestling with some thorny issues, and hackles had been raised. Davis clashed with several politicians, most notably his Texas nemesis, Senator Louis T. Wigfall. In the spring of 1863, Davis and Wigfall argued over a bill that would have given generals more latitude in selecting their staffs. Davis opposed it and won, but not without worsening already hard feelings. Other debates, most of them over issues that would have centralized more political power in Richmond, concerned Davis's right to suspend habeas corpus, the continuation of military conscription, impressment of slaves as military laborers, seizure of private property for military purposes, taxation, and inflation.[28]

All of these issues would erode public confidence and will over the next two years, but the most pressing problem in early 1863, and one that held serious practical implications for the army, was the runaway rate of economic inflation. The cost of living had risen tenfold since 1860, and prices continued to rise at an alarming rate. In Richmond, for example, flour sold for between $30 and $40 a barrel, although that was only a third of the price in many other places. Butter sold for $3 a pound, "bad bacon" went for $1.50 a pound, potatoes for $12 a bushel, and cornmeal for as high as $8 a bushel. According to one Richmond newspaper, the weekly grocery bill of a small family had risen from $6.55 to $68.25. Worst of all, people suspected that some merchants, manufacturers, shippers, financiers, and speculators were making "colossal fortunes" from the war, as, in fact, they were, at the expense of ordinary people.[29]

Two things most annoyed Confederate soldiers about life behind the lines, which they shared in common with Billy Yank. First, they disliked the speculative mania among civilians. "Everybody has gone crazy on the subject of money making," complained Dorsey Pender. Not only did speculation and greed drive up prices, but they also made the armies less effective. Railroads, for example, which seemed to have such a hard time supplying the nation's fighting men, never failed to deliver the freight of merchants and manufacturers who could afford to pay for speedy delivery.[30]

Second, Rebel soldiers worried about the South's peace movement. The protesters were not as well organized, vocal, or numerous as the North's Copperheads, but any agitation injured the pride and confidence of men who liked to think they had the nation's unquestioned support. In spring 1863, the most active and publicized antiwar movement occurred in North Carolina. Its high visibility could be attributed in no small part to the nurturing role of the state's governor, Zebulon Vance, and other "conservative" politicians. Dorsey Pender, a North Carolinian, also complained about the "treasonable articles" written by William W. Holden, editor of the state's leading newspaper, the *Raleigh Standard*. "Unless we can have a successful and early campaign," worried Pender, "there is no telling where it will stop."[31]

Less apparent to the average citizen and soldier but nonetheless worrisome, foreign affairs loomed large in the life of the Confederacy once again. President Davis had devoted fully half of his January address to Congress to the situation in Europe. If the government had been pessimistic about foreign intervention in December, it was downright fatalistic by the end of March. When the United States and Britain amicably resolved the *Peteroff* affair—the seizure of a British merchant vessel by the Union navy in February—Confederates were in despair. What would it take to shatter British complacency, to arouse the British lion from its slumbers?

But Southerners were being too shortsighted. The European balance of power was in a precarious state in the spring of 1863; potential trouble was brewing in Italy, Poland, and the German states. Britain had larger interests than the American war to consider. More than that, slavery still haunted the British conscience. The English working classes, ignoring the calculation inherent in Lincoln's Emancipation Proclamation, rallied in mass meetings to support the Union and denounce slavery. "Politically things go on swimmingly here," reported Henry Adams in late January while serving his father, the United States minister to Great Britain. "The anti-slavery feeling of the country is coming out stronger than we ever expected, and all the English politicians have fairly been thrown over by the people." Palmerston's government grew more comfortable in the belief that it could not—indeed, dared not—back the Confederacy too aggressively unless Lee or some other Rebel general could decisively demonstrate the strength of Confederate arms.[32]

France proved only slightly more helpful. Napoleon III was interested in gaining a foothold in Mexico, and the Confederate States provided a convenient buffer between his new North American empire and the United States, which firmly stood by the Monroe Doctrine. A French army invaded Mexico in January. That same month, the Davis government concluded negotiations with Frederick Emile Erlanger, director of a German-based French banking house, who was also close to the French emperor, for a $14.5 million loan. The Erlanger loan, using Southern cotton for collateral, provided Confederate contractors with enough credit to make military and naval purchases in Europe through the remainder of the year. It also shook the confidence of United States consuls in Britain, who called it the "Thieves Loan." Even so, the French government seemed no more willing than Queen Victoria to commit itself to a potentially losing cause. France would act only in direct concert with Britain. As one of Lee's soldiers put it, "Intervention from foreign powers is no longer to be expected and the only alternative left us is to persist in our course until our enemies find it is useless to pursue their determination to exterminate us." A Mississippi lad concluded, "I trust that all now are satisfied that our only help is to come from our strong arms."[33]

All these factors—domestic and foreign—doubtless entered the discussion when Lee met Davis in Richmond during the second week of March. The president felt better after being confined to his home with "neuralgia in the head" and an abscessed tooth for most of February, but a meeting was necessary in any case. President and general had to agree on a plan of action, for Lee's army must either advance or prepare to defend the Rappahannock line. Lee, like most of the president's confidants, probably found Davis preoccupied with the defense of the Mississippi River, a sharp reversal from his earlier lack of concern about the western and trans-Mississippi theaters. But mention of Virginia and potential danger to the capital always got Davis back on track, and on this occasion, he decided that Longstreet must press the enemy at Suffolk. Lee was reluctant to do so if it meant removing more troops from in front of Hooker. Indeed, Lee preferred that Hood and Pickett be prepared to rejoin him at a moment's notice.[34]

Before anything could be decided, Lee was abruptly recalled to the army by reports of the fight at Kelly's Ford. He immediately put the army on alert and worried anew that he had not yet divined Hooker's intentions. Stonewall Jackson's blood was already up. Having passed the winter patiently at Moss Neck Manor, the home of Richard Corbin, where he indulged in frequent worship services and delighted in the company of Corbin's six-year-old daughter Jane, the restless Jackson pitched his tent near Hamilton's

Crossing on the day of the Kelly's Ford fight. Three days earlier he had told his wife, Anna, "The time has come for campaigning."[35]

Lee still had no plan of action when he fell ill. "I have felt so unwell since my return," he told Mary Custis, "as not to be able to go anywhere." He blamed his condition, characterized by coughing, fever, and pain in his chest, back, and arms, on the trip to Richmond. His spirits rallied somewhat on March 27. The entire army, upon Lee's orders, respected that day of national "fasting and prayer," as proclaimed by President Davis. Army chaplains reported the largest congregations of the winter at worship services. A warm sun poured down on the men in the most beautiful day of the year, a good omen, some soldiers said. Yet so serious did Lee's condition become that on March 30 he moved from his tented headquarters some two miles from Hamilton's Crossing to the imposing Georgian-style house of Thomas Yerby, a little over a mile southeast of the depot.[36]

By then, Lee had more to worry him than poor health. On March 28, he learned that Burnside's IX Corps was again in motion, this time headed by transport and rail from Newport News to Kentucky. Its departure would relieve the pressure on Longstreet; perhaps he could now take Suffolk. Yet Lee remained cautious. Burnside would likely join Rosecrans for an advance against Bragg, thought Lee. Could Longstreet's two divisions better serve him by rejoining the army for an advance against Hooker? Or might it be best for Old Pete to threaten the Federals in North Carolina? If Lee could once more defeat the Army of the Potomac, and by so doing threaten Washington, Lincoln would likely reduce the concentration against Bragg by moving Burnside closer to the capital. That would free both the Army of Northern Virginia and the Army of Tennessee for offensive operations, perhaps even an invasion of the North. But Lee must decide—and soon. Spring had arrived. Expectations ran high in Richmond, although no one knew exactly what to expect.[37]

# CHAPTER EIGHT

# Practicing Strategy

April 2 passed quietly in the armed camps along the Rappahannock. Oliver Howard officially superseded Carl Schurz as commander of the XI Corps, while an angry Schurz stepped down to lead the Third Division. Lee informed President Davis that Burnside had left for Kentucky and speculated that Hooker would likely make a move as soon as weather permitted. A frustrated Lee could learn no more. "Their lines are so closely guarded that it is difficult to penetrate them," he explained. Still, he waxed confident. If Longstreet could exert pressure against the Federals in North Carolina and Gen. Robert H. Milroy could be neutralized in the Valley, Hooker might yet betray his intentions.[1]

By the time Davis read Lee's dispatch, he had endured a horrendous day. Inflation, hoarding, and rank speculation had caused widespread want and hunger among Richmond's working and middle classes. Women across the city had been threatening to protest for weeks. On April 2, shortly before 9 A.M., a crowd gathered before the home of Governor John Letcher to demand bread. Gaining no satisfaction, they marched to Capitol Square. From there, they moved into the city's main commercial district. By then the crowd had swelled to some one thousand women, children, and men. That is when the trouble started. The crowd became a mob, looting about twenty stores. When the looters ignored Mayor Joseph Mayo's threat to retaliate with armed troops, he arrested more than seventy people.

Not until President Davis hurried from the Executive Mansion to join an embattled Mayo near Capitol Square did the mob come to its senses. The president stepped gingerly onto an overturned wagon and appealed to his angry countrymen. Images of bread riots reported that week from towns in Georgia, North Carolina, and Alabama doubtless rushed through the president's mind. A similar riot had occurred just the day before in Petersburg. This sudden internal uprising was less threatening than the discontented Copperhead agitation Lincoln faced in the North, but it was bad enough. The social fabric of the Confederacy was being rent, and he must stop it. He tried to shame the crowd as lawless plunderers; he appealed to their patriotism. He would share his own bread with them, Davis said, but the violence must stop. It did, and sometime after 11 A.M. the crowd, more exhausted than cowed, slipped away.[2]

The episode impressed upon Davis the need for a quick military victory. Help from England or France could not be expected. Even so great a triumph as Fredericksburg had failed to inspire unwavering confidence in his own people, let alone convince Europeans that the Confederacy was a going concern. Lee had shown his ability to win in the East, but more headway must be made elsewhere, especially in the West. Over the next few days, Davis appealed again to Lee to transfer some part of the eastern armies to Joe Johnston in Mississippi and Gen. Pierre G. T. Beauregard at Charleston. Having come belatedly to appreciate the defensive needs of the West, Davis was now perilously close to underestimating the danger Lee's army would face should its numbers be further reduced.

So Lee tried to hold on to his men and worried about Hooker. Even Longstreet was asking for reinforcements that Lee could not spare. The commander knew that if Hooker suddenly advanced, he would be hard-pressed to stop him. "We are scattered," he confided to Mary Custis Lee, "without forage & provisions, & could not remain long together if united for want of food." Lee still suffered from his cold, diagnosed by the doctors as pericarditis, which he could relieve only by taking regular doses of quinine. He gratefully accepted gifts of apples, turkeys, hams, and sweet potatoes sent from as far away as the Valley by people concerned about his health. Unfortunately, all Lee could stand to eat was soup and tea, with sugar added to the latter. His principal problem, decided Lee's physician, was that he took too little care of himself, far less "than he ought to."[3]

Meantime, Lincoln grew impatient. On April 3, he told Hooker he was coming to Falmouth. The president's entourage, including Mary Todd Lincoln and their youngest son, Tad, arrived two days later, on Easter morning. They caused "quite a commotion" at headquarters with an unprepared Hooker "hustling off some of his female acquaintances in a most undignified way." The Lincolns stayed five days, much of their time spent reviewing Hooker's troops (Mary Lincoln seated in a carriage, the president and Tad on horseback). The soldiers marched proudly, confidently, vastly changed from January. "The army never looked better," confirmed Gen. Alpheus Williams, and Hooker had recently called it "the finest army on the planet." A few men complained about being turned out to "gratify the idle curiosity of visitors," but most of them understood that this grand display was intended as much for the benefit of the Rebels watching from across the river as it was for Lincoln.[4]

Lincoln expressed his pleasure, even though some of the soldiers mentioned how careworn he looked. But then Lincoln had always had faith in the army; it was his generals who gave him occasional fits. Indeed, Lincoln had traveled to Falmouth primarily to learn Hooker's plans for the upcoming campaign. President and general conferred at length privately on April 6, and they doubtless exchanged ideas over the next few days as Lincoln inspected camps, toured hospitals, and reviewed the army. Some of what Lincoln heard bothered him. Hooker seemed overconfident, and he spoke of capturing Richmond rather than defeating Lee. The general clearly needed guidance.

To clarify things, Lincoln, at some point during his visit, paused to write down his thoughts on strategy for Hooker. He reminded the general of Halleck's opinion, which he shared, that Lee's army, not Richmond, must be his target. Hooker must "fret" Lee, "continuously harass and menace him." Do not be distracted by his raids and patrols, do not be concerned with feints toward Washington, Lincoln emphasized. Hooker held the advantage in numbers and benefited from superior communications. Hooker should remain poised, his attention fixed on Lee. When Lee had weakened himself sufficiently by dispatching troops to Longstreet and elsewhere, Hooker should "pitch into him." After all, pointed out the president, only a "narrow river" separated the two armies.[5]

In his parting instructions, delivered orally to Hooker and General Couch, the president warned his commanders to avoid, at all costs, the mistake made by Burnside: "I want to impress upon you two gentlemen in your next fight . . . put in all your men." Lincoln was desperate. He wanted a victory and a decisive one. He understood that all the South need do was not lose the war; the North had to win. Every Union defeat like Fredericksburg, every half victory like Antietam, eroded confidence at home and morale within the army. They played into the hands of gleeful Copperheads and made the United States appear weak in the eyes of foreign powers. Some military campaigns, such as a botched effort to capture Charleston on April 7, had been inspired as much by political as military considerations. Lincoln wanted Charleston, the cradle of nullification and secession, as much as he wanted Richmond. But his navy had failed, and his armies along the Mississippi, in Tennessee, and in Virginia were not faring much better. That was why Lincoln counted so much on Fighting Joe. He knew that all the North, and perhaps all the world, had its eyes fixed on northern Virginia.[6]

The next day, April 11, Hooker, having apparently taken Lincoln's words to heart, finally committed a strategic plan to paper. He would move directly against Lee, although his precise tactical plan remained ill-formed. His only concern was that Lee, rather than standing his ground, might fall back toward Richmond before he could be "seriously crippled." To counter a possible retreat, Hooker would send Stoneman's cavalry—his "dragoon force"—on a grand sweeping march around Lee's left flank to sever his communications with Richmond and block his escape route.[7]

Lincoln approved the plan on the following day, and Hooker immediately dispatched a flurry of orders to mobilize the army. Infantry would march to block transit and communications at the Rappahannock's major fords—United States, Banks's, and Kelly's. Cavalry would ride upriver and prepare to cross above Kelly's Ford. Hooker had not yet decided when or at what points his infantry would cross the river, let alone what they would do once on the Rebel side. That would depend largely on how quickly the cavalry flanked Lee and how long it took Lee to withdraw toward Richmond. But Hooker was already confident enough at this stage of the operation to assure a group of officers, "My plans are perfect, and when I start to carry them out, may God have mercy on General Lee, for I will have none."[8]

As the Rappahannock line sprang to life, the military picture elsewhere came more sharply into focus, and much of it looked good for the Confederacy. The attempt to capture Charleston (with an ironclad attack on Fort Sumter) had been turned back. Grant remained stymied in his efforts to get at Vicksburg, and Rosecrans still sat idle in Tennessee. Meantime, Longstreet had struck the first Confederate blow of the spring. Having seen his command split into three separate departments on April 1, Old Pete was mollified to some extent when he received permission from Lee to advance against Suffolk. He started forward on April 8, and by April 11, as Hooker carefully composed his operational guidelines for Lincoln, Longstreet laid siege to the well-fortified town.

Lee did not immediately appreciate the significance of the movements on his front. His slowness may be attributed partly to continued poor health. His pulse on April 11 was still above ninety, "too quick for an old man," he kidded his daughter Agnes. On April 12, he felt better. His pulse rate had declined, and his nagging cough was less annoying. Still, it would be "a few

The new Union commander and part of his staff. This is one of several photographs that Burnside (standing Napoleon-like in center) posed for with different staff members at Warrenton, Virginia. Library of Congress.

A view of Fredericksburg from the east bank of the Rappahannock, or the Dare Mark. Library of Congress.

(*Left*) Confederate defenders slow the Union advance into Fredericksburg on December 11. Robert Underwood Johnson and Clarence Clough Buel, eds., *Battles and Leaders of the Civil War* (New York: Century, 1887), 3:87.

(*Above*) The devastation of war comes to Fredericksburg. National Archives.

(*Above Left*) The lower pontoon bridges at
Franklin's Crossing. The hills defended by
Stonewall Jackson's men line the horizon.
Library of Congress.

(*Left*) The assault on Marye's Heights,
December 13. Anne S. K. Brown Military
Collection, Brown University Library.

(*Above*) Confederate defenses in the
Sunken Road, December 13. Johnson and
Buel, *Battles and Leaders*, 3:80.

(*Left*) Joseph Hooker breathed new life into the Army of the Potomac in the early months of 1863. National Archives.

(*Below*) George Stoneman's cavalry gathers at Kelly's Ford before launching its raid in Robert E. Lee's rear. Library of Congress.

The Army of the Potomac heads for the
rendezvous at Chancellorsville on April 30.
Library of Congress.

(*Above Left*) Robert E. Lee and Stonewall Jackson discuss their flanking movement on the night of May 1. Johnson and Buel, *Battles and Leaders*, 3:204.

(*Bottom Left*) A view of the Plank Road from in front of Dowdall's Tavern. The Wilderness Church stands to the left. National Archives.

(*Above*) Federal wounded recuperate near Chatham as the fighting continues at Chancellorsville, May 1863. National Archives.

A destroyed Confederate artillery
battery on Marye's Heights, May 3.
National Archives.

days" more, he admitted to his wife, before he recovered completely. Lee had also convinced himself by mid-April that Hooker would stay on the defensive a while longer. He based this judgment solely on the transfer of Burnside's corps to Kentucky, and he seemed inclined during these days to interpret any movement of Hooker's troops as either a ruse or an effort to dispatch reinforcements to other theaters. He even talked of taking the offensive himself by moving into Maryland. This, he told a worried President Davis, would offer the twin advantages of forcing Hooker back across the Potomac and relieving the pressure on Johnston and Beauregard.[9]

Lee was lulled further by an elementary Federal stratagem. Having lived on intimate terms for so many months, each army had managed to interpret the other's signal-flag codes. The Federals now used their knowledge to feed Lee's signal officers false intelligence concerning the destination of Stoneman's cavalry corps. On April 14, Lee warned his forces in the Valley to beware: a Union cavalry movement upriver was aimed at them. Because Lee was convinced that Hooker had decided to stand pat for the moment, it made perfect sense. Hooker did not need his cavalry for reconnaissance because he was not going anywhere.[10]

On April 14, as ten thousand Union cavalry reached the river crossings opposite Culpeper, it started to rain, just as it had for Burnside in January. Rivers and streams rose rapidly. After five days, the weather cleared briefly, but the next day brought more rain, and it continued with slight interruption until April 24. All military operations ceased. The Army of the Potomac, which knew something was afoot, lived in a state of constant expectation. The Rebels, for their part, joked that the mud and rain were answers to Yankee prayers. "I believe they are afraid of the Rebel Army of Va," commented a Georgian, "and if they attack it at all, it will be deferred some time yet, and whenever done it will be with a great many misgivings."[11]

Hooker used the respite to reconsider his plans, but he mentioned no alterations to Lincoln and Halleck when they conferred with him at Aquia Landing on April 19. Meade complained that not even Hooker's corps commanders knew anything of his intentions. Two days after the president's flying visit, Hooker would go only so far as to tell Lincoln not to worry about apparent delays in the offensive. "As I can only cross the river by stratagem without great loss, which I wish to avoid," he explained, "it may be a few days before I make it. I must threaten several points, and be in readiness to spring when a suitable opportunity presents itself."[12]

Hooker modified his plan in part because he had learned from Sharpe's intelligence net that Lee's men blocked the two principal river fords where

he hoped to cross his infantry, Banks's Ford, five miles above Fredericksburg, and United States Ford, two miles farther on. Hooker decided to exploit these concentrations by sending half of his infantry—about three
corps—after the cavalry. The horse soldiers would gain Lee's rear as
planned, although in addition to cutting Lee's communications, they would
now serve as a giant raiding party, to "inflict a vast deal of mischief, and at
the same time bewilder the enemy as to the course and intentions of the
main body." The following infantry would cross the Rappahannock, swing
back downriver to cross the Rapidan, and move against Lee's left flank. To
distract Lee's attention from this daring maneuver, one infantry corps
would threaten a crossing at Fredericksburg while the two remaining corps
remained poised to strike across Banks's and United States Fords. When the
flanking movement crashed into Lee's left, he would be propelled backward, and the remaining infantry could cross the Dare Mark uncontested to
join the fun.[13]

Lee seemed sluggish and indecisive during these late April days. He remained convinced that Stoneman's target was the Shenandoah Valley. He
believed the new movement of Federal infantry upriver was meant to draw
him in that direction and so uncover Fredericksburg. He did not believe
Hooker would take the "aggressive" until his short-term volunteers—men
who had enlisted only for nine months or two years—could be replaced.
Lee, who estimated their number to be forty thousand, knew that would
take a few more weeks. Until then, Hooker would be undermanned. "It appears to me that he is rather fearful of an attack from us than preparing to
attack," Lee told Jeb Stuart on April 19, as Lincoln and Hooker consulted at
Aquia Landing. "His operations in front of you look rather to prevent your
moving against his right or getting in his rear." If Lee could advance his own
army by May 1, he believed he could force the Federals to fall back in all
parts of Virginia.[14]

Lee did take advantage of the threat posed by Stoneman on the upper
Rappahannock, however. Weary of warding off President Davis's urgings
that he send eastern troops to other parts of the Confederacy, Lee turned the
tables by asking the president to send additional cavalry to Stuart from
North Carolina, western Virginia, Alabama, and Georgia. Similarly, he told
Adj. Gen. Samuel Cooper that if Confederate troops were needed anywhere
it was along the Rappahannock line. "I believe the enemy in every department outnumbers us," he told Cooper, "and it is difficult to say from which
troops can with safety be spared. If it is determined to be best that the army
here should remain inactive, I doubt whether General Hooker will be quies-

cent." Yet privately, Lee continued to sound confident. "On every other point we are strong," he told his wife on April 19. "If successful this year, next fall there will be a great change in public opinion at the North. The Republicans will be destroyed & I think the friends of peace will become so strong as that the next administration will go in on that basis."[15]

So passed the damp, suspenseful days of late April. Yankees and Rebels alike knew something must happen soon. Strangely, the generals on neither side anticipated a direct attack by the enemy. Stuart's cavalrymen in Culpeper remained puzzled by the large force opposite them. "It does not seem disposed to cross," marveled a Rebel officer, "& we are at a loss to know what they are up to." Lee remained perplexed, too. Was Hooker still playing the Chinese game, or did he intend to fight? "Gen *Hooker* and *Lee* are *practicing strategy*," concluded a New England soldier. "When they get tired of that play most likely they will try their guns. The day is not far distant when the now quiet vale of the Rappahannock will again echo with the thunders of war."[16]

If anything other than the rain served to dampen the enthusiasm of the Federals it was the recently published report on Fredericksburg by the Committee on the Conduct of the War. "Everybody is reading [the report]," remarked Colonel Wainwright, who was appalled by "its unfairness, partiality, and in very many cases absolute falseness." Meade so disliked its "terribly severe" portrayal of General Franklin that he said a few words on Franklin's behalf to Lincoln during the president's April 19 visit. He was heartened to learn that Lincoln shared his opinion. Meade had become convinced that the failure of Franklin's grand division at Fredericksburg "turned on a misapprehension, Burnside thinking he was saying and ordering one thing and Franklin understanding another." Franklin had not been "fully advised as to Burnside's plan," Meade told his wife. "I am sure if he had been so advised, his movements would have been different." This same potential for misunderstanding worried Meade about the current campaign. Hooker was being too secretive about the operation.[17]

Hooker satisfied Lee's doubts, if not Meade's, to an uncomfortable degree on April 28–29, when his army surged across the Dare Mark. His plan, if not perfect, was entirely sound, and it began brilliantly. The army began its advance on April 27, and by early morning on April 29, 134,000 men and some four hundred guns were poised to strike. The army traveled light. Officers and men carried most of their own equipment, rations, and ammunition. Pack mules rather than wagons bore extra rations and ammunition. The few precious wagons carried mostly forage for the animals. Hooker even limited the number of ambulances and artillery batteries in the advance. By the evening of April 28, Lee still had not reacted. Hooker had stolen a two-day march on the Gray Fox.

Problems with short-term volunteers—one of Hooker's chief concerns and one of Lee's fondest hopes—proved negligible. Had all left, Hooker would have lost not only forty thousand men but several of his best fighting regiments. He was saved by administrative confusion. The War Department insisted that most of these veterans had another month to serve. The men claimed to have done their duty, and not a few balked at the thought of dying in one last battle. Hooker tried to defuse the situation by allowing corps commanders to assign short-timers to duties behind the lines. Even so, many of the men claimed they would not accompany the army or, if accompanying it, would refuse to fight. A few regiments did, in fact, lay down their arms. Still, only a portion of one New York regiment ultimately refused to advance, and when those men were court-martialed within twenty-four hours, the rest seemed to be chastened.

The hardest march was conducted by the nearly forty thousand men in Hooker's "flying column," bound for Kelly's Ford. The right wing consisted of Howard's XI Corps, Slocum's XII Corps, and Meade's V Corps. Hooker selected these three units because they were encamped the farthest from Lee, near Aquia Landing, between Stafford Court House and Brooke's Station, and between Brooke's Station and Falmouth, respectively. Their movement was less likely to be detected by the Rebels, especially since Lee had pulled back his cavalry from between Stafford and Kelly's Ford to watch for Stoneman's anticipated move toward the Valley. Further to shield the movements of his right wing, Hooker had the III Corps reviewed by Secretary of State Seward and some foreign ministers at Falmouth on April 27.

The remaining three corps, two of which had encamped around Falmouth, further protected the right wing's march by moving straight toward Lee. Sedgwick's VI Corps, the largest corps in the army with 23,600 men, advanced to Franklin's Crossing, two miles below Fredericksburg, where it would lay pontoons on the site of Burnside's lower bridges and reenact the December crossing of Franklin's Left Grand Division. Reynolds's I Corps moved to Fitzhugh's Crossing, nearly two miles farther downriver. Sickles's III Corps, after being reviewed, would form a reserve for Sedgwick and Reynolds, while Couch left John Gibbon's division of the II Corps near Falmouth and led his remaining two divisions to Banks's Ford.

Stoneman's cavalry, ready to advance from its camps around Warrenton Junction, received slightly altered instructions. This third cavalry plan retained more of the focus of the original scenario, which called for Stoneman to destroy Lee's supply lines and block his retreat. The horse soldiers would advance in two columns so as to inflict the widest possible damage and chaos. After crossing at Kelly's Ford, one column would push Stuart's cavalry out of Culpeper while the second, larger force headed straight for the Rapidan. The columns would eventually reunite on the Pamunkey River.

All of these movements were achieved under the strictest security ever seen in the Army of the Potomac. None of Hooker's corps commanders, including Stoneman, were told their ultimate objective. Each knew only that they were to cross the Rappahannock sometime between the evening of April 28 and the morning of April 29. Hooker provided Lincoln with a fairly precise sketch of his plan on April 27, but conceded, "It almost makes me tremble to disclose a thing concerning it to anyone except yourself." That same evening, Hooker shared his plan with Couch (his second in command) and Slocum (senior officer on the right wing). Fighting Joe seemed willing to risk whatever confusion and lack of initiative his secrecy might breed.[18]

Another burst of cold, rainy weather hit the Federal columns as they marched on April 27–28. The days were gloomy, the roads muddy. Many infantrymen, finding their heavy loads of fifty to sixty pounds too much to bear, tossed aside everything but rations and ammunition. Nor did they disencumber themselves without leveling a volley of curses at "those that got up the brilliant idea of making men asses." But for all that, they seemed ready to fight and had been for some time past. "This army is in excellent condition," a Maine artillerist had reported two weeks earlier, "& the feeling of partial discouragement in some instances has subsided and all seem cheerful & confident of success." He fully expected that he and his comrades would "flog the rebels sweetly & show them that the Army of the Potomac is a good army if dexterously handled." The men had never been in better shape or had more faith in themselves, insisted a New York officer. "I have always believed this Army would defeat General Lee's Army and take Richmond and I still believe so," he elaborated, "but just now I am more hopeful of reaching this end soon than I have been for some time." Even the cautious Meade playfully warned his wife, "Look out for 'Fighting Joe's' army. . . . Joe says we are to do great things when we start."[19]

Other men, more resolved than enthusiastic about soldiering, simply wanted action. They were "tired of so much preparation and doing nothing." Whether Hooker attacked next week or next year, the Rebels would be waiting for them. "This army is now in good order to commence operations," concluded an artillery officer. "Neither officers nor men are quite as anxious for a fight as they were last spring," he conceded, "[but] both are much better seasoned to the hardships and know much more about their business."[20]

Hooker accompanied the crucial right wing as far as Morrisville, a few miles east of Kelly's Ford. He wanted no mishaps there, and none occurred. Stoneman's horsemen crossed the river by 5 P.M. on April 28. Stoneman and John Buford led about two-thirds of the riders straight toward Raccoon Ford, on the Rapidan. Averell led the second column toward Brandy Station and Stuart's unsuspecting cavalry. This cleared the way for the infantry of the XI Corps, which crossed on pontoon bridges a few hundred yards below Kelly's Ford. Unlike December's fiasco, the pontoons arrived on schedule from Washington by way of the Orange and Alexandria Railroad. Rebel pickets along the river were so taken by surprise that they could manage only a few volleys before scattering. Stuart, encamped near Culpeper Court House, did not learn of the crossings until 9 P.M.

By the time Lee learned of this bold move the next morning, a portion of Sedgwick's and Reynolds's corps had crossed on his immediate front. Gen. William T. H. Brooks sent his division over the upper bridges with minimal opposition, but a picket force of the Sixth Louisiana and Twenty-third Georgia stopped the pontoniers at Fitzhugh's Crossing in the early morning fog. As the fog lifted at about 9 A.M., the Twenty-fourth Michigan and Sixth Wisconsin, reflecting the lessons of December 11, leaped into boats and, under a covering fire from their artillery, paddled across the two-hundred-yard moat to establish a bridgehead. "When we got across the river," reported one Badger, "we jumped into the mud and water, waist deep, waded ashore, crawled and scrambled up the bank, laying hold of the bushes. Very few shots were fired before the rebels were throwing down their arms or running over the plain." By 10:30 A.M., the pontoniers had completed their work, and Gen. James S. Wadsworth's division rushed to secure the Federal position.[21]

Jubal Early informed Stonewall Jackson of the crisis, and Jackson dispatched an aide to tell Lee. Jackson had established his personal headquarters at the home of Thomas Yerby, where Lee had convalesced earlier in the spring, so as to enjoy the company of his wife, Anna, and their new daughter, Julia. Within hours, mother and child, who had joined him nine days earlier, had been sent to Richmond. Lee stirred in his sleep briefly in the predawn darkness when he heard gunfire near his camp, along the Mine Road three miles below Franklin's Crossing, but not until Jackson's urgent message arrived did he arise. Shortly thereafter, the Episcopal church bell in Fredericksburg tolled the alarm.

Early responded minimally to the threat by placing his division along the Richmond, Fredericksburg, and Potomac Railroad. His line stretched from Massaponax Creek, on the right, to Deep Run, on the left. By then it was early afternoon, and the two Federal divisions were safely planted below the Rappahannock. As in December, the Yankees enjoyed the advantage of covering fire from Stafford Heights. Lee responded by ordering up his own artillery, requesting reinforcements from Richmond, shifting troops in Fredericksburg to the heights above the town, and asking Longstreet to rejoin him as soon as possible. By evening, Lee knew that both Union cavalry and infantry had crossed into Culpeper County and that at least a portion of both arms had crossed the Rapidan. "Their intention, I presume," he informed Jefferson Davis, "is to turn our left, and probably to get into our rear."[22]

Lee's final orders of the day came around 6:30 P.M. He instructed Lafayette McLaws, whose division commanded the heights above Fredericksburg, to guard against an attack on his left. He told Richard Anderson, who had been shielding the army's left at United States Ford, to pull back and use a portion of his division to block the turnpike between Fredericksburg and Chancellorsville, about eight miles to the west. "We may be obliged to change our position," he warned both McLaws and Anderson, "in consequence of the enemy's having come in between us and General Stuart."[23]

With his upriver troops safely across the Rappahannock, Hooker had returned to Falmouth on the morning of April 29. He assumed that those troops would proceed as planned, and most of them did. Only Averell's column stalled, when Confederate skirmishers blocked its path at Brandy Station and a fine sleet began to fall. Stoneman's column reached the Rapidan, while Meade's corps crossed the river at Ely's Ford. By midnight, both Slocum and Howard had crossed on pontoons at Germanna Ford. All that remained for the infantry was to follow the roads to Chancellorsville, less than ten miles away, where Hooker would rejoin them the next day to coordinate the attack on Lee's left.

Chancellorsville, unsuspecting of the pivotal role it was about to play in the war, sat on a vital crossroads midway between Fredericksburg and Germanna Ford. Despite its name, Chancellorsville was not a village but a two-story brick house owned by the Chancellor family. It faced the Orange Turnpike, where several other roads converged at or near it. Most important was the Orange Plank Road, which ran as one with the turnpike between Chancellorsville and Wilderness Church, two miles to the west, before breaking off at Chancellorsville and looping southward to rejoin it five miles from Fredericksburg. Sixteen people occupied the house. A widow, Frances Pound Chancellor, resided there with seven of her nine children. Of those seven, six were unmarried daughters who had spent the winter flirting with Confederate soldiers encamped nearby. The remaining occupants were refugees from Fredericksburg.

On Thursday, April 30, everything fell into place for the Federals. Hooker had already bettered Burnside's efforts, and as the day progressed, he methodically closed in on Lee's flank. Meade's men left the Rapidan at 4 A.M. and reached Chancellorsville at noon. They encountered only token resistance from Confederate pickets and even stopped to pillage a country store along the way. Meade was in high spirits when Slocum and his vanguard joined him in midafternoon. "This is splendid, Slocum," he rejoiced; "hurrah for old Joe! We are on Lee's flank and he does not know it." Meade's hopes for an immediate advance were dashed, however, when Slocum told him they must wait for Couch and Sickles. Couch, with the divisions of Hancock and French, would arrive that night, having moved upriver from Banks's Ford to cross on pontoons at United States Ford. When McLaws and Anderson pulled back, they had left the ford unprotected. Sickles's corps expected to cross there the next morning. Hooker would also arrive soon, and until then, Slocum and Meade were to prepare defenses around Chancellorsville.[24]

The Chancellor family had hidden its silver and other valuables by the time Meade arrived. They greeted the growing assemblage of Yankee officers on their doorstep coolly. Their attitude did not improve when they were informed that Chancellorsville would be army headquarters and that they must confine themselves to a single room in the rear of the house. "From the windows we could see couriers coming and going," recalled Sue Chancellor, just fourteen years old in 1863, "so we knew that the troops were cutting down trees and throwing up breastworks. I know now that they were very well satisfied with their position and seemed to be very confident of victory."[25]

Other civilian families in the area had their homes invaded, too. Less than two miles west of Chancellorsville on the turnpike, Oliver Howard occupied the home of a forty-eight-year-old Baptist preacher, Melzi Chancellor. Still referred to in the area as Dowdall's Tavern, the one-and-a-half-story structure had not served its public function since 1859, when the Chancellors purchased it. The family was pleased with the courteous treatment accorded it by the pious Howard, a sharp contrast to earlier dealings with Union soldiers. At nearby Fairview, about seven hundred yards southwest of Chancellorsville, the Moxley family had abandoned its home by the time Alpheus Williams knocked on the door. James Moxley, who worked as Frances Chancellor's overseer, believed the sturdy ironworks at nearby Catharine Furnace promised more protection in any impending battle than his three-room wooden house. When the Wellford family heard the "shouting and shooting" of Federal pickets approaching their substantial brick home, less than a mile south of the furnace on a lonely wilderness road, Charles Wellford and his teenage son took to the woods. The family, including four women, had moved to the house only a short time earlier from Fredericksburg.[26]

Stoneman's cavalry made less progress on April 30 than did the infantry. While some horsemen had crossed the river on the previous night, most of the Gregg-Buford column, led by Stoneman, slept above the Rapidan. Not until 4 A.M. did it splash across at Raccoon and Mitchell's Fords, about five miles apart. Not until dark did the entire column reach the south side, and then reports that Rooney Lee's brigade of Rebel cavalry lurked in the vicinity made Stoneman cautious. He would proceed no farther that night. Averell failed even to cross the Rapidan. As the morning fog cleared on April 30, he discovered that both the Rebels and the sleet had melted away. His division advanced unopposed to Culpeper Court House, where it cut telegraph wires and confiscated needed provisions. Another cold rain fell as the column continued toward Rapidan Station, however, and by the time the Federals reached the river, after dark, Rooney Lee's men and two pieces of artillery had sealed off the ford. His horses were exhausted and his men tired and hungry so Averell bedded down for the night.[27]

John Sedgwick, senior commander on the Union left, had the day's hardest assignment. Having gained the Rebel shore, his men had to sit nervously through a day punctuated by a casual exchange of artillery fire. Sedgwick also had to deal with Hooker's only lapse into indecisiveness on April 30. Early that morning, Hooker told Sedgwick to make a "demonstration" on Lee's front. Three hours later, he changed his mind and instructed Sedgwick to "make tremendous demonstrations of camp-fires" that night, evidently hoping to impress Lee with the strength of Sedgwick's force without risking a fight. The left wing was not to advance any farther unless Lee fell back or moved against the Federal right. If all went well, Hooker hoped, Sedgwick would not have to commit his two corps until the right wing reached Chancellorsville.[28]

"Great excitement" ran through Confederate camps across the Rappahannock by 3:30 A.M. on April 30. The men who took positions opposite Sedgwick's vanguard were as edgy as their Union counterparts. No one who had witnessed the carnage on that plain in December could help but wonder if "the same dreadful scenes" might soon be repeated. "The field is literally covered with graves now," a man who had been wounded there informed his wife on April 30. "I saw the arm of a dead Yankee sticking out of a grave that had not decayed." The corpse might have been his own, he mused, had the stray bullet that hit him struck a more vital spot. Impressed forcefully by the fragility of life, he added, "Do not grieve for me, even if I should fall, but remember me as one dying to save his country."[29]

R. E. Lee, who had been bothered by dull chest pains upon waking, discussed the tactical situation with Jackson and rushed engineers and additional artillery to Anderson. The South Carolinian had already pulled back from his position of the previous night near the Chancellorsville crossroads. He believed himself vulnerable to a flanking movement there, and the woods had been so dense that he could not deploy his artillery. Anderson returned nearly four miles to open ground near Zoan Church, a Baptist meeting place on the turnpike. His left extended beyond another house of God, Tabernacle Church, nearly a mile away on the Mine Road. Dig in, Lee told him in midafternoon: "Set all your spades to work as vigorously as possible. . . . Hold your position firmly, and prepare your line for them."[30]

Lee was not fooled by Sedgwick's halfhearted advance; he knew that Anderson's spartan force faced the principal threat to his army. Indicative of his concern, Lee's orders to Anderson marked the first time the "King of Spades" ever constructed fortifications in the open field. Jackson had wanted to attack Sedgwick at once, but he relented after examining the ground and Federal positions to his front. His inspection led him to share Lee's opinion that it would be extremely difficult to push Sedgwick back across the river. Anyway, Lee knew how to deal with Sedgwick. He would leave Early with 11,100 infantry and less than a third of the army's 228 guns to defend the heights while he marshaled the remaining 42,000 infantry against Hooker. McLaws's division, less Barksdale's brigade, would move to Anderson's aid "as soon as possible." Jackson's corps, less Early's division, would follow at first light on May 1. When he reached Anderson's position, Stonewall would "make arrangements to repulse the enemy."[31]

It was dangerous for Lee to divide his force in this way. All the tactical manuals forbade it, but for someone who had graduated second in his class at West Point, Lee showed a curious disdain for manuals. He had divided his forces before, during the Seven Days, at Second Manassas, and at Antietam, yet he had never done so to this degree, and never when he faced such overwhelmingly superior numbers. The safer move would have been retreat, but Lee believed he must hold the Rappahannock line. Federal occupation below the Dare Mark could well cripple Confederate communications and transportation in northern Virginia and give the Yankees too many strategic options. Besides, Lee knew war is a "risky" business that requires a "very bold game" to win. "I determined to hold our lines in rear of Fredericksburg with part of the force and endeavor with the rest to drive the enemy back to the Rapidan," he wired the War Department at midnight.[32]

Far on the Confederate left, Stuart had divided his force in accordance with Lee's instructions. He assigned Rooney Lee with a thousand men to "protect public property" on the railroads by harassing and, if need be, pursuing Stoneman. Rooney's primary mission was to block any movement toward Gordonsville and the Virginia Central Railroad. Consequently, it was Lee's men that Averell encountered at Rapidan Station. Stuart raced with his remaining two brigades to rejoin Robert Lee and the main body of the army. The commanding general would need him for reconnaissance.[33]

Hooker spent the day collecting as much information as possible about Lee's reaction to his movements. "It is hard to estimate their forces, for they are partially concealed in pine woods," Thaddeus Lowe reported from the *Eagle*, stationed at Banks's Ford, but it appeared to him that fully three-fourths of Lee's men remained near Fredericksburg. Hooker rode out of Falmouth around 4 P.M. to command his right wing, although he would be connected by telegraph and signal flag to all parts of his army by an excellent system of communications at Falmouth, maintained and directed by Dan Butterfield. Hooker found spirits high at Chancellorsville. Couch arrived on schedule, and hundreds of officers mingled and congratulated one another on their brilliant maneuver. "It was a gay and cheerful scene," Alpheus Williams reported. "We had successfully accomplished what we all supposed would be the great work of the campaign. Everybody prophesied a great success, an overwhelming victory."[34]

But how did Hooker intend to win? It is impossible to know with certainty because he revealed so little about his plans. He did not inform Lincoln of the rendezvous at Chancellorsville, and he kept newspaper correspondents in the dark as much as possible. His last communication to Lincoln, on April 27, had been singularly vague about his movements below the Rappahannock. Some historians insist that on the evening of April 30 he knew only that he wanted to advance. "God Almighty could not prevent me from winning a victory tomorrow," he swore with typical bombast. In a congratulatory order to his men that night, Hooker praised the skill and fortitude with which the army had maneuvered. He assured them that Lee must now "either ingloriously fly, or come out from behind his defenses and give us battle on our own ground, where certain destruction awaits him."[35]

At least one historian believes Hooker intended to destroy Lee by baiting him, taking advantage of the Rebel's aggressive nature and luring him into the teeth of a strong Federal defense. The issue turns on what Hooker meant by "our own ground." Did he mean the ground at Chancellorsville, where he had already ordered Slocum and Meade to entrench? Or did he mean ground to be claimed when he advanced the next morning, the day on which he defied even the Almighty to deny him victory. The most compelling evidence suggests the latter. In his late afternoon directive to Sedgwick, delivered by Butterfield after the commander had left for Chancellorsville, Hooker said he intended to drive Lee backward the next day and that Sedgwick should be prepared to strike from the opposite direction. "He [Hooker] expected, when he left here," Butterfield explained, "if he met with no serious opposition, to be on the heights west of Fredericksburg to-morrow noon or shortly after, and, if opposed strongly, to-morrow night." Nearly two years later, appearing before the Committee on the Conduct of the War, Hooker testified to his intentions on May 1: "I went out to attack the enemy."[36]

# CHAPTER NINE

# Days of Hard Marching and Derring-Do

George Meade wrote to his wife on the night of April 30, "There is as yet but a little skirmishing; we are across the river and have out-maneuvered the enemy, but we are not yet out of the woods." Meade meant that figuratively and literally. When Hooker awoke on Friday, May 1, to begin his attack, he found himself engulfed by wilderness. Indeed, he was in the middle of the Wilderness, a seventy-square-mile maze of uneven terrain honeycombed with boggy ravines, thick undergrowth, and "tangled thickets of pine, scrub oak and cedar." To one soldier it was "the most god forsaken looking place I ever saw." The only significantly open portions of the region were along the main roads, a fifty-acre clearing around Chancellorsville, and a few open spots on neighboring farms. Both communications and the movements of massed troops would be difficult. For all his careful reconnaissance and elaborate intelligence system, Hooker was unprepared for this. He would later admit that he had crossed the Rappahannock with "no adequate conception" of how rugged this terrain would be. "It was impossible to maneuver," he said.[1]

May 1 dawned overcast and foggy. Lowe's balloons were useless, and Hooker hesitated to advance without knowing the enemy's position. He would not receive an aerial report until early afternoon, but by 11 A.M., with the skies clearing, the apparent pall over Hooker's confidence also lifted. He ordered portions of three corps to advance by three different routes. Meade's V Corps held the left as it sauntered along the River Road toward Banks's Ford. Once the Federals secured that river crossing, reinforcements could safely and speedily join the main body by that route. By using Banks's rather than United States Ford, Hooker could shorten his lines of communication by a half dozen miles. Sykes's division of Regulars, normally attached to Meade's corps, headed down the Orange Turnpike toward Zoan Church, where Hooker intended to make his new headquarters. They were followed in close order by Hancock's division of Couch's II Corps. Slocum, on the right, started his corps down the Plank Road with Howard trailing him.

The forty thousand men who formed these three columns exhibited a marked cheerfulness and easy confidence. As they advanced with their two dozen guns, they covered a mile-wide front, and they fully expected to thrash any graycoat in their path. "I never saw my troops in better condition, never more anxious to meet the enemy," reported Alpheus Williams from Slocum's column. "Such, I believe, was the condition of almost every corps of the army." No one expressed regrets or misapprehension about Hooker, his strategic vision, or the tactical plan. "Surely," asserted Williams, "we had promise of success."[2]

Unhappily for Hooker, he advanced a day late. To have seized Zoan Church ridge, located in a reasonably clear area on the fringes of the Wilderness, would have given him a formidable position for either offense or defense. But Richard Anderson, showing no amateur's eye for terrain, had settled in that exact spot, and he and McLaws had been digging in for twelve hours. By failing to take this position on the previous day, as Meade and Slocum had anticipated doing, Hooker squandered four days of hard marching. He would have to fight for the ridge now. Jackson reached the Anderson-McLaws line at about 8:30 A.M., nearly three hours before Hooker advanced and ahead of both Lee and his own corps. Good as this position promised to be for defense, Lee had given Jackson authority to attack. That is what Stonewall would do.

Jackson wisely selected the brigades of Gens. William Mahone and Carnot Posey to lead the way. Their men, having spent the winter encamped on this ground, knew the region and its roads. Mahone headed up the Orange Turnpike, followed by McLaws's three remaining brigades. The Third Virginia Cavalry covered the right flank, and twenty-four guns were made available to that wing. Posey led the left wing up the Plank Road, which cut through a densely wooded area. Gen. Ambrose Ranson "Rans" Wright's Georgia brigade followed Posey's men, and fourteen guns accompanied the column. The Fourth Virginia Cavalry protected the left flank. Counting reserves, Jackson had twenty-seven thousand men when he ordered the advance at 10:30 A.M. His own corps still had not arrived.

Blue and gray skirmishers exchanged musket fire, and the boom of artillery soon followed. As main lines collided, men fighting near the turnpike, where the ground was largely cleared, found it easiest to maneuver. But cleared ground also made them good targets. "Whew, the shells come thick as they whiz near," commented a Union surgeon accompanying the advance. "The impulse is irresistible to duck, and the whole line bows very frequently." Sykes's division garnered the first gains, driving back Rebel skirmishers at least a mile. But the farther the Regulars advanced, the faster they outpaced supporting units on their flanks, and the more exposed those flanks became. No sooner had they slammed headlong into Mahone's Virginians than the Confederate lines closed in from both sides. By 1 P.M., Sykes was in danger. Hancock's division advanced to relieve the pressure on him, but with no little apprehension. "We began to meet the wounded returning from the fight," reported one of Hancock's infantrymen, "some on foot and some in ambulances. The more gritty ones call out to give it to them boys, others more faint hearted would assure us we would soon get enough of it."[3]

Slocum, on the Federal right, could not be expected to help Sykes. He had his hands full with both the Rebels and the terrain. Posey and Wright had progressed rapidly down the Plank Road while Slocum's men, arranged in line of battle rather than in columns, fought their way through the undergrowth. "Our brigade was taken through swamps, woods and brush thickets almost impossible for human beings to get through," complained a Buckeye in Gen. John W. Geary's division. Another of Geary's men, this one a Pennsylvanian, grumbled, "my Clothes were nearly torn from my back by the Briars and Brush." Consequently, the Federal right lagged nearly two miles behind where Sykes was heavily engaged.[4]

Meade, who had almost reached Banks's Ford, might well have pitched in to help, but he had no instructions to do so. This was the first serious instance when Hooker's failure to provide his corps commanders with the bigger picture hurt him. Meade had been told only to advance; he had to assume that his principal goal was to cover the ford. Though not usually one to lack initiative, Meade on this occasion proved strangely lethargic. He sent out skirmishers to probe in the direction of Sykes, but they went only halfway before turning back.

Then Hooker apparently panicked. He had not expected such delays or such stout resistance from nature and the Rebels. At 2 P.M., having been advised that Jackson's corps was approaching from Fredericksburg, he had to make a decision. He must either continue to fight against growing odds—as many as forty-eight thousand men, he thought—or pull back and allow the Rebels to advance against his entrenched and superior numbers. Fighting

Joe chose to recall all three columns and establish a defensive position around Chancellorsville. Perhaps he remembered Lincoln's admonition of April to "beware of rashness." Certainly caution is evident in his orders earlier that day to establish strong picket lines for the "safety of this army."[5]

The Confederates felt the tide turn. An infantry sergeant in Wright's brigade marveled at the ease with which they gained the Federal flank. "We pushed forward as quickly as possible," he explained, "soon checked their advance, and following them up, drove them over a half mile." It remained only for the artillery to move up and throw canister into the retreating blue ranks. Another Confederate described the fighting as nothing more than a "heavy Skirmish," in which most of the Yankees fired too high to cause serious damage. Not that some Rebels did not pause to consider what was happening. As wounded Confederates passed to the rear and other men lay crumpled and unmoving on the battlefield, a member of the Richmond Howitzers reflected, "I am beginning to see the horror of war in earnest."[6]

The final thrust of the Confederate attack seemed even easier when the Federals voluntarily fell back, although only Meade complied immediately with Hooker's order. Couch, who had moved forward with Hancock's division, received Hooker's instructions to retreat at about 2 P.M., just as Sykes's exhausted Regulars fell back behind Hancock's line. Sykes, Hancock, and Gen. Gouverneur K. Warren, Hooker's chief engineer, agreed with Couch that it was a mistake to withdraw. Even if failing to reach their target, they had secured a good piece of high ground a mile from Chancellorsville that, if abandoned, could be used with effect against them by enemy artillery. Couch dispatched a staff officer with an appeal for Hooker to reconsider his decision, but this only produced a second "positive order" to disengage by 5 P.M. On the right, Slocum disliked the order, too, as did his soldiers when given the word to withdraw. Alpheus Williams remarked, "The men went back disappointed, not without grumbling."[7]

The confident Federal advance ended quite differently from the way it began. By the time Couch pulled back Hancock and Sykes, the Rebels were pressing hard. It became necessary to conduct a fighting withdrawal, although Hancock's proud division of New Englanders, New Yorkers, and Pennsylvanians provided a sense of orderliness. Hooker told his four corps commanders to strengthen defenses along the lines they had occupied the previous night "without a moment's delay." Now, far from claiming the hills above Fredericksburg, Hooker wanted only to hold the ground he occupied. Artillery exchanges continued until dark, and the "constant popping" of rifles sounded throughout the night. So did the ring of axes and shovels as

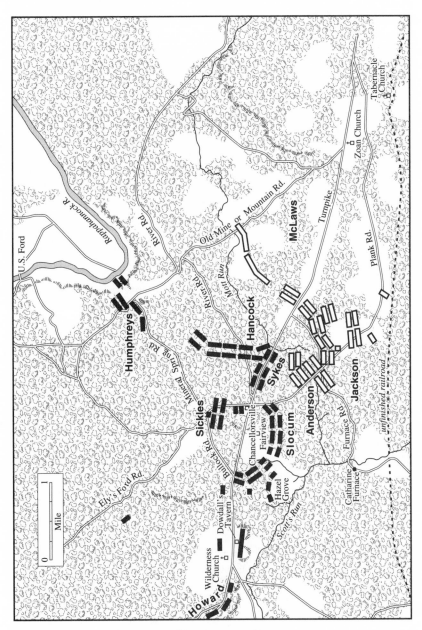

Chancellorsville, afternoon of May 1, 1863

men labored to construct breastworks and abatis. Hooker cast the changed situation in the best possible light by announcing to the army that he *wanted* Lee to attack them on this, their own ground.[8]

By evening, the Chancellor house had become a hospital. The wounded arrived in every variety of wagon because ambulances, as a result of Hooker's marching orders, were in short supply. A division field hospital stood near Chancellorsville, but as the number of wounded grew and the Federal line became more constricted, most of the casualties were taken to the Chancellor house. Assistant Surgeon John S. Billings found "everything . . . in confusion" there, with wounded men lying on the veranda, in the halls, and anywhere else space could be found. Teamsters, orderlies, runaway slaves, and assorted soldiers milled about and filled the outbuildings. "I immediately broke open the doors," reported Billings, "had the furniture carried out; and the wounded taken into the parlors; cleared out the kitchen, and ordered a cook to prepare soup." The surgeons had few operations and amputations to perform, but the bandaging of wounds continued through the night.[9]

Amid all this hubbub, Hooker met with his staff and subordinate commanders to review their options. They could either resume the attack next morning, he said, or wait for Lee to attack them. General Warren did not think their position particularly advantageous for defense, but Hooker had seemingly made up his mind. He had seventy thousand men and 208 guns, and he directed General Reynolds to bring up the I Corps at once. Reynolds would strengthen the right flank and extend the line of Howard's corps from the Orange Turnpike all the way to Ely's Ford on the Rapidan. Their lines already formed a six-mile-long perimeter. The XI Corps anchored the extreme right flank along the turnpike about a mile west of Dowdall's Tavern, where the Plank Road joined the turnpike. Birney's division of the III Corps, which had arrived that afternoon, covered Hazel Grove, a valuable piece of high ground a mile to the southwest. The XII Corps covered the line between the Plank Road and Fairview. Two divisions of the II Corps stretched out from that point to the Chancellorsville crossroads before curling back toward the Rappahannock. The V Corps extended the line northeast along Mineral Springs Road, and two more divisions of the III Corps formed a reserve behind the Chancellor house.

May 1 ended nervously on the Federal left, where Sedgwick and Reynolds still had two extremely vulnerable divisions on the Rebel side of the Rappahannock. Early's men continued to strengthen their defenses, and, while the steep riverbanks helped to shield Yankee pontoons from Rebel cannon, those Union lifelines seemed threatened. Left to speculate, Reynolds believed the Confederates were more numerous than it appeared. He worried that should he and Sedgwick expose their men in an offensive movement, they would be overwhelmed. These Federals also felt isolated, cut off from the army's right wing by a combination of distance and frequently disrupted or delayed telegraphic communications. Hooker depended heavily on his telegraph to bind the two wings, but telegraphic machines are delicate instruments, and they would malfunction repeatedly during the campaign. Besides that, the wires used to connect stations were all too frequently dislodged from their poles by passing wagons and artillery limbers, and, finally, not all telegraphers were equally skilled.

Then, as on the previous day, came a string of conflicting orders that confused Sedgwick and Reynolds about Hooker's intentions and their own responsibilities. At 4 P.M., they received an order written two hours earlier telling them to attack if they thought success likely. An hour later, while still considering the possibility of an attack, they received a second message, this one written at 11:30 A.M., asking them to stage a "demonstration" at 1 P.M. Sedgwick could not begin to guess the reasons for the change or to decide if the demonstration should be offered before an attack. Deciding to follow the earlier directive, he told Reynolds to "assume a threatening attitude." A few hours later, a relieved Sedgwick received instructions to postpone all offensive movements.[10]

Sedgwick and Reynolds would have worried less, and perhaps even smiled, had they known that the Rebels across the river were just as puzzled as they. The Confederates were especially perplexed by the Federals in their immediate front. What was their game? "Expect the battle to open every moment," asserted an Alabamian. "It had been a beautiful day after the morning fog had dissipated. Drums rolled in the Yankee camps all day, and their balloons, clearly seen for miles, could only be assumed to be transmitting valuable information for an imminent attack. Guns could be heard booming upriver, and yet before Fredericksburg nothing."[11]

Cavalry operations had little impact on the day's events. Averell was still in Culpeper, unable, it appears, to push through the two regiments of dismounted Virginia cavalry that faced him across the Rapidan. Stoneman's column, finally satisfied that Stuart's men did not lie in wait, cautiously advanced toward Louisa Court House on the Virginia Central Railroad. The horse soldiers stopped to pillage every "smokehouse and farmyard" along their route, so it was 6 P.M. before they departed the village of Orange Springs, still nine hours away from Louisa Court House. The Confederates were lucky that Averell and Stoneman carried out their missions so casually, for no Rebel cavalry remained to interfere with them. Stuart, who had fought his way through a Union cavalry screen to join Lee the previous night, now provided reconnaissance for the army and protected its flanks. Rooney Lee, having sufficiently delayed Averell, received orders on the night of May 1 to burn the railroad bridge at Rapidan Station and fall back to protect Gordonsville.[12]

"The problem presented to General Lee's mind on Friday night, May 1st," recalled Fitzhugh Lee of his uncle, "was to decide how best to attack Hooker's army on the morning of May 2d." No statement better summarizes the shift in momentum and initiative. Yet as Hooker's men tumbled back before his advance, Lee could not help but be suspicious. Why, he asked, was Hooker giving way so easily? Lee rode forward with Jackson to see for himself on May 1. He quickly learned from personal inspection that Hooker's left flank was well anchored, a judgment later confirmed by his engineers. But as he discussed the situation with Stonewall that evening at the junction of the Plank Road and a road running west toward Catharine Furnace, Stuart galloped up to report that Hooker's right flank was "in the air," not secured in any way, either by terrain features or by a secure defensive line. Hooker had not even assigned cavalry to expose or thwart an advance against the inviting target. The right could be turned.[13]

Even though a formidable force sat on his immediate front, Lee decided to risk the flank attack. Having already divided his force once, he would do so a second time. He saw no alternative; he must act before Hooker reclaimed the initiative. True, the Federals could strike unexpectedly, in the midst of the Confederate movement, but Lee's instincts told him that was unlikely. Hooker seemed to be daring Lee to attack—here, along the Dare Mark. It was a gamble, but Lee was a gambler. Careful examination of a rough sketch map and consultation with Jackson's chaplain, Beverly Tucker Lacy, who knew the region, convinced him that a flanking movement across Hooker's front, screened by the Wilderness, was possible. Jackson said he would be ready to advance at 4 A.M. The meeting broke up at about midnight, and the weary soldiers laid down for a few hours of rest.

Jackson arose shortly after 2 A.M. to consider his line of march more carefully. After examining a pocket map with Lacy, Stonewall decided to move parallel to the Union lines as far as Catharine Furnace, then loop away from the Yankees to follow a system of roads and trails that would shield his progress around their flank. This twelve-mile route was longer than the one originally proposed, but it would be safer. With Charles Wellford's son to guide the column, he hoped to have his entire corps, approximately twenty-eight thousand infantry and 108 guns, in position to attack before noon. Jackson had a very imperfect idea of the strength and position of his target, but that did not seem to concern him. If Lee struck the Federal left with the divisions of Anderson and McLaws, approximately fifteen thousand men and twenty-four guns, at the same moment he hit the right, he knew they could drive Hooker into the Rappahannock.

But Jackson had already made a critical error. He had slumped down to sleep for the night without alerting his officers and men that they must march before dawn. Consequently, his movement began three hours late, a delay that changed the entire complexion of the battle, perhaps even the war. The morning was chilly as the column moved out. The soft, damp, narrow road could accommodate no more than four men abreast so that the tail of the column did not fall in line until 11 A.M. The men marched silently, in businesslike fashion. Jackson remained "grave & silent," except for occasional reminders to avoid straggling and to "press forward, press forward." It was a hard march, the pace at times being more a "dogtrot" than a route step. Occasionally, men fell out of line, jerked off their knapsacks or bundles, and discarded all but their most precious possessions before rejoining the column. Still, most men "felt entire confidence and that it would come out all right."[14]

Hooker seemed to anticipate Jackson's maneuver. An hour before Stonewall began his march, Hooker, Sickles, and some staff officers galloped west along the turnpike to inspect their lines. Men cheered as Hooker passed astride his white charger Colonel, a modest rank for the steed of Fighting Joe. He rode as far as Dowdall's Tavern, looked at Howard's and Slocum's deployments, and pointed to several weak points in their defenses. An engineer on Hooker's staff, Col. Cyrus Comstock, told Howard how to strengthen them, but Howard seemed uninterested. He believed the terrain too densely wooded for enemy troops to launch a coordinated attack.

By the time Hooker returned to his headquarters, about 9 A.M., the ball, as his soldiers would say, had opened. Most men remained confident. The previous day's losses did not seem severe, and they held a strong position. "I never knew our army to be in better spirits than it is to-day," one of Meade's men assured his mother that morning. "And if *Men* can gain a victory, we shall have it." They were called to action when Federals at Hazel Grove reported the head of a Rebel column—Jackson's—turning south past Catharine Furnace, less than a mile away. Sickles, whose men occupied Hazel Grove, rode forward to see for himself. By 10 A.M., he had opened on the gray-clad intruders with two rifled cannon, and he soon had six guns in action.[15]

Lee ordered the batteries of Anderson and McLaws to respond against Hooker's left. He sent out skirmishers, too, although he cautioned them not to draw the Federals into a genuine fight. Lee wanted only to hold the Federals' attention while Jackson rambled across their front. The odds were already stacked precariously against him. "It is plain that if the enemy is too strong for me here, I shall have to fall back," he informed Jefferson Davis, "and Fredericksburg must be abandoned. If successful here, Fredericksburg will be saved and our communications retained."[16]

Casualties mounted rapidly. Sometime during the morning, Hooker sent the civilians in the Chancellor house to the basement and out of harm's way. As she moved through the house in obedience to orders, Sue Chancellor was appalled by the number of wounded men. "They had taken our sitting room as an operating room," she reported, "and our piano served as an amputating table." Two of the amputees were wounded Confederates. When Mrs. Chancellor saw their gray uniforms, she requested that her family be allowed to attend them. Given permission, she had the soldiers taken below stairs. So many wounded men had arrived at the hospitals by early afternoon that a train of twenty ambulances carried all who could bear to be transported back to United States Ford.[17]

Hooker had additional problems on this pleasant but breezy May day. Lowe's balloons, posted at Falmouth and Banks's Ford, were jostled and buffeted to such an extent that his observers could not clearly see the Confederate positions or Jackson's column. To Sickles it looked as though Jackson was retreating "in great confusion" toward Gordonsville. Hooker could see a portion of the column through binoculars from his headquarters, and another possibility occurred to him. Recalling the gaps in Howard's unsecured line, he sent word for both Howard and Slocum to beware of secesh tricks. "We have good reason to suppose that the enemy is moving to our right," he told Howard. He advised the XI Corps commander to advance his pickets and watch for an attack against his flank. Howard, with the smallest—and, some said, least reliable—corps in the army, responded that he would see to it, but he only posted a signal officer a mile farther west. He repositioned none of the troops or cannon in his front lines to face in that direction.[18]

The action was less heated below Fredericksburg although just as confusing as on the previous day. At 7 A.M., Reynolds received orders to withdraw his corps and join the main body at Chancellorsville. Hooker had decided to stack his right wing while abandoning any thought of an offensive strike against Early. Unfortunately, the order had been sent five hours earlier, and the withdrawal was supposed to have been completed under cover of night. Reynolds moved at once to comply, even though his column was subjected to Confederate artillery fire all that morning. His corps did not arrive at United States Ford until sunset. That left Sedgwick holding an inexplicable dispatch, also received five hours late, directing him to take up the pontoons at Franklin's Crossing before daylight. To comply, he would have to cut off his two divisions south of the river. The sun was already well up, so Sedgwick ignored the order. He was left to ponder his role in the campaign, which apparently now would be purely defensive, and to wonder what new orders he might receive too late to act on.

Then, remarkably, Jubal Early abandoned his position, save for a single brigade. Lee had asked him to rejoin the left wing if he thought the force opposite him posed no danger. Unfortunately, the messenger, Col. Robert H. Chilton, delivered Lee's discretionary order orally and gave it such a preemptory sound that Early, after some fussing and a good deal of cursing, formed his men in column and headed upriver. He left three thousand men and fifteen guns to defend Fredericksburg and the heights.[19]

By noon, no general engagement had yet developed along the Rappahannock. Word began to spread through Union ranks that the Rebels were retreating, but Hooker, finally acceding to Sickles's desire to strike the Confederate column in his front, would only allow the New York politician to "advance cautiously . . . and harass" the Rebels. Stonewall had already redirected his regimental artillery and the bulk of his wagons down another road—the Catharpin Road—farther to the east of Hazel Grove, but his infantry, divisional artillery, and "fighting trains" continued to push down the furnace road in sight of Sickles. Acting immediately on Hooker's order, Sickles rushed forward Birney's division and Col. Hiram Berdan's sharpshooters, only to find the tail of Jackson's column nearly out of sight. Jackson's rear guard, the Twenty-third Georgia Infantry and a Virginia artillery battery, blocked Federal pursuit. A brief but intense fight ensued near the furnace before the Georgians fell back and reformed in an unfinished railroad cut. Berdan's men soon outflanked them and took three hundred prisoners, but the artillery escaped along with the rest of Jackson's men. It was nearly 4 P.M.[20]

Sickles and Hooker threw men into the fighting around the furnace all afternoon. Emboldened by Sickles's repeated and confident declarations of a Rebel retreat on his front, Hooker ordered Howard and Slocum to pitch in with some of their troops to assist Sickles. He might have done much more. If the Confederates marching away from Hazel Grove were, in fact, retreating, Hooker might well have attacked the troops that remained on his left— Lee's men. Instead, Howard moved forward at about 4 P.M. with his reserve brigade—Gen. Francis C. Barlow's—to reinforce Birney, who had already engaged two of Anderson's brigades in the tangle of woods east of Catharine Furnace. Sickles also moved up part of Gen. Amiel W. Whipple's division to cover Birney's left. Part of Geary's division also tried to join the fight, but it was cut off and forced back by McLaws's men. Pleasonton, who would have been far more useful reconnoitering in front of Howard, arrived at Hazel Grove with three cavalry regiments but declined to engage the enemy because of the uneven and wooded terrain.[21]

So extended was Jackson's line of march that the head of his column came within sight of Howard's unsuspecting corps at about the same time Sickles engaged his rear guard. From a knoll less than a mile from the junction of the turnpike and the Plank Road, Jackson could see the blue lines. The Yankees had stacked arms while they played games, smoked pipes, and prepared supper. Jackson grew excited. If he continued his march just two miles farther north, across the Plank Road and to the turnpike, his men would be completely out of sight and directly on Howard's flank. By 2:30 P.M., his lead regiment, the Fifth Alabama Infantry, had reached the turnpike. Shortly before 3 P.M., Jackson scribbled a note to Lee: "I hope as soon as practicable to attack."[22]

Jackson required another two hours to form the divisions of Colston and Gen. Robert E. Rodes into three lines, which extended about a mile on either side of the turnpike, a half mile from the enemy. At least three reports from Howard's pickets had been sent to XI Corps headquarters since 2:30 P.M. warning of large numbers of the enemy massing to the west, but, with Howard himself gone to assist Sickles, none of the staff officers credited them. Some eighty-six hundred infantry (with sixteen guns) continued to face south; only twenty-two hundred infantry (and eighteen guns) protected the exposed western flank. "Are you ready, General Rodes?" Jackson asked the commander of his lead division at 5:15 P.M. When Rodes responded promptly and decidedly that his Alabamians, Georgians, and Tar Heels were, indeed, ready, Stonewall calmly replied, "You can go forward then."[23]

Unaware of the impending doom on his right, Hooker's thoughts for the moment were all about Sickles and Sedgwick. At 4:10 P.M., he informed Butterfield, still serving as his communications conduit at Falmouth, to have Sedgwick move his whole force across the Rappahannock as soon as

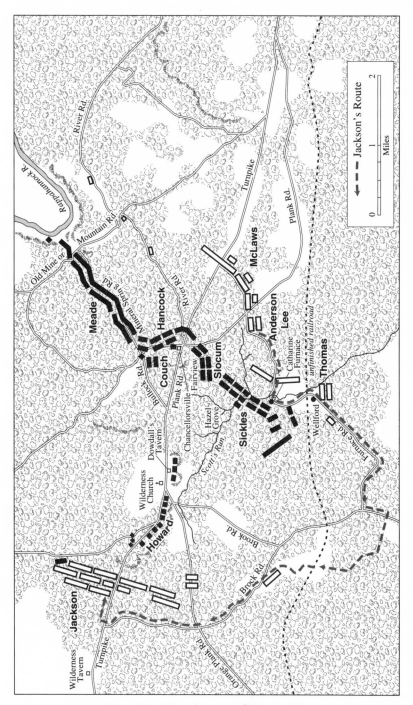

Chancellorsville, afternoon of May 2, 1863

possible. Lee's army was in flight, he said. Now was the moment to take Fredericksburg and "vigorously pursue the enemy." Hooker had evidently forgotten that he had ordered the pontoon bridges disassembled only fourteen hours earlier. Sedgwick, who had witnessed the westward procession of Confederate troops on his front all day, could not have been much surprised when the message arrived. Unhappily, yet another unaccountable delay in dispatching the order from Falmouth meant that he did not receive it until 6:30 P.M.[24]

By that time, Hooker had forgotten entirely about Sedgwick, for Stonewall Jackson was about to demolish his XI Corps. Even without the most recent frantic warnings to XI Corps headquarters, there had been signs of danger all afternoon. Rebel cavalry pickets had collided with Howard's infantry pickets on several occasions that day, and Howard's officers could catch glimpses of Jackson's column crossing the Plank Road. "We could see the rebels moving to our right all fore noon," confirmed an Ohio infantryman. "And all the men could see them plain." A surgeon at Dowdall's Tavern thought he saw a "silent anxiety" in men's faces. Yet Howard and his staff interpreted these movements to mean a Confederate retreat, that seed having been planted by Sickles. Howard never doubted the soundness of his deployment. "We had not a very good position, it is true," he said later, "but we did expect to make a good strong fight should the enemy come."[25]

The final, fatal warning came when an assortment of forest creatures—deer, turkeys, rabbits—raced wildly ahead of the advancing Confederates. It was not long before men in blue uniforms scattered just as frantically. Here and there brave pockets of veterans stood against the waves of screaming, seemingly crazed Rebels that stormed over them, but too many men were green recruits without combat experience. Most of them raced for safety toward United States Ford, many others back to Chancellorsville. The panic began in two German regiments posted on the turnpike about half a mile from Dowdall's Tavern. Facing south along the turnpike, they were hit so hard and so swiftly that they simply dropped their rifles and ran. Two other regiments in the same brigade, facing west when the volleys of musketry first rolled over them, managed a few ineffective blasts at a brigade of Georgians, but they too broke within minutes. Half of these four regiments simply surrendered, and as their comrades ran pell-mell through the corps' camps, other troops panicked without ever considering the source or proximity of the danger.

"Our corps was completely routed," admitted one man. "In 15 minutes we were all cut to pieces," estimated a New York artillerist. An Ohio infantryman reported: "To the right or left or in front as far as I could see, every-thing was fleeing in panic. . . . It seemed to me that the whole army had gone to pieces." By 6 P.M., the center of Jackson's foremost lines had reached a clearing around the Wilderness Church, home to Melzi Chancel-lor's flock and located about 150 yards north of the intersection of the Or-ange Turnpike and Plank Road. All that stood between them and Chancel-lorsville were Schurz's division and one brigade from Gen. Adolph von Steinwehr's division, and the latter unit, commanded by Col. Adolphus Buschbeck, faced south.[26]

It might have been worse had not Howard, just recently returned from Hazel Grove, organized some semblance of resistance. "Such a mass of fugi-tives I hav'nt seen since the first battle of Bull Run," exclaimed the stunned corps commander. He grabbed the national colors from in front of his head-quarters, thrust the staff under the stump of a right arm lost at Fair Oaks, and rode forward to rally his men. Much of Schurz's division had retreated by then. Several artillery batteries worked feverishly to slow the Rebel ad-vance, but they lacked infantry support. Howard managed to wheel Busch-beck's brigade to face west, which, along with the remains of Schurz's and Gen. Charles Devens's divisions, gave him about four thousand men in all. But Buschbeck's troops, who had only shallow rifle pits for cover, soon broke, and with them went the entire Federal flank. Howard ordered his remaining artillery back to Chancellorsville. This stage of the retreat seemed less fran-tic. An Ohio sergeant compared it to the Federal withdrawal at Shiloh rather than Manassas. Still, he admitted, there was "a good deal of disorder."[27]

The Confederates could hardly believe the ease with which they pushed back the Federals. "You never saw such a grand sight in your life," a Vir-ginia infantryman assured his brother. "You never saw such a charge as we made upon them, we soon got them routed and then it was a perfect foot race." Indeed, so swiftly did the Rebels crack the Union flank that they be-came somewhat disorganized and scattered, which slowed their advance and reduced the impetus of the attack. Gen. Alfred Colquitt actually halted his brigade when he thought he saw Federal reinforcements advancing from the south. Surprisingly few men stopped to plunder the Federal camps. The aroma of fresh beef simmering in kettles or the sight of a new pair of shoes beside a tent proved too great a temptation for some hungry or barefooted soldiers, but most of them plunged on after the enemy.[28]

Before Hooker could respond to this crisis on his right, Lee attracted his attention. The Confederate commander had passed some nervous hours waiting for Jackson to complete his overlong march. "He sat on his horse a great deal of the time," observed one officer, "and you could see a shade of anxiety . . . on his face." His men had held Hooker's attention all day, beginning with skirmishers and sharpshooters peppering the Union lines at sunrise. At 7 A.M., the Rebel artillery warmed up, and it continued to exchange fire with Federal batteries through the day. But once Lee heard the muffled sounds of fighting to the west, he had to feign an attack. Most of Anderson's division was at the furnace, engaged in brisk skirmishing with Sickles. Only McLaws's division, with Mahone's brigade in support, was left to advance as skirmishers while the artillery stepped up its bombardment. Lee had no intention of challenging Hooker's defenses; he wanted only to persuade him that an assault was possible and so prohibit Hooker from shifting troops to his right. The demonstration worked. When McLaws's men fell back to their defenses at sunset, about 7 P.M., Fighting Joe's left had not budged.[29]

The army around Chancellorsville awakened to the full extent of the XI Corps's collapse around 6:30 P.M., and by then, Hooker's headquarters was in chaos. One infantryman marveled at the "blaze and roar of cannon and musketry, troops marching to and fro, . . . officers riding at full speed along the lines shouting their commands to their men; shells . . . screeching and howling over our heads and bursting and crashing among the trees, dense rolling clouds of battle smoke." Sue Chancellor called it a "terrible time," and it was about then that the first of Devens's panicked mob raced into camp. They came without rifles, without knapsacks, without accoutrements. They shouted in German and English and some mixed version of the two languages as they pleaded for directions to the river and the pontoons. "They were like a flock of scared sheep," thought Alpheus Williams, "the first really frightened mass of men I ever saw." "Men on foot on horseback on mules & in teams were pushing & piling back for dear life telling all kinds of yarns," verified an enlisted man, "& we began to think that there was another Bull Run." Again, the comparison was made to Manassas, where Hooker, only a witness to the scene, had been so critical of Irvin McDowell and the other Union officers and had later assured Lincoln that he was much superior to all that lot.[30]

Once he grasped the situation, Hooker responded decisively to organize a new defensive line. He ordered artillery at Fairview wheeled to bear on the surging Rebel attackers. He brought up two brigades of Gen. Hiram Berry's division, once commanded by Hooker himself, from its reserve position and told them to rush the Rebels with fixed bayonets. He directed Williams's division to fall back from Hazel Grove to its original position at Fairview.

When the overdue John Reynolds galloped up, Hooker greeted him warmly and told him to push forward his corps, only to have his hopes dashed when Reynolds reported that his men had not yet crossed the river. Even so, with Howard rounding up the more steadfast members of his command, a total of ten regiments, Hooker had enough men to plug the dike scarcely a half mile from his headquarters.

It was 8 P.M. The sun had set an hour earlier. Yet a bright full moon combined with a cloudless sky to provide an unusual amount of light, enough light for Jackson to push the attack. Stonewall had followed his men impatiently into battle while periodically shouting encouragement. "Press on, press on!" he told his soldiers, and warned them not to let the Federals reach the river fords. His persistence and the spirit of his men had produced a remarkable military achievement, but Jackson knew the victory was not yet complete. The three hours lost in starting the march that morning were looming larger. An aide asked him if it was wise to be so near the enemy. Stonewall replied that the danger had passed. At about 8:45 P.M., Jackson ordered Powell Hill's fresh Light Division to push through to United States Ford while he and his staff followed the lead brigade of James Lane's North Carolinians.[31]

At about 9 P.M., the impatient Jackson led his entourage of eight riders through the advancing infantry to look for a soft spot in the Federal defenses. Hill, who had followed Jackson to the front accompanied by nine members of his own staff, started out some fifty yards behind them. As men picked their way cautiously through the undergrowth and the night, the fighting seemed to have ceased for the moment. A wicked artillery exchange of fifteen minutes duration had occurred a half hour earlier, but now "all was quiet" except for the shouting of military commands and the "mournful cry of a whippoorwill."[32]

But if the sounds of combat had been stilled, many soldiers, North and South, along the lines this night were nervous. Lines had become so snarled that Lane's Tar Heels surprised and captured some two hundred members of a trapped Pennsylvania regiment, and a Union general nearly suffered the same fate. All of this occurred several hundred yards to the right of Jackson's party, which continued along a narrow woodland road about sixty yards north of the Orange Plank Road. As Confederate skirmishers drew near the Federal lines—as close as two hundred yards in some places—anxious young soldiers started and flinched at sudden sounds and movements. "We could distinctly hear the commands of the officers and the steps of the troops," reported a Union artillery officer. Nineteen-year-old Sgt. Thomas

A. Cowan, Company A, Thirty-third North Carolina Infantry, shouted a challenge to some men in front of his skirmishers: Were they Yanks or Rebs? They were Yanks, came the reply. Cowan told his men to open fire.[33]

A single shot in response to Cowan's command ignited a succession of fusillades that rolled north along the entire skirmish line, soon to be echoed by the main Confederate force. Jackson, having advanced midway between that main line and his skirmishers, had completed his inspection and was returning to safety when the crossfire hit him. He was struck three times, once each in his right hand, left forearm, and left upper arm near the shoulder. The third shot shattered a bone. The shots likely came from the Eighteenth North Carolina. A similar volley scattered Hill's party. Following the immediate confusion of horses rearing, men shouting, and soldiers diving for cover, Hill and his cohorts, who had stuck to the Plank Road, rode to assist Jackson. Stonewall's staff rapidly bandaged his wounds, which did not bleed excessively, and carried him gingerly to the rear.[34]

As Jackson rode to meet his destiny, Hooker had already devised a plan for the morrow. He would outflank and strike Jackson before Stonewall could resume his attack. To support this maneuver and protect his left flank, Hooker ordered Sedgwick at 9 P.M. to move toward Chancellorsville with the utmost speed. He should "attack and destroy" any force he encountered and fall on Lee's rear. Only Gibbon's division would remain behind to occupy Fredericksburg. It was a preemptory order, to supersede all previous orders. Butterfield underscored the need for speed when he replied to Sedgwick's request for a guide: "Seize the mayor of Fredericksburg or any citizen. Put them ahead as guides, on pain of death for false information." Butterfield finally found a contraband to lead the column.[35]

Hooker had assumed that Sedgwick had already taken Fredericksburg, as he had been instructed to do that afternoon. But by the time Uncle John received the commanding general's 9 P.M. directive at 11 P.M., he had barely gained a foothold against light Rebel resistance. He had moved Brooks's division below Deep Run, Gen. Albion P. Howe's division between Deep Run and Hazel Run, and Newton's division to the outskirts of Fredericksburg. What was more, unknown to either Hooker or Sedgwick, Jubal Early had returned to the hills behind the town. Shortly before dark, as Early's column had marched to Lee's summons, a courier intercepted him to say it was all a mistake; Lee had not intended him to abandon the town if it was in danger. No sooner had Early finished with an impressive fit of heated profanity than a second messenger, this one from Fredericksburg, informed him that the Federals were marching in force toward the town. With his token force below and on the heights facing certain disaster, a still infuriated Early turned his column around and headed back.[36]

The last action of May 2 around Chancellorsville came near midnight. Fearful of being cut off at Hazel Grove by Jackson's advance, Dan Sickles decided to lead a night attack back through Fairview and against Stonewall's right flank. Not only would this reestablish the Federal line, but it would also allow him to recapture some Union artillery lost earlier in the day. Unfortunately, Sickles, who had no idea where the enemy lines might be, advanced without scouts or skirmishers. The results, were it not for the nearly two hundred casualties the episode cost him, might be considered comical. As his men crashed through the woods, they attracted the fire of both Federals and Confederates, and they returned the fire equally into both sides. The Third Michigan Infantry even "captured" a Union battery. The affair, which a Maine volunteer generously described as "a bad thing," ended quickly, and Sickles's men returned to the vicinity of Hazel Grove. Surgeons worked through the night to repair the damage.[37]

A final disappointment for Hooker on this bizarre day involved his cavalry. Informed that Averell had yet to cross the Rapidan, the commanding general angrily ordered him to report with his column to United States Ford. In compliance, Averell slipped downriver to cross at Ely's Ford, only to be attacked by Confederate cavalry and infantry under Jeb Stuart. He would not cross the river until the following morning. Hooker would have been even more annoyed had he known how far short of expectations Stoneman's column had fallen. According to Hooker's calculations, Stoneman should have completed destruction of the Richmond, Fredericksburg, and Potomac Railroad at Hanover by May 2. In fact, he had advanced only as far as Thompson's Crossroads, over twenty miles west of Hanover. He had managed to tear up five miles of track on the Virginia Central Railroad around Louisa Court House, but Rooney Lee, advancing from Gordonsville, had captured about two dozen of his men.[38]

Yet the apparent failure of Stoneman's raid was the least of Hooker's worries by early May 3. At about 3:30 A.M., he learned that Sedgwick could not reach him before daylight. "General Sedgwick just reports three regiments threaten his left flank now and have engaged his pickets," Butterfield informed Hooker at 2:25 A.M.; "there is still a force in Fredericksburg; that he is marching as rapidly as possible." And that was the most optimistic report Hooker would receive from his left wing for several hours. Having begun the campaign with seventy-two hours of near perfection, he had seen nothing but failure in the next forty-eight hours.[39]

# CHAPTER TEN

# The Hardest Battle Ever Fought

John Sedgwick's confusion matched the fog that blanketed the Rappahannock in the predawn hours of Sunday, May 3. Hooker had assured him that only a token Confederate force held the hills above Fredericksburg. Yet, as he moved his corps upriver along the Old Richmond Road from Deep Run, enemy infantry impeded his every move. His advance brigade, part of Newton's division, finally secured the town, but these men, too, met stiff Rebel resistance. "Everything in the world depends upon the rapidity and promptness of your movement," Butterfield had notified Sedgwick at 2:35 A.M. "Push everything." Still mindful of these orders, Sedgwick directed Gen. Frank Wheaton's brigade, also from Newton's division, to initiate a reconnaissance toward Marye's Heights.[1]

Wheaton's men, supported by two batteries, deployed a quarter mile in front of the infamous stone wall. As they advanced at 4 A.M., the Second Battle of Fredericksburg began. The opening phase did not last long. Halfway to their objective, the Federals buckled under the "sudden destructive fire" of Barksdale's Mississippians behind the wall and the Washington Artillery on the heights. Wheaton's line fell back, halted, and laid down behind the protective crest that had saved so many Union lives in December. Sedgwick, who had ridden forward to inspect the damage, exclaimed to his adjutant general, "By Heaven, sir, this must not delay us." He ordered up more artillery to punish the Rebels and directed that all available pontoons be laid opposite Fredericksburg so that Gibbon's men, already in position to cross the Dare Mark, could join him south of the river.[2]

As the skies brightened above Chancellorsville, Hooker prepared to fight without Sedgwick. The center of his defenses, formed by the corps of Sickles, Slocum, and Couch, nearly encircled the Chancellor house.

Meade's corps secured Hooker's immediate right, spread out along the road to Ely's Ford. Reynolds's corps, having finally arrived, extended Meade's line at a right angle along a creek that ran to the Rappahannock. Howard's corps extended Hooker's left along Mineral Springs Road to the river. The night had reverberated to the sound of axes and falling trees as Union soldiers strengthened their defenses along every part of the line.

Two aspects of this deployment are worth noting. First, three of Hooker's corps—Meade, Reynolds, and Howard—confronted no Confederate troops, and Reynolds's line was two miles from Chancellorsville. Second, and most important, Sickles's seven infantry brigades and thirty-eight guns no longer held Hazel Grove. Sickles had understood the importance of the position. He had urged Hooker during the night to extend his lines to encompass it. By doing so, he argued, Hooker could keep Lee's left wing divided and dismantle it piecemeal. But Hooker, fearing that Sickles might be cut off after the failure of his night attack, pulled him back to Fairview shortly before daylight. It was his most fateful decision since halting the advance toward Fredericksburg two days earlier.

For all these potential Federal weaknesses, Lee's force still remained dangerously divided, his strategic situation little changed from the day before. If Hooker suddenly became aggressive, he could overwhelm either of Lee's two wings in front of Chancellorsville. The Confederate commander, above all else, had to reunite those two wings. He would have to depend on Early to protect his rear, but Lee knew that the bulk of the Union forces were in front of him. The Federals still held the advantages of numbers and position, but then, they had held those advantages from the outset. If Lee could not defeat Hooker here, both he and Early must abandon their positions. He could still block a Federal advance toward Richmond, and perhaps, by then, Longstreet would rejoin the army. Yet, having spent so many lives and believing he was close to victory, Lee never considered not attacking.

Tactically, Lee knew precisely what to do. Jeb Stuart now commanded in Jackson's place. A. P. Hill normally would have succeeded to command, but he, too, had been wounded in the crossfire that downed Jackson. Stuart's nearly thirty-two thousand men of all arms occupied the same position astride the Plank Road where they had halted the night before. His twenty-six thousand infantry, positioned less than half a mile from Williams and Berry, were crouched and ready to spring. Lee still commanded personally on the right, where he had about fifteen thousand men. He was "much distressed" over the loss of Jackson, but he had great confidence in Stuart. All Stuart need do was push straight ahead against Hooker "so as to drive him

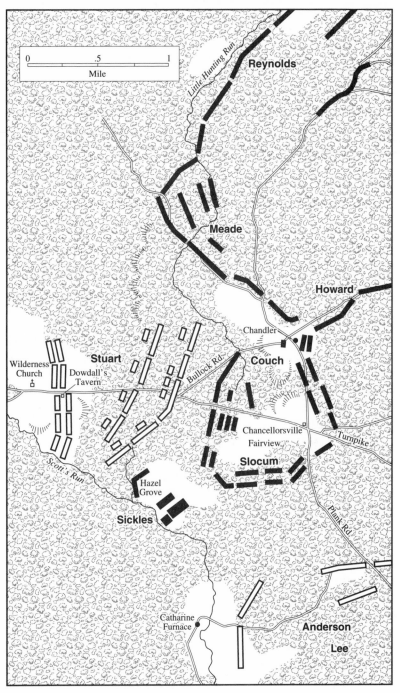

Chancellorsville, dawn of May 3, 1863

from Chancellorsville." Lee would drive simultaneously against the Union left, his grand object being to reunite his divided wing. Lee's left flank sat just over two thousand yards from Stuart's right flank, separated, he still believed, by the Union salient at Hazel Grove. But they must strike at first light, Lee warned Stuart in two predawn messages, before Hooker recovered from the previous day's blow and realized how few men faced him.[3]

Stuart, decked out in a new—blue—uniform coat and with fresh red and black plumes adorning his hat, eagerly ordered his infantry forward at 5:30 A.M. The cavalryman never doubted for a moment, commented one officer, that he could "just crash his way wherever he chose to strike." Three brigades of Powell Hill's division, now commanded by Henry Heth, led the way across a mile-wide front below the Plank Road. The men met slight resistance initially, as they plowed through the underbrush and woods. The right flank, especially, had an easy time. But as the center of the line drew to within seventy yards of the Federal entrenchments at Fairview, the attack on that part of the field spent itself and the Rebels drew back before heavy fire.[4]

Both the strength of the Fairview defenses and the unusual ease with which Stuart's right flank advanced can be explained by Sickles's withdrawal from Hazel Grove. Stuart's attackers encountered only the Federal rear guard at Hazel Grove, and when Porter Alexander realized what was happening, he urged Stuart to claim the abandoned position. He could enfilade the entire Federal line from that elevation, Alexander told Stuart, even bombard Chancellorsville, only a mile away. Stuart directed Willie Pegram to bring up two batteries, and within two hours, thirty more guns crowded the plateau. The speed with which the guns were delivered testified to the efficiency of Lee's new artillery system, which would shortly make possible the finest offensive use of artillery in the war. "The position turned out to be one of great value," Alexander later commented with studied understatement. In fact, by abandoning Hazel Grove, Hooker would soon lose the battle.[5]

The next few hours witnessed some of the most ferocious fighting of the war. By 9 A.M., three successive waves of Confederate attackers had hurled themselves "with the impetuosity of an avalanche" against a stout blue wall on both sides of the turnpike. The wall bent in places and occasionally cracked, but it did not break. The Federals twice leaped forward in courageous counterattacks, only to scamper back to the safety of their earthworks and log parapets. Back came the Rebels, racing, screaming, "more like fiens than men," toward the invaders. Men who had fought at Antietam and

Fredericksburg called this the toughest combat they had ever seen. "It was an ugly give and take," vouched a Pennsylvanian; "the hardest battle that ever was fought," swore another soldier. "It would be useless . . . to attempt to describe the fighting," submitted a New Yorker. "It was desperate beyond the power of description." Most simply, a Michigan infantryman testified, "That was a awful day."[6]

The dominant impression of the men fighting at Chancellorsville was the horrible sound, the "din," the "variety of hideous noises," the screeching shells and whizzing bullets. "It was the most frightful shelling ever I was in," reported a Union surgeon. Men wondered at how the bullets "sung" and flew "thick almost as hail," as the "intense" firing, "continuous & deep," produced a "perfect gauntlet of shot and shell." "The musketry fire . . . was for an hour to-day, as heavy and incessant as I ever heard," claimed a midwesterner. "The firing was the heaviest I ever was in," verified a Georgian. "The men were dropping all around me, shot down." An Alabamian recalled, "The ping of the minnie ball, the splutter of cannister, the whistling of grape, the 'where are you' 'where are you' of screaming shells and the cannon's roar from a hundred mouths went to make up the music for the great opera of death."[7]

The battle took an unexpected turn shortly after 9 A.M., when a Rebel cannonball split a porch column where Hooker had been standing. The heavy timber struck the general on the right side and knocked him senseless. Hooker recovered sufficiently in a few minutes to realize that Chancellorsville was no fit place for a headquarters. He mounted Colonel with assistance, partly to assure his men that he had survived the blow, and was escorted to the rear. Still groggy from the pain and probably in mild shock, Hooker stopped at the farmhouse of Oscar Bullock, a half mile toward the Rappahannock. A sip of brandy revived him, but he still felt unsteady. At 10 A.M., he put Couch in command of the army and ordered him to pull back from Chancellorsville.

Lee chose the same moment to press the attack. He had set his men in motion shortly after Stuart moved forward. By 10 A.M., having pivoted Anderson's division to the south by way of Catharine Furnace, his wing formed a single line of advance. As he sat on Traveller at Hazel Grove, roughly the center of the line, Lee grasped the situation in a moment. Fairview and the Chancellor house would be his next targets. He ordered both flanks to move forward and throw Hooker back across the Dare Mark.

The Chancellor house was already battered and in flames. Surrounding fields, woods, and Federal abatis were likewise ablaze. "Oh the horror of that day!" exclaimed Sue Chancellor. She would never forget the hellish scene that greeted her when Federal officers called the family out of the cellar and escorted it to the rear. Piles of arms and legs testified to the frantic work of the surgeons; rows of corpses tallied their failures. Deadly shells screeched around them; terrified horses reared and screamed; determined men ran in all directions. A constant dirge of moans, curses, shouts, and prayers underscored the confusion, and intense heat and smoke added to the sense of an inferno. As the family hurried along the road to United States Ford, Miss Chancellor looked back to see her home "enveloped in flames."[8]

The sounds of battle subsided around Chancellorsville just as the contest for Marye's Heights began in earnest. Having learned in his initial reconnaissance that the Rebels in his path could not be swept away lightly, Sedgwick informed Hooker at 5:30 A.M. that his entire corps was "warmly engaged on Sumner's old ground." The commanding general should not expect him to arrive anytime soon. Sedgwick had already decided to assault Early in three columns. Howe's division, aligned to the left of Hazel Run, would attack Telegraph Hill and Marye's Heights obliquely. Newton's division would join with Gen. Hiram Burnham's Light Division to stage a demonstration on the plain in front of the stone wall. Gibbon's two brigades would cross the river and assemble in Fredericksburg, file out of town to the right, and hit Gen. Cadmus M. Wilcox's brigade. Wilcox, who had been guarding Banks's Ford since the morning of May 2, had already pulled back to the defenses on Stansbury's Hill. Downriver, on the extreme left, William Brooks would hold in check those Rebels entrenched between Deep Run and Hamilton's Station.[9]

Early had just thirteen thousand men and forty-six guns to oppose Sedgwick's twenty-six thousand men and sixty-six guns, and most of his command was in the wrong place. Early did not believe that Sedgwick, an old West Point classmate, would dare repeat Burnside's mistake and assault Marye's Heights. He expected the brunt of the attack to come from Howe and Brooks. Accordingly, he assigned only twelve hundred men and eight guns to defend the heights directly behind the town. In truth, Early had read Sedgwick correctly, for Uncle John did not want to hit the stone wall head-on. He had envisioned a turning movement, with Gibbon crashing down on the Rebel left flank. But things went wrong. First, Gibbon took longer than expected to get his division across the river. Sedgwick had hoped to launch his assault by 8 A.M., but at 9:30 A.M. many of Gibbon's men were still filtering through Fredericksburg. Then, when Gibbon tried to move into position west of town, he was slowed by a thirty-foot-wide

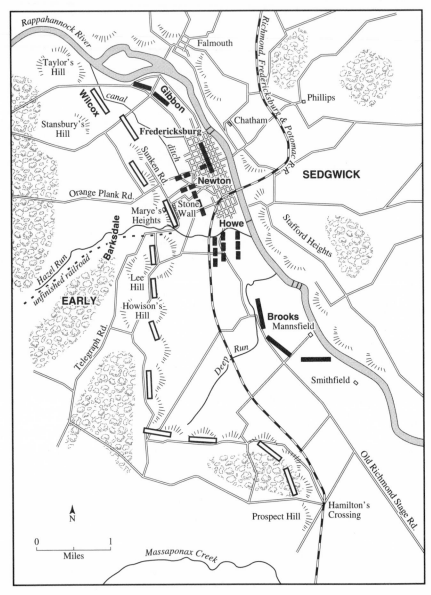

Fredericksburg, morning of May 3, 1863

canal and Rebel artillery. Similarly, Howe's division found it impossible to cross the stream and gully at Hazel Run without exposing its flank and rear to the enemy. All of these delays led Sedgwick to believe that he had no choice but to have Newton and Burnham "carry the works by direct assault." Sedgwick had not been there in December. He had heard about what happened, but he could not know.[10]

The attacking columns had been waiting on the edge of town listening to the supporting artillery bombardment, which had begun at 6 A.M. When the big guns paused at about 10:30 A.M., the infantry, ten regiments in all, moved forward. Burnham sent two regiments in columns of four up the Orange Plank Road, followed by two of Newton's regiments. On their left, two more of Newton's regiments moved up Hanover Street while, on the far left, another of Newton's regiments advanced with the remainder of Burnham's Light Division directly against the stone wall. It looked like another Union disaster. Rebel artillery blasted Burnham's men on the Plank Road when they came within three hundred yards. At fifty yards, Barksdale's infantry—the Eighteenth and part of the Twenty-first Mississippi Infantry—opened up from behind the stone wall on both the center and left columns. Burnham fell wounded from his horse. Chaos reigned as the Federals dropped "like leaves in autumn."[11]

Then, suddenly, everything changed. Two of Howe's brigades finally got across Hazel Run to pressure Barksdale's right flank. Col. Thomas W. Allen, who had been leading the Fifth Wisconsin against the left end of the wall, rallied his Badgers. "You have got to take them," shouted Allen. "You think you cannot do it, but you can and you will." The regiment had already lost a third of its number, but the survivors rose on Allen's command and rushed forward with a shout. The Seventh Massachusetts, which had taken 40 percent casualties, rallied in like fashion on Allen's right. Blue infantrymen stormed the wall. Bayonets flashed and dripped blood; rifle butts struck heads, backs, and shoulders with sickening thuds and cracks. The Rebels fought like "mad men," the Yankees like "lions." The gray line collapsed on both flanks as the Federals continued to surge over the wall and up the steep slope of Marye's Heights. In fifteen minutes of ferocious mayhem they claimed the prize they had sought for five months. "We drove the rebs like sheep from the trenches," exalted one infantryman.[12]

It had been a costly fight for all, this brief brawl behind Fredericksburg. The Rebels lost 475 men, but the winners sacrificed 1,100. Barksdale escaped with most of his brigade. His line had been pierced but not the spirits of his men. "We'll be all right in a little while," he declared. The pugnacious

Mississippian had done it again. On December 11, he had bought Lee an entire day to prepare for Burnside's army. Now, at the wall where Georgians had won glory at First Fredericksburg, he gained valuable time for Lee by delaying Sedgwick's advance. The capture of Marye's Heights took Early, who had been keeping Brooks at bay, by surprise. After venting his frustration in yet another of his famous tirades, he pulled back his right wing along the Telegraph Road to join Barksdale in establishing a new defensive line two to three miles southwest of town.[13]

Sedgwick had to make a decision. Should he regroup and finish off Early or move immediately toward Chancellorsville? He had no idea of the situation to the west, but Hooker's latest directives had made it clear that he needed the VI Corps. It would be dangerous to leave a large force in his rear, but Gibbon's thirty-five hundred men could hold the heights. If Sedgwick moved expeditiously, he probably would have little to fear from Early's apparently battered and beaten command. Besides, his own men were in the best of spirits; some even wanted to march on Richmond. So at 2:15 P.M., Brooks's division, which had by then rejoined Sedgwick, headed up the Plank Road.

But Sedgwick had not counted on Cadmus Wilcox, who made a virtue of necessity. Cut off from Barksdale by the broken Confederate line, Wilcox found it nearly impossible to reunite with Barksdale and Early. Instead, he withdrew his Alabama brigade up the River Road and prepared to intercept Sedgwick on the Plank Road three miles west of town. "I felt it a duty to delay the enemy as much as possible in his advance," he explained. He spread his main line along the Salem Church ridge, a position similar to that occupied by Anderson and McLaws three days earlier at Zoan Church. Artillery, infantry skirmishers, and the Fifteenth Virginia Cavalry, attached to his command, would slow Federal progress to that point. A member of the brilliant West Point class of 1846, Wilcox had seen his share of combat in Mexico and since First Manassas. He knew Sedgwick's intentions, and he knew that only his brigade of fewer than 2,000 men stood between Sedgwick's 22,500 and Lee's rear.[14]

Lee was poised to polish off Hooker with one more assault when, at about 12:30 P.M., he learned of the Fredericksburg debacle. Lee calmly postponed his attack and prepared to divide his command a third time in as many days. He ordered McLaws to send two brigades—Mahone and Kershaw—to stop Sedgwick. McLaws would follow shortly thereafter with his two remaining brigades—those of Gen. Paul J. Semmes and Gen. William T. Wofford. Lee then directed Anderson's division to block the junction of the River Road and the Mine Road, thus preventing Hooker and Sedgwick from joining forces along either of those routes. Lee's response to this crisis was daring and decisive, yet he had few other options. He could not leave so large a force as the VI Corps in his rear, and he apparently never considered retreat. He had to act, and the quiescent Hooker made the gamble seem safe enough.

McLaws had not expected to find Wilcox at Salem Church, but each man must have been relieved to see the other. They completed their deployments, which called for McLaws to divide his four brigades on either side of Wilcox's centrally placed men, just in time. At 3:25 P.M., Brooks's division, mostly men from New Jersey, New York, and Pennsylvania, engaged Wilcox's skirmishers and advanced artillery. The Federals dislodged them easily and continued forward at a steady pace. The terrain, with alternating patches of clearings and forests, presented the only obstacle in their path. A "strange sort of quiet," without a hint of "any impending calamity," prevailed as the Federals pushed ahead for another ninety minutes before striking the main Confederate line.[15]

Pressing their attack manfully, the Federals concentrated on the left-center of the Rebel defenses, held by Wilcox and Semmes. "We just did have time to form our lines," reported a member of Semmes's Georgia brigade, "before the Yanks drove our skirmishers in." His regiment was lucky. Some units had to be "double-quicked into the fight," not even having time to align themselves. "The struggle became furious," Semmes's Georgian continued. "I never heard such a noise in all my life. It sounded like a large cane break on fire and a thunder storm with repeated loud thunder claps, one clap following another."[16]

Some of the most ferocious fighting swirled around the red-brick Salem Church and a nearby log schoolhouse south of the Plank Road. Two companies of the Ninth Alabama Infantry had turned the buildings into miniature fortresses; the Eighth and Tenth Alabama were formed in battle lines behind them. Charging Federals nearly broke through at this point. The volleys of rifle fire that ripped holes in their lines staggered the Federals, but they continued to bull ahead, surround the schoolhouse, capture its small garrison, crash into the Tenth Alabama, and send that regiment reeling backward.

The rampage was slowed when a portion of the Eighth Alabama, on the right flank of the retreating Tenth, wheeled to fire into the side of the intruding Yankees. Then came a vengeful cry from the remainder of the Ninth Alabama, which had been standing in reserve behind the Tenth. They saved the line by rolling over and through the Federals to reclaim the schoolhouse and rescue their captured comrades. All this time, the company of the Ninth posted in the church delivered a "harassing and deadly fire" into Federal ranks. As the Federal charge gradually wavered and stalled, Rebels all along the line delivered "one of those wild shouts so terrible to the Yankees" and leaped forward to counterattack. The enemy "staggered . . . and fled in great confusion" for nearly a mile before finding sanctuary behind its own artillery, which raked the oncoming Rebels with canister. The pursuing graybacks, exhausted and disorganized, soon retreated.[17]

Yankees and Rebels fought at Salem Church with nearly equal numbers, about 4,000 men each, but the results were very uneven. Sedgwick lost 1,523 men, the Rebels only 674. Sedgwick had been caught in the open and unprepared, and he probably ordered Brooks forward too soon, before the rest of his command was in position to lend support. Wilcox, in contrast, held the advantages of terrain and perhaps surprise, for Sedgwick had not expected to encounter so many Rebels or such "determined resistance" on the Salem Church ridge. Sedgwick and his men rested uneasily that night. "We slept in line," reported one man, "with the dead of the day's battle lying near us. The stretcher bearers with their lamps wandered here and there over the field. . . . The night was inexpressibly gloomy. Fires were not allowed."[18]

Back at Chancellorsville that afternoon, Hooker had waited impatiently to be saved by Sedgwick. By 1:30 P.M., his wing was hemmed in. With Slocum's left flank resting on the Rappahannock, Hooker had placed Howard to his right, followed by Couch along the Mineral Springs Road. Sickles's corps defended the apex of the line at the Bullock house. Only Slocum, Couch, and Sickles faced appreciable numbers of Rebels. To the right of Sickles, Meade's and Reynolds's little-used troops formed the other half of the perimeter. They faced virtually no Rebel threat but kept busy strengthening breastworks, cleaning rifles, and clearing fields of fire.

The remainder of the day around Chancellorsville settled into an exchange of artillery fire and efforts to recover the dead and wounded. There were lots of dead and wounded. Lee had lost nine thousand men, killed, wounded, and missing in five hours of fighting, not much less than he had lost in twelve hours at Antietam. Hooker had suffered about eighty-six hundred casualties, a large portion being victims of Confederate artillery, but a third, too, being captured. The end was particularly grim for wounded men trapped in patches of woods that had caught fire. "You could plainly hear the poor fellows scream and yell," testified a Federal. Men in immediate danger cried out to be saved; those momentarily safe from the flames called piteously with parched throats for water. Many blackened bodies were recovered from the smoldering trees and charred underbrush. "I cant give you any idea what a sight it was to walk the Battle Field and see men lying with their cloths burnt off their hair burnt close to their head their arms and legs all drawed up with fire," a North Carolinian confided to his family. "I never saw such a distressing sight."[19]

In the midst of all this chaos and suffering, Lee planned for the morrow. Toward sundown, while listening to the final stages of combat at Salem Church, he encouraged Early to join forces with Wilcox and McLaws and "demolish" the enemy. Dark had descended by the time Early received the message, but Jubal had a better idea anyway. He had been outgeneraled that day, and he knew it. He was responsible for the army's perilous position, and he wanted to redeem himself. An exchange of messages with McLaws and Lee determined Early to strike Gibbon at first light and retake Marye's Heights. Having thus divided the Federal left wing, he could then turn and hit Sedgwick from the east while McLaws, acting as senior commander at Salem Church, clobbered him from the west. Lee, betting that Hooker would continue to sit tight, approved.[20]

Hooker remained groggy most of the day. He rallied long enough at one point to ride out and inspect his lines, but most men who saw him described the general as worn, nervous, and in pain. He also thought to inform Lincoln of the situation. There had been "desperate fighting," he said in his first communication to the president in six days, and a new defensive line had been established. "If Sedgwick could have gotten up," Hooker emphasized for the president's benefit, "there could have been but one result." Still, he did not "despair of success," and the army remained in "good spirits." Hooker went to bed early, but at II P.M., Gouverneur Warren woke him. Warren had just returned from Sedgwick's column and thought it essential that he brief the commanding general on the fortunes of his left wing. Hooker roused himself long enough to acknowledge Warren's report, mumbled that he now awaited Lee's attack in the morning, and implied that Sedgwick "would have to depend upon himself." He then dismissed Warren and went back to sleep.[21]

Warren, uneasy about both Hooker's seeming lack of concern over Sedgwick's predicament and his imprecise explanation of his own plans, took a bold step. Uncle John, he knew, was desperate for orders, so Warren composed his own version of the instructions he thought Hooker intended. Everything was "snug" at Chancellorsville, he began. Hooker had easily repulsed Lee that day, and he was eager to meet the next attack. Then, somewhat amazingly, Warren told Sedgwick that Hooker did not want him to attack Wilcox in force unless he, Hooker, was able to attack "at the same time," though who Hooker intended to attack, whether Lee or Wilcox, was unclear. "Look well to the safety of your corps," Warren concluded. Sedgwick could fall back to either Banks's Ford or the river crossing at Fredericksburg if he thought it necessary, but the former would put him in closer communications with the main army. Warren later admitted that the dispatch was ill-advised and poorly worded but added that he was "exceedingly exhausted" after twenty-four hours in the saddle when he composed it.[22]

An anxious Lincoln received the commanding general's 1:30 P.M. dispatch at 4 P.M. He immediately wired back to ask Hooker's position, as well as those of Sedgwick and Stoneman. And what of Stoneman? Where was the elusive cavalryman? He was finally in action and doing considerable damage. The previous night, May 2, after disabling several bridges and railroad depots, his column had advanced southward as far as Thompson's Crossroads, about twenty-five miles southwest of Chancellorsville and twenty-five miles northwest of Richmond. There he divided his thirty-five hundred men into six raiding parties. Having reached a point in Lee's rear where he believed he could wreak havoc, Stoneman had decided "like a shell, . . . to burst in every direction." He directed the raiding parties to destroy their assigned targets by midafternoon on May 3. Stoneman, who was suffering from hemorrhoids, the bane of all cavalrymen, would remain at Thompson's Crossroads with five hundred men.[23]

Stoneman's raiders had a wonderful time sacking depots, tearing up track, destroying bridges, cutting telegraph wires, even capturing a train filled with wounded Rebels, but they fell far short of severing Lee's Richmond supply lines. What was worse, Stoneman remained as silent as ever so that Hooker knew even less of Stoneman than Lincoln knew of Hooker. The commanding general vented his frustration on another cavalryman, Averell. When Averell reported to Hooker for instructions that afternoon, Fighting Joe learned that his column still lingered along the Rapidan. He betrayed nothing of his disgust in Averell's presence, but that evening, he relieved the cavalryman of his command and transferred his troops to Pleasonton.

May 4 started well enough for the Rebels. Jubal Early's morning attack took Gibbon completely by surprise, and by 7:30 A.M., Marye's Heights was swarming with "gray-backed devils." Gibbon, uncertain of his own role and of Sedgwick's plans, had failed to fortify the heights. His orders had been to guard the river crossings, and that he did. His men also succeeded in holding Fredericksburg. They had dug rifle pits along the edge of town and loop-holed the houses. Heavy skirmishing continued through the day, and luck-ily, the Rebels opposing them had no artillery. In any case, Early had a more important target. He sent Gen. John B. Gordon to test Sedgwick's left flank, anchored by Howe's division. Sedgwick's line, like Hooker's, now resem-bled a horseshoe, and the western portion rested a scant half mile from McLaws.[24]

But McLaws seemed to be in no hurry. Early thought he had convinced the Georgian on the previous night of the need for concerted action. He as-sumed that as he moved to retake the heights, McLaws would strike Sedg-wick. With Sedgwick's escape route via Fredericksburg cut off, Early be-lieved they could squeeze the Federals in a deadly vice. But McLaws wanted more men and had asked Lee for reinforcements. Lee had been thinking along the same lines, and a short time before receiving McLaws's request had dispatched Richard Anderson's remaining three brigades to assist the right wing. That left just three divisions—Heth, Colston, and Rodes—to face sixteen Federal divisions, twenty thousand men against seventy thou-sand. Lee had taken yet another gamble, perhaps his biggest one of the cam-paign. Yet he believed he now had to destroy Sedgwick before dealing with Hooker. To expedite matters, he mounted Traveller and headed for Salem Church.

Hooker graciously accommodated Lee's daring design. He was perfectly content to sit out the dance of May 4, in part because of mixed intelligence reports that suggested Longstreet's command might soon arrive from Suf-folk. He heard rumors, too, that Stonewall Jackson was on the move again. Jackson had crossed the Rappahannock, said one report, circled Hooker's rear, and burned the supply depot at Aquia Creek. Another report insisted that Jackson had moved downriver and gained Sedgwick's rear. Stonewall seemed to be everywhere but on his sickbed near Guiney Station. Some evi-dence suggests that Hooker contemplated an offensive move for the next day. According to this plan, he intended to slip a portion of his men back across the Rappahannock at United States Ford, march seven miles to Banks's Ford, recross the Dare Mark, and strike Lee's flank. In fact, Hooker went nowhere on May 4 and so disappointed many of his men. "Our troops were ready for a fight and we did nothing but remain in position," complained General Patrick. "I can only hope that Hooker has something very wise and deep on hand for tomorrow," sighed an equally frustrated ar-tillerist. Hooker summoned Dan Butterfield to join him from Falmouth, but an "ominous" quiet prevailed along the Chancellorsville line.[25]

Meanwhile, Sedgwick wondered what to do. He had received Warren's message at 6:30 A.M., about the time Early's men moved toward Marye's Heights. His misfortune the day before had led Sedgwick to overestimate his own losses and the strength of the Rebels between him and Hooker. Warren's caution that he should look to the safety of his corps froze him even before he learned that Early had closed in from behind. "I think they will attempt to drive me back," he cautioned Hooker at 8:30 A.M. "I await instructions." At 11 A.M., he warned Hooker that the enemy was pressing him "hard" and again mentioned the possibility of a withdrawal. By 11:15 A.M., Sedgwick realized the Rebels had him on two sides. Could Hooker help him should he be attacked? By 1:40 P.M., Sedgwick was near panic. He believed he faced no fewer than forty thousand men, and he had already sent engineers to select a defensive position near Banks's Ford. At 2:15 P.M., he alerted the commanding general, "I shall do my utmost to hold a position on the right bank of the Rappahannock until to-morrow."[26]

Hooker sent a string of messages to Sedgwick in return, but apparently none arrived before 1:40 P.M. Certainly none was optimistic. He would send no assistance, Hooker said, unless he heard "heavy firing" from downriver. Sedgwick must, in any case, take "a commanding position near Fredericksburg" and hold Banks's Ford for at least another day. This, Hooker emphasized, was of "vital importance." Hooker also said he intended to advance the next day, but he divulged nothing more of this plan, if, indeed, there was anything more to divulge. He also endorsed Warren's dispatch from the night before, even though it contradicted the spirit of his own orders.[27]

By early afternoon, Sedgwick was living on borrowed time. Lee arrived at Salem Church at 11 A.M., shortly ahead of Anderson's men. He assigned positions to the new brigades, although the men had trouble reaching them through the woods and undergrowth. Then Lee learned that McLaws had not yet conducted a reconnaissance to determine the strength and location of the Federal positions. He was not pleased. This trouble in his rear had already interrupted his plan to strike Hooker; additional delays now made him testy. Seeking to quell his growing anger, Lee rode to see Early and verify his understanding of the plan. When he returned at 2 P.M., Lee was still not satisfied with the placement of the troops. He frowned and replied to well-intended advice in icy tones. Not until 6 P.M., an hour before sundown, was his wing ready to attack.

Lee wanted Early and Anderson to drive against the left side of Sedgwick's horseshoe. As it collapsed toward the river, McLaws should shove the right into the retreating left. Things started fine. Six Confederate bri-

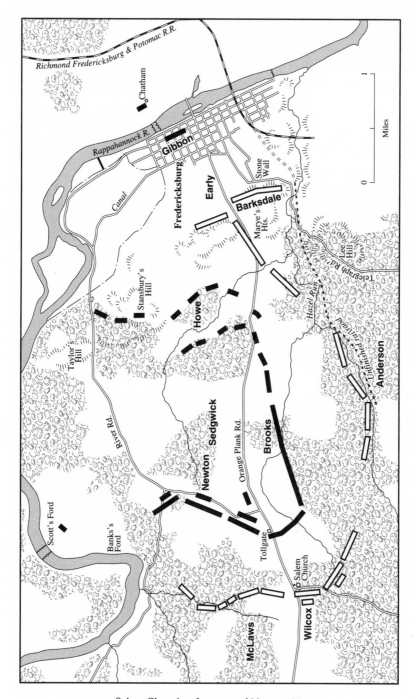

Salem Church, afternoon of May 4, 1863

gades swept forward "with deafening yells." "The whole hillside was alive with men," marveled a Union officer. "A magnificent sight." Fighting along some parts of the line grew as fierce as anything witnessed at Chancellorsville on the previous day. Early's men exerted most of the pressure, but ultimately, even this line failed to dislodge the Federals. Anderson's attack failed utterly when his brigades, through misdirection and confusion caused by the darkness and terrain, became entangled.[28]

Lee's anger had subsided into frustration, but he refused to let this opportunity pass. From his headquarters at the Downman house, in the rear of Anderson's division, he sent a message to McLaws, warning him that if the attack was broken off, the Federals would entrench that night, and all the day's work would have to be redone on the morrow. Press the attack, he said, regardless of the hour, and drive Sedgwick into the river. Gradually, Lee's troops responded; slowly, and in good order, the Federal line receded. "Surrender! Lay down your arms!" shouted jubilant Rebels. The Yanks replied, "Go to hell," delivered a volley of rifle fire, and continued their retreat. Sedgwick ordered his troops to pull back and form a tighter perimeter around Scott's Ford, about a mile downriver from Banks's Ford, where two pontoon bridges awaited them. The time had come, he thought, to save his corps. The Rebels collared a large number of prisoners through the night, but Uncle John escaped disaster.[29]

Hooker received the alarm about 11 P.M., and another confused exchange of messages followed into the early hours of May 5. Sedgwick stressed his perilous position. Hooker at first gave him permission to withdraw but reversed that decision twenty minutes later. He was too late. By the time Sedgwick received the new instructions, at about 3:20 A.M., most of his command had already crossed the Rappahannock. He had also ordered Gibbon to evacuate Fredericksburg.

In the interim, Hooker held a midnight meeting in his tent with five of his corps commanders, Butterfield, and Warren. Slocum could not immediately be located. Hooker wanted advice on whether to retreat or attack, and after some discussion of the options, he, Butterfield, and Warren exited the tent to allow the corps commanders to discuss matters. When Hooker returned, he asked for a vote. Howard, Meade, and Reynolds wanted to attack. Couch and Sickles advised retreat. Hooker, somewhat surprised by the majority decision, revealed that he had already decided to withdraw. Meade had predicted he would do so.

May 5 was a day to communicate with presidents. Unlike Hooker, Lee had been briefing Davis or Seddon daily on the progress of the battle, so his telegram to Davis on May 5 dealt primarily with the fighting near Fredericksburg. He provided no details of his next move, but he had decided what must be done. He sent Early and Barksdale back to Fredericksburg to keep Sedgwick at bay. At noon, he sent McLaws's division back to Chancellorsville. Anderson would follow. Lee returned to his headquarters at Fairview and prepared to deal with Hooker. McLaws and Anderson would strike from the east on the next day, Stuart from the west. Lee was tired of sparring with Fighting Joe. He would have rid of him.

Hooker's message to Lincoln was less buoyant, his plan less bold. It had become "expedient," he told the president, for the army to "retire" north of the Rappahannock, and he blamed nearly everyone but himself for this necessity. Averell had botched his assignment utterly, Lincoln learned. Sedgwick had "failed in the execution of his orders." Hooker judged his own position to be a "strong" one, but he expected Longstreet to arrive at any hour, and his two-year and nine-month volunteers had already begun to go home. Finally, the terrain had not been conducive to offensive operations. Lee might still attack him, but he could no longer afford to wait. The army would recross the river that night.[30]

Meanwhile, the people of Fredericksburg sighed in relief. Citizens, most of whom hid in their cellars during the fight of May 3, had been flabbergasted to discover the Federals in possession of Marye's Heights. Undeterred, they had put on "a bold front" as long as Gibbon's men occupied the town. They told the Yankees that they did not doubt the "final result" of the war. Southerners had a righteous cause, asserted one particularly feisty woman, "& we trusted God & our skillful leaders & brave men." "Sesesh damsels" spurned Yankees they met in the streets. The soldiers laughed and claimed there was not one of them they would look at twice anyway. Brief as it was, the Yankee occupation still produced Rebel losses. "Nearly all the negroes left of the last invasion of the Yankees went off this time," complained a woman, "so neither love nor money (if you had it) can secure servants." Even many free blacks left this time, especially when they heard that Barksdale was returning. They claimed the Mississippian had forced them to clean the streets without paying them when he occupied the town, and they would have no more of that treatment.[31]

But if thrice saved, Fredericksburg could not easily hide the scars of war. As Lee's men strengthened defensive works on Marye's Heights, the old town below them looked "sad and desolate." A Georgia infantry officer lamented the stark bareness of the entire countryside. Large groves and natural parks of mature trees had been wiped out by the needs of the army. Military roads, breastworks, and trenches bisected farms. "The man who has fled from the approach of the enemy and returns after we have driven him off," he sighed, "will hardly recognize his old home that is if his home be standing." Then, in a caution ripe with irony, he told his mother, "We in Georgia know as little of war, or of an invaded territory as the Yankees."[32]

Upriver, not a few men were embarrassed by the "organized skedaddle" from Chancellorsville. General Patrick marveled, "This was most extraordinary, as there was not the slightest cause for it, the Troops being in the best of spirits & double the enemy in number." Many Federals confessed to being "nearly played out," and all had a "tired look," but that was very different from being defeated. "You may rely upon it that this Army will do something great before long," a sergeant had insisted just two days earlier. "Hooker seems determined to conquer or be whipped." The army certainly had not been whipped. Before receiving orders to evacuate, a New Jersey infantryman told his parents, "Our Army is licking the Rebels . . . got the Rebels entirely surrounded & . . . I expect this will be the crushing of the Rebellion." A Pennsylvanian and his mates felt "heartsick" when given the word to pull out. "And then," he added, "the thought, *must* we lose the battle?" A Union major, still "sanguine of success," could think only that part of the army was being dispatched to assist Sedgwick. Colonel Wainwright recorded in his diary, "All appeared to feel that our retreat was a disgrace, and . . . each conversation concluded the same: 'If Little Mac had been here we never should have gone off this way.'"[33]

The carefully laid plans of both armies were undone when the rain came. It started sometime after 2 P.M., paused briefly in midafternoon, but then fell hard at intervals through the night. The landscape became a quagmire. Anderson's division was delayed several hours in its return to Chancellorsville, and Lee found it impossible even to move units at hand along sloppy roads and through flooded ravines. Lee suspended his attack until the following morning. Hooker's well-planned retreat, which might have rivaled Burnside's escape from Fredericksburg, became a comedy of errors and a far more perilous undertaking than it ought to have been. The Rappahannock rose over its banks and covered the bridges. Hooker, who had been among the first to scurry across to safety, halted the crossing at 9 P.M. to let the water subside and have his engineers secure the bridges. "It required *all* our skill and *all* our energy," recalled one engineer. "A single false move of ours would have lost us the bridges and the Army." That was no exaggeration. Troops were painfully vulnerable, spread out in columns for miles, with many thousands more—"a perfect sea of men"—crowding the plain along the river.[34]

Not until after 1 A.M. were the bridges deemed safe enough to resume the crossing. For seven hours, soggy and silent soldiers filed back to the camps they had left so confidently just a few days before—or had it been weeks? It must have seemed so to many. Puzzlement over why the army should retreat turned to despair in the gloomy weather. "One hundred thousand miserable and discouraged men are wading through this terrible mud and rain," a Wisconsin officer recorded in his journal. "We cannot understand it in any other way than as a great disaster."[35]

So Hooker escaped, and Lee was furious. Stuart sent a messenger around dawn on May 6 to give Lee the news, but the commander refused to believe him. When Dorsey Pender confirmed reports of a Union withdrawal later that morning, he found Lee ill-prepared for the truth. "That's the way you young men always do," exclaimed the exasperated commander. "You allow those people to get away. I tell you what to do, but you don't do it!" Pender, frozen to the spot, could not respond. "Go after them!" Lee exclaimed. "Damage them all you can!" But it was no use. They were gone. Lee had been similarly surprised when Burnside limped away on a cold December night, but now he felt not a little embarrassed. In anticipation of costly yet necessary assaults, he had notified President Davis earlier in the morning that Hooker held a "strong position" in his front. Not until the following day would Lee tell Davis what had happened. Also on May 6, Longstreet's two divisions, having abandoned their siege of Suffolk three days earlier, boarded the cars for Richmond.[36]

Nothing remained for the Confederates but to bury the dead, tend the wounded, and pick the battlefield clean, all of which had been going on, in any case, since at least Sunday, May 3. Federal surgeons who had stayed behind when Hooker withdrew cared for their wounded; Rebel surgeons helped them when possible. Some Federals claimed that the Confederates, in desperate need of medicine, bandages, and dressings, seized U.S. medical supplies, but injured Yankees praised the care they received from doctors in gray. A Georgia infantryman's description of Salem Church fit many a place for miles around. "Every available foot of space was crowded with wounded and bleeding soldiers," he gasped. "The floor, the benches, even the chancel and pulpit, were all packed almost to suffocation with them. The amputated limbs were piled up in every corner almost as high as a man could reach."[37]

The spoils of war lay strewn over acres and miles, thicker even than the dead and wounded. "I never saw such quantitys before," marveled a Virginian. A Georgian agreed: "I never have seen so large a space intersperced

[with] the dead and guns and accoutrements: knapsacks haversacks canteens &co. Our brigade, I think, nearly all supplied themselves with oil clothes." An artillerist reacted similarly. "We captured enough Knapsacks and oil cloth to give every man in our army one I verily believe," he said. "I have never on any battle field seen so much plunder, or so many evidences of a complete defeat." Officers watched silently as men stripped the dead of cash and valuables and pulled off their shoes and useful clothing. Officially, Lee's army reaped 19,500 small arms, tons of ammunition, and piles of coats, blankets, and rations.[38]

Most of the dead were buried by May 7, and the last of the Federal wounded were evacuated across the Rappahannock a week later. The final tally of killed, wounded, and missing amounted to more than seventeen thousand for the Army of the Potomac. That was five thousand more than Burnside had lost at Fredericksburg, although nearly six thousand of Hooker's losses were men missing or captured. And, of course, Burnside had lost most of his men in a single day. Many Federals fell into Rebel hands during the final retreat, when confusion reigned and stragglers filled the woods. Some of these men had been sleeping separated from their regiments and did not hear the command to withdraw. "Many, too," noticed a Union surgeon left behind to tend the wounded, "straggled for the purpose of being taken prisoners and to be paroled." The Army of Northern Virginia lost thirteen thousand men, twice as many as at Fredericksburg. Judged proportionately, Lee suffered more severely. About 22 percent of his army was gone, as opposed to 13 percent for Hooker.[39]

But there remained Stoneman. Fanning out west and north of Richmond, the Federal raiding parties, despite several setbacks and false starts, inflicted an immense amount of physical damage and threw panic into Rebel civilians. They destroyed some twenty bridges, scores of miles of railroad track and telegraph wires, three railroad depots, four supply trains, hundreds of wagons, and tons of supplies, mostly food. In addition, they captured scores of Rebel soldiers and confiscated significant "plunder," including hundreds of horses and mules (though few good cavalry mounts) and as much flour, bacon, grain, and tobacco as they could carry. Although they had fought several brief actions against guerrilla bands and Rebel patrols, the only serious combat came at Shannon Hill, less than ten miles to the southwest of Thompson's Crossroads, when Rooney Lee's brigade clashed on May 4 with a small regiment of Federal vedettes. "On the whole," concluded a New England trooper, "we had a big time." Col. Hugh Judson Kilpatrick's column terrified the capital city when it passed within sight of

Richmond's outer defenses on May 3–4. Thousands of militia, convalescent soldiers, public officials, and ordinary citizens turned out to face what they feared for a few tense hours would be an assault on the city. Reports said the Yankees had as many as six thousand men. When Kilpatrick suddenly veered to the northeast, relieved Richmonders returned to their shops, businesses, and homes to await word of the fighting at Chancellorsville.[40]

His work done, Stoneman next had to extricate himself from Rebel territory. Four of his six columns gathered on May 5 along the South Anna River. The men and horses of Kilpatrick and Lt. Col. Hasbrouck Davis, having penetrated deepest into enemy territory, were too far gone to return to the rendezvous point. They headed for Union lines on the Peninsula. Stoneman waited for them until the evening of May 5–6. Then, unable to linger any longer, he ordered his men to retrace their steps to the Rapidan. By the end of May 8, men and horses, both utterly spent, had recrossed the Rappahannock at Kelly's Ford. Their losses amounted to about two hundred men, mostly captured, and a thousand horses. The horses would be judged the more serious loss in the coming weeks.

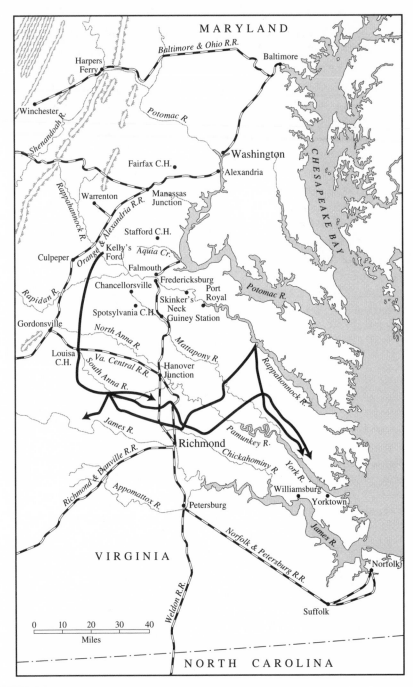

Stoneman's Raid, April 29–May 8, 1863

# Luck Favored Pluck and Skill

It ended in May, and it ended in confusion. The mud, rain, and frustration of Hooker's retreat initially left North and South uncertain about who had won. Lee's army had turned back the Union challenge for the Dare Mark, but it had not destroyed Hooker's army. Lee believed he had been within a few hours of doing so, just as he had come within a day of demolishing Burnside. Yet Hooker still sat opposite him, just as he had for the past four months. "It would seem that Hooker has beaten Lee and that Lee has beaten Hooker," one Federal officer explained. "Everything seems to be everywhere, and everybody all over, and there is no getting at the truth." Another Union soldier remarked, "I should like to see [a newspaper] to hear if the Battle was a victory or a defeat."[1]

The Confederates had a better claim to victory, but it still took several days for them fully to appreciate the magnitude of their triumph. Their surprise at finding the Federals gone, the foul weather, and the exhaustion produced by days of continuous combat had left men more concerned about finding something to eat and a dry place to sleep than with celebrating. "I had fought until I was worn out," asserted one soldier. It was not like First Fredericksburg, where they could see at a glance how much they had punished the enemy and where they had lost far fewer of their own comrades. Yet the realization did slowly come, and the Rebels savored it. "The enemy has been badly, ignominiously whipped, at a time and upon ground of his choosing," a Virginian reported gleefully to his wife in mimicking Hooker. Artillerist Willie Pegram told a sister on May 11, "The more we think of our recent victory, the grander it seems. Every one, high & low, considers it the greatest victory of the war."[2]

Lee may have been the hardest case. He congratulated his men on May 7 for displaying, once again, "the valor that has triumphed on so many fields," but he could not help being depressed, just as he had been after First Fredericksburg. He still held the Rappahannock line, but he had not finished off the invader. It had been a dearly bought victory, too, and when Stonewall Jackson died on May 10, it felt all the more costly. Lee was frustrated; he longed for an opportunity to grab a Union army by the throat and finish it off. His blood was up; he wanted action. On May 14, Lee traveled to Richmond to press his case for a raid into the North with President Davis. Two days later, he had the backing of the entire cabinet.[3]

The Southern press and public celebrated even if the army was too tired to join them. Newspaper reports of the victory, often referred to as the "Battles of the Rappahannock," were actually few in number, and many of those were drawn from Northern papers. As late as May 11, the *Charleston Mercury* complained that it had no complete account of the fighting. The disruption of telegraphic communications from Fredericksburg explains much of the delay. Then, too, most of the reports detailed events on Lee's right wing, rather than the more important fighting upriver. But as word spread, none doubted the significance of the campaign. The word "great" was used frequently to describe the victory, "which all admit to be a glorious one," added a North Carolina woman. It cast the triumph of First Fredericksburg "in the shade." Nor did people share Lee's disappointment. On the contrary; Chancellorsville made both Lee and his men seem invincible in the public's eyes. If one general and one army could win the war, Southerners said, it was Lee and the Army of Northern Virginia.[4]

Few of Hooker's men felt beaten, however, although they knew they had been in a tough fight. Like the Rebels, they frequently compared the battle to the first duel on the Dare Mark. "This fight was very hard," judged a Pennsylvanian; "if anything it was hotter than it was at Fredericksburg before." A Union surgeon thought Fredericksburg had been "comparatively child's play," and an infantry sergeant agreed: "Soldders says that these was the hardest battles ever was fort and thay ware all at frericksburg." A realistic artillery officer acknowledged the "failure" of the campaign, but he did not think it was as disastrous as some people feared. In yet another comparison to December's battle on the Rappahannock, he decided, "The defeat at Chancellorsville was bad enough but not so bad as Fredericksburg."[5]

Certainly words like "demoralized" and "disheartened" circulated through some camps, but the tone differed markedly from the days after First Fredericksburg and the Mud March. Men were disappointed, even mortified, but they betrayed little of the earlier gloom and despair. "Although we fell

Back accross the river we gave them Rebels one of the worst thrasings they ever got from our army since the war commenced," crowed a Michigan infantryman. If they had been soundly whipped, or if they had not inflicted such heavy casualties, or if they had failed again to take Marye's Heights, men would have reacted differently. But they had not failed in those respects. They were glum for much the same reason that Robert E. Lee remained dissatisfied: they had nothing to show for their efforts. "A victory is no victory at all unless you can show some great advantage to compensate for so many lives lost," submitted a midwesterner. "We marched, we fought, we failed," agreed a Hoosier. "We were not defeated but we did not defeat." A New Englander agreed: "Patriotism is not on the wane, but we feel as if we had wasted our strength . . . and fought all in vain."[6]

Officers took it worse than enlisted men, and the higher their rank, the more disappointed they seemed to be. They knew they could have beaten Lee, and most of them, unlike the average enlisted man, blamed Hooker for their failure. "We have lost physically and numerically," believed Alpheus Williams, "but still more morally, not by being dispirited, but by a universal want of confidence in the commanding officer. . . . I have not met the first officer who does not feel this, from the highest to the lowest." Everyone thought the army "might have done better," and they were neither impressed nor fooled by the braggadocio of Hooker's congratulatory order to the army. If they had not accomplished all "that was expected," Hooker had said, the reasons were "well known" and "were of a character not to be foreseen or prevented by human sagacity or resource." The officers laughed bitterly at that assessment. "It is these very reasons that everyone I have met is looking for," Wainwright protested; "what they are no one seems able to conceive." Naturally, the pro-McClellan men cried the loudest.[7]

The Northern public did not know what to make of it. Rumors swirled at first: Hooker was under arrest, they were told; Stanton had resigned, Halleck would command the army. Then, too, Hooker's continuing news blackout, reinforced by government censorship between May 3 and 7, ensured that the story reached the reading public only in bits and driblets. People could not make "head or tail of it." All the newspapers told a different story, and no one knew what to believe. Eventually, the story received enough positive spin to reassure Northerners that it was not, at least, another Fredericksburg. A Massachusetts soldier told his wife as early as May 10, "From later accounts of the whole afair i believe we have the best side of it." These reports irritated R. E. Lee. "The *northern* papers are labouring very hard to prove to themselves & the world that Genl. Hooker has gained a great victory," he told Mary Custis Lee on May 14. "It will be incomprehensible news to those engaged in the battle."[8]

Lincoln took it far worse. Despite the lack of news from his commanding general during the fighting, Lincoln had drawn hope from what information he gleaned from Confederate newspapers and Union intelligence. But when Hooker reported on May 6 that the army had retreated across the river, an ashen-faced president could only ask, "What will the country say? Oh, what will the country say?" Friends had never seen him "so broken up, so dispirited, and so ghostlike." Lincoln left with Halleck that same day for Hooker's headquarters, where he arrived the next morning. Everyone expected the president to ask what had gone wrong and why. Instead, he inquired about the condition of the army. Was it still willing to fight; could it rebound? He wanted Hooker to advance as soon as possible, to "help to supersede the bad moral effects" of Chancellorsville. It was imperative, Lincoln believed, that the country and foreign observers see that Chancellorsville had injured neither the resolve of the government nor the spirit of the army. He acknowledged the defeat, but he also submitted, as he had after Fredericksburg, that it "could not be helped." He returned to Washington that same day, satisfied that the army was in sufficiently good condition to carry on. Nevertheless, he also left Halleck behind with instructions to learn all he could about the "disaster."[9]

When Halleck met with Lincoln and Edwin Stanton upon his return from Virginia, he reported that Hooker had mismanaged the operation and urged his removal. Many cabinet members and congressmen agreed, and Lincoln must have been tempted to oblige them. Confidence in all of his commanders was near a low ebb in the first half of May. Even Grant, who was now tantalizingly close to the gates of Vicksburg, seemed to have stalled. Besides those generals who were failing him in the field, Burnside, now commander of the Department of the Ohio, had recently stirred a political controversy when he arrested Clement Vallandigham for disloyalty to the government. A furor over civil liberties had ensued, and Lincoln had yet to calm those waters. But in Virginia, he would give Hooker another chance. After all, he told one journalist, he had tried McClellan "a number of times," so he saw no reason why he should not try Hooker at least twice.[10]

Lincoln had misgivings almost immediately. He had stood by Hooker, in part, because the general had hinted at a new plan to take on Lee. When a week passed without any action or elaboration on the grand scheme, Lincoln feared he must have another McClellan or Burnside on his hands. The president began to make excuses for not allowing Hooker to advance the army. Lee had probably been reinforced by now, the president told his general, and his lines of communications restored. It might be best for Hooker to rebuild and put the "army in good condition again" before venturing out against the Rebels. Lincoln had also heard disturbing rumors, quite likely as a result of Halleck's inquiries at Falmouth. "I have some painful intimations that some of your corps and division commanders are not giving you their entire confidence," the president told Hooker plainly. "This would be ruinous, if true."[11]

It was true. Not only did Hooker's senior officers blame him for the defeat, but some of them schemed briefly to have him removed. While Butterfield, Sickles, and Stoneman stood by their patron, nearly everyone else wanted Hooker out. Even officers favorably disposed toward him, like Meade, admitted that Hooker had "disappointed all his friends by failing to show his fighting qualities at the pinch." Couch and Slocum, veterans of the Byzantine political world of the Army of the Potomac, led the revolt. They and Sedgwick agreed that Meade should command the army, even though he was their junior in rank. When Meade refused to become embroiled in their intrigue, the other men hesitated to press the issue, but the discontent could hardly be kept a secret. "General Couch does not talk freely," observed General Heintzelman, "but I can readily see that he doesn't think we took advantage of our opportunities." Within a week, Hooker had fallen out with most of his senior commanders, and he was at "open war" with Meade.[12]

Interestingly, the Committee on the Conduct of the War did not feel the same sense of urgency to investigate Chancellorsville as it had Fredericksburg. Perhaps it delayed because spring offered hopes of another campaign. Perhaps the insistence by some newspapers that the campaign had, in fact, succeeded impressed the committee. Perhaps it was swayed by the fact that no politicians or army officers were clamoring for an investigation. More likely, the committee kept quiet because its most influential members— men like Chandler and Wade—were Hooker partisans. Some committee members visited the Army of the Potomac and made inquiries, but they avoided talking to people like Couch, Slocum, and Meade. They seemed more interested in interviewing Hooker's known friends. Chandler, in writing of Hooker immediately after his visit to Falmouth, said, "I believe he can & will whip the Rebels in the next fight." The committee did not begin a formal inquiry until late February 1864. The hearings continued for fourteen months.[13]

No one would deny that Hooker had opened the operation with a brilliant strategic plan, but from the moment he pulled back from his initial advance on May 1, he let all initiative pass to Lee. Indeed, he handled his army so poorly after that point, judged a Confederate officer, that he scarcely deserved credit for his opening gambit. Hooker's most recent defender insists that the general had intended to fight on the tactical defensive all along and that his advance on May 1 was meant to draw Lee into reckless and bloody frontal assaults. There is plenty of evidence from Hooker himself to cast doubt on that theory, but be that as it may, even defensive commanders must know when to take advantage of offensive opportunities. Hooker missed several openings over the next four days, including the May 1 advance and possible counterattacks on May 3 and 4. Hooker made a great show of leadership throughout the battle, issuing confident statements and congratulatory orders, riding up and down the lines to inspire his men, but ultimately he lacked the confidence and will to seize victory when it beckoned. He waited for Lee to hand him victory, and Lee declined to do so.[14]

Hooker blamed the defeat on everyone and everything but himself. He never submitted an after-action report so it was not until many years later that Fighting Joe insisted, "The trust I had reposed in commanders was not executed in a manner satisfactory to myself, and in a way that would have been done could I have given the operations of these commanders my personal supervision." The Committee on the Conduct of the War said the same thing. It blamed defeat primarily on the "stampede" of the XI Corps, the injury to Hooker, Sedgwick's failure to strike Lee's rear on May 3, and Stoneman's inability to cut Lee's communications. Yet, just as Burnside must bear ultimate responsibility for the actions of Franklin and Sumner at Fredericksburg, so Hooker cannot be absolved from mistakes made by his corps commanders. In any case, those mistakes were not irredeemable.[15]

Howard, it is true, should have been more vigilant. Hooker had warned him of possible danger. The commanding general could have been more assertive or preemptive, as he was with Sedgwick, but Howard should have shown more common sense. The Howard controversy is complicated by the need to separate his decisions as a commander from the actions of his corps. Many contemporaries, even if acknowledging other reasons for Union defeat, put the "cowardice" of the XI Corps at the top of their lists. Howard's men were an easy target. Many were foreign-born, a fact that could be used to explain the rout of Hooker's right flank without sullying the army's honor. Yet at least one non-German member of the corps, while resenting the stigma placed on his unit by the "New York dutch," also pointed to the skedaddle of many short-time volunteers and insisted that the entire corps had been placed in a "very poor" position. He also marveled at the way his officers ignored the presence of Rebel troops on their front all that day. "I don't know who to blame, whether Hooker, Howard, Devens, or who, but whosoever fault it was they have brought disgrace to our corps." Yet the Union right ultimately held. The army was not defeated on May 2.[16]

Stoneman, despite his success in destroying large amounts of Confederate war material and scaring the population of Richmond, inflicted little lasting damage. The railroads he wrecked were back in operation within two days. Supplies continued to roll into Hamilton's Crossing. And Stoneman never did position himself to block a possible retreat by Lee. But then Hooker's orders were not very precise about specific objectives and the cavalry's relationship to the main force. The commanding general instructed Stoneman to get between Lee and Richmond (which he did), "isolating him from his supplies" (which he thought he did), and "inflicting on him every possible injury" (which begs interpretation). Yet the flow of supplies to Lee was not very great to begin with, and Stoneman disrupted it to some extent, at least. More to the point, the cavalryman's supposed failures did not cause Hooker to retreat.[17]

Two further points about Stoneman's raid deserve consideration. Many students of the campaign stress that Hooker made a fatal mistake in sending off most of his cavalry with Stoneman. Pleasonton's brigade could not provide the reconnaissance Hooker needed, say these critics, even in conjunction with Lowe's balloons and Sharpe's intelligence network. Other historians have answered these charges by saying Hooker kept sufficient cavalry to do the job but admit that he misused the cavalry. Even Hooker's most staunch defenders acknowledge that he should have struck a better balance between his own reconnaissance needs and Stoneman's raiders.

The second point is not necessarily important in determining why Hooker lost at Chancellorsville, but it does suggest an unappreciated benefit of Stoneman's raid. Whether or not his cavalry accomplished all that Hooker intended, the raid did boost the confidence of the Union cavalry. Federal horse soldiers were widely thought to be inferior to Confederate horsemen until the Saint Patrick's Day fight at Kelly's Ford and Stoneman's raid. The latter event, in particular, opened an entire new scope of offensive operations for Union cavalry in Virginia. "For the first time the cavalry found themselves made useful," explained a New Jersey horse soldier. "It gave our troopers self-respect, and obliged the enemy to respect them." Hooker failed to recognize the value of this new spirit.[18]

Sedgwick could have shown more initiative, but he was not the pivotal figure Hooker or the committee made him out to be. Sedgwick did what was asked of him, when he could determine what Hooker wanted. Part of this confusion derived from the tardy arrival of messages, often caused by imperfections in Hooker's telegraphic system. But Hooker sent some contradictory and irrational orders, too. Sedgwick might have been able to push through to Chancellorsville on May 3 had he moved more quickly and struck Wilcox in force before the arrival of McLaws. Yet Hooker's secrecy and less than precise orders left Sedgwick, like Stoneman, with an imperfect vision of what the commanding general expected of him. Some of Sedgwick's men thought it strange that he, with 22,500 soldiers, should be expected to rescue Hooker, who had three times that number. They fully expected Hooker to reinforce *them* once they took the heights. A Pennsylvania infantryman even blamed the defeat on Sedgwick's efforts to join Hooker.[19]

Nor did Hooker ever employ his entire force. By his own admission, three full corps saw little if any action. He had ignored Lincoln's advice—very nearly an order—to use all available men, and he failed to follow his own instructions to Stoneman, which were to "fight, fight, fight." He need not have flung his men into deadly frontal assaults to do that. He could have maneuvered, gotten on Lee's flanks, even bolstered his defensive lines to a formidable degree. Perhaps Hooker, a fine division commander, was simply out of his depth when asked to maneuver an army. Perhaps one of his officers diagnosed the problem correctly when he concluded, "Hooker had more [men] than he could manage." A lesser figure, a cavalry private, agreed. "Gen Hooker is a bold and a fighting Genl," he concluded, "but not one to plan out manuvering of a large army."[20]

Hooker claimed that the Wilderness prohibited movement, but Lee did not find the terrain too tough. Both men had the same opportunities to maneuver. One took advantage of them, the other did not. Hooker even misused terrain when he had the advantage, his sacrifice of Hazel Grove being the most obvious example. As long as he held that high ground, he kept Lee's left wing divided. True, it became a vulnerable salient, but, as Sickles suggested, Hooker could have moved his lines forward to embrace it. Once the Confederates occupied Hazel Grove, they commanded the field. Darius Couch, Hooker's second in command, thought Hooker had a bad eye for terrain. Couch was particularly skeptical of the defensive possibilities of the original Chancellorsville position. "There was no commanding positions for artillery," Couch pointed out, "and but little open country to operate over; in fact, the advantages of ground for this arm were mainly with the attacking party."[21]

Confederate dominance on Hazel Grove suggests an inherent weakness in Hooker's organization of his artillery. Lee's new battalion system produced "effects unknown [and] unhoped before" at Hazel Grove. Yet the heavier and more numerous Union guns might have neutralized the Rebels from Fairview. The Union batteries failed because Hooker lacked a chief of artillery to concentrate the guns and direct their fire, functions performed with superb effect by Henry Hunt at Fredericksburg. When told on May 3 how disorganized his artillery had become—"no one seems to know where to go," reported Wainwright—Hooker called up General Hunt from across the river to set things right; but by then, Fairview had been lost and the battle with it.[22]

Hooker himself downplayed his knock on the head as a determining factor in the campaign—one emphasized by the Committee on the Conduct of the War—but the injury was unfortunately timed, and it probably did produce some ill effects. After losing Hazel Grove, it was critical that Hooker shore up his line and retreat no farther. Yet when his dazed and unsteady condition forced him to place Couch in charge, he saddled his subordinate with a definite order to pull back. Equally important, Hooker's grogginess led to General Warren's misleading directive to Sedgwick early on May 4. Sedgwick based his movements all that day on Warren's appraisal of the situation at Chancellorsville, which also convinced him that his corps might be in peril. The seriousness of Hooker's concussion also explains the oft-mentioned, yet false, charge that he was drunk at Chancellorsville.[23]

Hooker missed one chance after another to win the battle, right up to the sixth day. "In forcing us back, the enemy became much exhausted, and why General Hooker did not take advantage of this fact is more than I can tell," worried a Union artillery officer. This man liked Hooker and retained full confidence in him, but he believed the general had "failed in this great battle to take advantage of all the opportunities which were open to him." If Hooker had really wanted Lee to attack him on his own ground, he never had a better chance than on May 5, the day he ordered the retreat. He had a compact defensive line, at least double Lee's numbers in men and guns, and a fortified position that Porter Alexander called *"impregnable."* Yet rather than face Lee one more time, he turned tail. Alexander could not understand Hooker's action. "He ought to have known Lee's aggressive audacity enough to at least wait a day or two more & see if he could get him to attack," asserted the Rebel artillerist. Alexander called this Hooker's biggest "blunder."[24]

This perspective on Chancellorsville provides a potent reminder that

Hooker also failed because he faced Robert E. Lee, and Lee simply out-generaled him. To be sure, Lee made mistakes. Hooker's bold turning movement caught him by surprise, and Lee should have ordered Long-street to return to the Rappahannock long before the first of May. Lee did not always get the best from his lieutenants, either. There was, for instance, his frustration with McLaws and Anderson at Salem Church and Banks's Ford. Some people—though not Lee—thought Jubal Early should have held Marye's Heights. Indeed, Barksdale and Early were feuding publicly within days of the battle over who had lost the heights. Lee was lucky, too. His bold maneuvers—dividing his force not once but three times—required Hooker's passive cooperation, and his inability to strike on May 5, as he wanted to do, might have spared his army. But then, even Napoleon prized luck as a desirable quality in his generals.

More to the point, Lee took action and outmaneuvered Hooker on the battlefield. Whatever his errors, and however much good fortune may have helped in the pinch, he won because he improvised, took the initiative, and created circumstances favorable to victory. Even some Federals understood that. "Our valor was wasted by poor generalship," fumed a Michigan soldier. "What business had he [Hooker] in letting them out maneuver him?" Lee made brilliant use of interior lines, just as he had at Fredericksburg. He made so bold as to divide his forces because he believed he could swiftly rejoin the parts if required. This confidence fed Lee's boldness, and in the end boldness was what counted. Titanic battles turn on the offensive, for either success or failure. Too timid to take the offensive himself, Hooker had to stop Lee's offensive design. He failed.[25]

Porter Alexander came closest to the truth when he called Chancellorsville "a marvelous story of how luck favored pluck & skill." Lee may have been fortunate, but he also devised "the boldest & most daring strategy of the whole war" during those five days in May. Darius Couch agreed. "In looking for the causes of the loss at Chancellorsville," he considered after the war, "the primary ones were that Hooker expected Lee to fall back without risking battle. Finding himself mistaken he assumed the defensive, and was outgeneraled and became demoralized by the superior tactical boldness of the enemy."[26]

Lee's worst turn of luck in the campaign was the loss of several senior officers. Jackson's death would have the most serious consequences, but the casualty list also included twelve brigade commanders killed or wounded. Some Confederates thought this "unparalleled" loss of officers the most significant blow suffered by the army. Even Jackson's loss, submitted one Virginian, was not as telling as it might have been earlier in the war, before Jackson had helped to ingrain notions of the Rebels' invincibility in both the Army of Northern Virginia and the Army of the Potomac.[27]

The heaviest burden of victory for Lee and the lasting legacy of the Dare Mark campaign was the continuing belief within the Army of Northern Virginia that it would never taste defeat. "Victory will be ours," insisted one soldier. "We have drove old Hooker and his blue coats over the Dare Mark, but thousands of them will never get back. They will moulder on the south side of the River. The Rappahannock River is the Dare Mark [and] with General Lee they can't stay on this side." A Georgian boasted: "This is the best army in the world. We are all satisfied with Gen. Lee and he is always ready for a fight." Indeed, he was, and even Lee had come to suspect his army might be "invincible." He believed his men could go anywhere and accomplish any task. He believed they could march north, even into Pennsylvania, even without Jackson.[28]

The Rappahannock remained crucial to Confederate strategy in the East. Lee might have drawn his dare mark at any number of places in order to defend Richmond and northern Virginia. The North Anna River, for example, loomed large in his strategic thinking as early as November. But in the end, Lee chose the Rappahannock as the most effective place to throw down his gauntlet. Even when justifying his Pennsylvania campaign after the fact, Lee emphasized that a major consideration in moving north had been the difficulty of attacking Hooker "to advantage" as long as the Federals hugged the northern side of the Rappahannock. To defeat Hooker and discourage enemy hopes of nesting below the river, Lee knew he had to "draw him from it."[29]

Lincoln also remained "wedded" to the Rappahannock, too much so, thought George Meade. "For my part," Meade confided to his wife, "it would seem that all projects based on pursuing this line of operations having been tried and failed, we should try some other route." But it was not that easy. By "route," Meade betrayed old strategic thinking, defined as "the road to Richmond." Yet ever since Fredericksburg, Lincoln had stressed that Lee's army was the prime target in the East. "I think *Lee's* army, and not *Richmond*, is your sure objective point," the president told Hooker a month after the fighting at Chancellorsville. The Rappahannock, therefore, became important because Lee had chosen to defend the interior of Virginia and the Confederate capital on that line.[30]

Hooker would not be given an opportunity to redeem himself against Lee. When Fighting Joe tried to respond to the early stages of Lee's Pennsylvania campaign in June, Lincoln urged caution. Influenced by Halleck's constant grumbling about Hooker and his own experience with the general, Lincoln gradually lost faith in any strategic plan Hooker proposed. Indeed, Lincoln, Halleck, and Stanton had likely agreed to remove Hooker after Halleck's return from Falmouth in May, but the general's Radical political patrons had forced them to handle the removal delicately. When Hooker, frustrated by Lincoln's refusal to authorize any of his suggested movements with the army, asked to be relieved of command on June 27, the president leaped at the opportunity. He replaced him with the reluctant heir apparent, the man who had been waiting in the wings since January, George Gordon Meade.[31]

There would be a final struggle to control the Rappahannock. Meade pursued Lee out of Pennsylvania in July until he ran him to ground in Culpeper County, just as McClellan had shown promise of doing a year earlier. Following an engagement at Rappahannock Station on November 7, 1863, Meade, who had twice watched his commanding generals fail on the Dare Mark, led the much maligned Army of the Potomac south of the river never to be dislodged. And yet that contest was almost anticlimactic. The real duel on the Dare Mark, the one remembered by history and the soldiers, had long since ended.[32]

# Notes

## ABBREVIATIONS

ACW      *America's Civil War*
B&L      *Battles and Leaders of the Civil War*
CWH      *Civil War History*
CWMC     Civil War Miscellaneous Collection, USAMHI
CWR      *Civil War Regiments*
FSNMP    Fredericksburg and Spotsylvania National Military Park, Fredericksburg VA
H        Harrisburg Civil War Round Table Collection, USAMHI
HC       Harrisburg Civil War Round Table Collection—Gregory A. Coco Collection, USAMHI
LC       Library of Congress, Washington DC
OR       *Official Records*
SHSP     *Southern Historical Society Papers*
UMB      Bentley Historical Library, University of Michigan, Ann Arbor
USAMHI   United States Army Military History Institute, Carlisle PA
VHS      Virginia Historical Society, Richmond
VMHB     *Virginia Magazine of History and Biography*

## I. OF GENERALS AND POLITICIANS

1. Clifford Dowdey and Louis H. Manarin, eds., *The Wartime Papers of R. E. Lee* (New York: Bramhall House, 1961), 323–24, 328.

2. Stephen W. Sears, *George B. McClellan: The Young Napoleon* (New York: Ticknor & Fields, 1988), 322–23, 330–36; U.S. War Department, *The War of the Rebellion: A Compilation of the Official Records of the Union and Confederate Armies*, 128 vols. (Washington DC: Government Printing Office, 1880–1901), ser. 1, vol. 19, pt. 2, 102, 497–98, 504 (cited hereafter as OR, and all references are to Series 1 unless otherwise indicated).

3. Allan Nevins, *The War for the Union*, 4 vols. (New York: Charles Scribner's Sons, 1959–71), 2:326, 328–31; Sears, *George B. McClellan*, 333–34, 337; Stephen W. Sears, ed., *The Civil War Papers of George B. McClellan: Selected Correspondence, 1860–1865* (New York: Ticknor & Fields, 1989), 507, 518.

4. Daniel E. Sutherland, "Abraham Lincoln, John Pope, and the Origins of Total War," *Journal of Military History* 56 (October 1992): 567–86, and *Seasons of War: The Ordeal of a Confederate Community, 1861–65* (New York: Free Press, 1995), 117–29; James M. McPherson, *Drawn with the Sword: Reflections on the American Civil War* (New York: Oxford University Press, 1996), 70–71, 77–80; Mark Grimsley, *The Hard Hand of War: Union Military Policy Toward Southern Civilians, 1861–1865* (Cambridge: Cambridge University Press, 1995), 74–75, 85–92, 105–6.

5. John G. Nicolay and John Hay, *Abraham Lincoln: A History*, 10 vols. (New York: Century, 1890), 4:155–56; Earl S. Miers et al., eds., *Lincoln Day by Day*, 3 vols. (Washington DC: Lincoln Sesquicentennial Commission, 1960), 3:88; Roy Basler, ed., *The Collected Works of Abraham Lincoln*, 8 vols. (New Brunswick NJ: Rutgers University Press, 1953), 5:460–61.

6. Nevins, *War for the Union*, 2:145–46; James M. McPherson, *Battle Cry of Freedom: The Civil War Era* (New York: Oxford University Press, 1988), 494–500; Mark E. Neely Jr., *The Fate of Liberty: Abraham Lincoln and Civil Liberties* (New York: Oxford University Press, 1991), 51–54.

7. David H. Donald, *Lincoln* (New York: Simon & Schuster, 1995), 362–67; Howard K. Beale, ed., *Diary of Gideon Welles*, 3 vols. (New York: Norton, 1960), 1:70–71; David H. Donald, ed., *Inside Lincoln's Cabinet: The Civil War Diaries of Salmon P. Chase* (New York: Longmans, Green, 1954), 99–100.

8. Nevins, *War for the Union*, 2:240.

9. Philip Shaw Paludan, *"A People's Contest": The Union and Civil War, 1861–1865* (New York: Harper & Row, 1988), 97–102; Nevins, *War for the Union*, 2:299–322; Basler, ed., *Works of Lincoln*, 5:493–94; Allan Nevins and Milton Halsey Thomas, eds., *The Diary of George Templeton Strong*, 4 vols. (New York: Macmillan, 1952), 3:271–72.

10. Kenneth P. Williams, *Lincoln Finds a General: A Military Study of the Civil War*, 5 vols. (New York: Macmillan, 1949–59), 2:469–70.

11. Edward H. C. Taylor to sister, November 27, 1862, Edward H. C. Taylor Letters, UMB; David S. Sparks, ed., *Inside Lincoln's Army: The Diary of Marsena Rudolph Patrick, Provost Marshal General, Army of the Potomac* (New York: Thomas Yoseloff, 1964), 173.

12. Donald, *Lincoln*, 387–90.

13. William Marvel, *Burnside* (Chapel Hill: University of North Carolina Press, 1991), 99–100, 110–11, 159–60.

14. OR, vol. 19, pt. 2, 695–98, 701–3.

15. Herman Hattaway and Archer Jones, *How the North Won: A Military History*

*of the Civil War* (Urbana: University of Illinois Press, 1983), 304; Steven E. Woodworth, *Davis and Lee at War* (Lawrence: University Press of Kansas, 1995), 206–10.

16. OR, vol. 19, pt. 2, 696–98, 701–3.

17. Vorin E. Whan Jr., *Fiasco at Fredericksburg* (University Park: Pennsylvania State University Press, 1961), 5–6.

18. Beale, ed., *Diary of Gideon Welles*, 1:182–83; John Niven, ed., *The Salmon P. Chase Papers*, 4 vols. (Kent OH: Kent State University Press, 1993–97), 3:319; Sparks, ed., *Inside Lincoln's Army*, 174–75; Russell Duncan, ed., *Blue-Eyed Child of Fortune: The Civil War Letters of Colonel Robert Gould Shaw* (Athens: University of Georgia Press, 1992), 259–60; James I. Robertson Jr., ed., *The Civil War Letters of General Robert McAllister* (New Brunswick NJ: Rutgers University Press, 1965), 219; Rufus B. Dawes, *Service with the Sixth Wisconsin Volunteers* (Marietta OH: E. R. Alderman & Sons, 1890), 107.

19. Howard K. Beale, ed., *The Diary of Edward Bates, 1859–1866* (Washington DC: Government Printing Office, 1933), 220.

20. OR, vol. 19, pt. 2, 552.

21. Hattaway and Jones, *How the North Won*, 334–35, 371–72; OR, vol. 19, pt. 2, 552.

22. Whan, *Fiasco at Fredericksburg*, 19–23; OR, vol. 19, pt. 2, 579.

23. OR, vol. 19, pt. 2, 553.

24. OR, vol. 19, pt. 2, 521, 559–67.

25. Douglas S. Freeman, *R. E. Lee: A Biography*, 4 vols. (New York: Charles Scribner's Sons, 1934), 2:428–29; Janet B. Hewett et al., eds., *Supplement to the Official Records of the Union and Confederate Armies*, 41 vols. (Wilmington NC: Broadfoot, 1994–97), 3:605 (cited hereafter as *Supplement*); Barbara P. Willis et al., eds., *The Journal of Jane Howison Beale of Fredericksburg, Virginia, 1850–1862* (Fredericksburg: Historic Fredericksburg Foundation, 1979), 64–65.

26. Robert E. Lee to George Washington Custis Lee, November 10, 1862, Robert Edward Lee Papers, Perkins Library, Duke University, Durham NC; OR, vol. 19, pt. 2, 714–15.

27. Freeman, *R. E. Lee*, 2:429–30; OR, vol. 19, pt. 2, 717.

28. OR, vol. 19, pt. 2, 706, 711, vol. 21, 1013.

29. Richard Lewis, *Camp Life of a Confederate Boy of Bratton's Brigade, Longstreet's Corps, C.S.A.* (Charleston SC: News and Courier, 1883), 34–35; Henry M. Talley to mother, November 9, 1862, Henry M. Talley Papers, VHS; Charles W. Ramsdell, "General Robert E. Lee's Horse Supply, 1862–1865," *American Historical Review* 35 (July 1930): 759–60; OR, vol. 19, pt. 2, 706, 709, 710, 712, 716–17, 718.

30. A. J. Gillespie to Susan Gillespie, November 13, 1862, Randall Family Papers, Alderman Library, University of Virginia, Charlottesville; Robert E. Lee to Mary Custis Lee, November 13, 1862, Robert E. Lee Papers, VHS; Charles R. Adams Jr., ed., *A Post of Honor: The Pryor Letters, 1861–63, Letters from Capt. S. G.*

*Pryor, Twelfth Georgia Regiment, and His Wife, Penelope Tyson Pryor* (Fort Valley GA: Garret Publications, 1989), 290.

31. OR, vol. 19, pt. 2, 722.

32. Whan, *Fiasco at Fredericksburg*, 23–24; Marvel, *Burnside*, 110, 165–66.

33. OR, vol. 21, 84–86, 101–2; Robert G. Carter, *Four Brothers in Blue; or, Sunshine and Shadows of the War of the Rebellion* (1913; rpt. Austin: University of Texas Press, 1978), 170; J. Franklin Mancha Diary, November 22, 23, 1862, USAMHI (CWMC).

34. OR, vol. 21, 85–86, 102; *Supplement*, 3:683; Sutherland, *Seasons of War*, 186–88. There is some controversy over whether Sumner could—or should—have forded the Rappahannock above Fredericksburg on November 17. Some sources say he attempted a crossing but was turned back by the Fifteenth Virginia Infantry, four companies of Mississippi infantry, and an artillery battery. See Alfred M. Scales, "Battle of Fredericksburg," *SHSP* 40 (September 1915): 203–4.

35. OR, vol. 21, 104–5, 773–74; Walter H. Hebert, *Fighting Joe Hooker* (Indianapolis: Bobbs-Merrill, 1944), 151, 153–54.

36. Allan Nevins, ed., *Diary of Battle: The Personal Journals of Colonel Charles S. Wainwright, 1861–1865* (New York: Harcourt, Brace & World, 1962), 128.

37. OR, vol. 21, 1014–15, 1019.

38. George C. Rable, *The Confederate Republic: A Revolution Against Politics* (Chapel Hill: University of North Carolina Press, 1994), 170–73; Steven E. Woodworth, *Jefferson Davis and His Generals: The Failure of Confederate Command in the West* (Lawrence: University Press of Kansas, 1990), 179–81; William C. Davis, *Jefferson Davis: The Man and His Hour* (New York: HarperCollins, 1991), 471–81.

39. OR, vol. 21, 1019–22.

## 2. RIGHT IN THE WRONG PLACE

1. Woodworth, *Davis and Lee*, 107; Gary W. Gallagher, ed., *The Fredericksburg Campaign: Decision on the Rappahannock* (Chapel Hill: University of North Carolina Press, 1995), 148–52; Douglas S. Freeman, *Lee's Lieutenants: A Study in Command*, 3 vols. (New York: Charles Scribner's Sons, 1942–44), 2:313.

2. Freeman, *R. E. Lee*, 2:434–35; Betty Herndon Maury Diary, December 28, 1862, LC; Elizabeth W. Roberson, *Weep Not for Me Dear Mother* (Gretna LA: Pelican Publishing, 1996), 93; James D. Nance to Laura, November 30, 1862, James Drayton Nance Letters, South Caroliniana Library, University of South Carolina, Columbia; William H. Tatum to Tee, November 23, 1862, William Henry Tatum Papers, VHS; William R. Stillwell to Molly, November 23, 1862, Letters from Confederate Soldiers in Georgia, 14:101–2, Georgia Department of History and Archives, Atlanta.

3. John T. Goolrick, *Historic Fredericksburg: The Story of an Old Town* (Richmond: Whittet & Shepperson, 1922), 40; Thomas C. Elder to wife, November 23,

1862, Thomas Claybrook Elder Papers, VHS; Halsey Wigfall to Louis T. Wigfall, November 23, 1862, Wigfall Family Papers, LC.

4. Thomas C. Elder to wife, November 23, 1862, Elder Papers.

5. OR, vol. 21, 148–50, 793–95; Ed Malles, ed., *Bridge Building in Wartime: Colonel Wesley Brainerd's Memoir of the 50th New York Volunteer Engineers* (Knoxville: University of Tennessee Press, 1997), 94–98, 134.

6. Willis et al., eds., *Journal of Jane Beale*, 67; William H. Tatum to Tee, November 23, 1862, Tatum Papers.

7. W. R. Montgomery to mother, December 7, 1862, W. R. Montgomery Papers, South Caroliniana Library, University of South Carolina, Columbia; Thomas C. Elder to wife, November 23, 1862, Elder Papers; Catherine S. Crary, ed., *Dear Belle: Letters from a Cadet and Officer to His Sweetheart, 1858–1865* (Middleton CT: Wesleyan University Press, 1965), 169.

8. Frank Longstreet to sister, November 29, 1862, Frank Longstreet Letters, USAMHI (CWMC); Samuel S. Partridge to Edward Partridge, November 30, 1862, Samuel Selden Partridge Letters, vol. 146, FSNMP; Carter, *Four Brothers in Blue*, 170–71, 178.

9. Carter, *Four Brothers in Blue*, 171, 177–79; Arthur A. Kent, ed., *Three Years with Company K: Sergt Austin C. Stearns, Company K, 13th Mass. Infantry* (Rutherford NJ: Fairleigh Dickinson University Press, 1976), 141–43; Stephen W. Sears, ed., *For Country, Cause and Leader: The Civil War Journal of Charles B. Haydon* (New York: Ticknor & Fields, 1993), 293.

10. Sears, ed., *For Country, Cause and Leader*, 292–93; Lawrence F. Kohl and Margaret C. Richard, eds., *Irish Green and Union Blue: Civil War Letters of Peter Welsh, Color Sergeant, 28th Regiment Massachusetts Volunteers* (New York: Fordham University Press, 1987), 37; U.S. War Department, *Medical and Surgical History of the Civil War*, 12 vols. (1870–83; rpt. Wilmington NC: Broadfoot, 1990–92), 1:174, 176.

11. Carter, *Four Brothers in Blue*, 164, 169–70, 180–81.

12. Henry H. Walling to sister, December 9, 1862, William Henry Walling Letters, USAMHI (CWMC); Sears, ed., *For Country, Cause and Leader*, 295; Edward H. C. Taylor to sister, November 29, 1862, Taylor Papers; Carter, *Four Brothers in Blue*, 174, 176, 183.

13. Robert G. Scott, ed., *Fallen Leaves: The Civil War Letters of Major Henry Livermore Abbott* (Kent OH: Kent State University Press, 1991), 146; Kohl and Richard, eds., *Irish Green and Union Blue*, 33, 35, 37; Curtis C. Pollack to mother, December 9, 1862, Curtis C. Pollack Letters, USAMHI (CWMC).

14. Thomas J. Morrison to mother, November 30, 1862, Thomas J. Morrison to father, December 8, 1862, John R. Morrison to father, December 9, 1862, Morrison Letters, vol. 237, FSNMP.

15. William R. Stillwell to Molly, November 30, December 7, 9, 1862, Letters from Confederate Soldiers, 14:104–5, 107–8.

16. William R. Stillwell to Molly, November 30, 1862, Letters from Confederate Soldiers, 14:104–5; Marion H. Fitzpatrick, *Letters to Amanda from Sergeant Major Marion Hill Fitzpatrick to His Wife, 1862–1865* (Nashville: Champion Resources, 1982), 33; James A. Wilson to wife, December 1, 6, 1862, James Albert Wilson Letters, vol. 206, FSNMP.

17. Thomas C. Elder to wife, November 23, 1862, Elder Papers.

18. OR, vol. 21, 1029; Warren W. Hassler, ed., *The General to His Lady: The Civil War Letters of William Dorsey Pender to Fanny Pender* (Chapel Hill: University of North Carolina Press, 1965), 190–91.

19. Williams, *Lincoln Finds a General*, 2:508, 516–17; Hattaway and Jones, *How the North Won*, 329–30; Basler, ed., *Works of Lincoln*, 5:514–15.

20. Mark E. Neely Jr., *The Last Best Hope of Earth: Abraham Lincoln and the Promise of America* (Cambridge MA: Harvard University Press, 1993), 74–75; Basler, ed., *Works of Lincoln*, 5:509–10; Worthington C. Ford, ed., *War Letters, 1862–1865, of John Chipman Gray and John Codman Ropes* (Boston: Houghton Mifflin, 1927), 33–34.

21. Malles, ed., *Bridge Building in Wartime*, 107.

22. James I. Robertson Jr., *Stonewall Jackson: The Man, the Legend, the Soldier* (New York: Macmillan, 1997), 645–48; George F. R. Henderson, *Stonewall Jackson and the American Civil War* (1898; New York: Grosset & Dunlap, 1949), 571–73; OR, vol. 21, 1037.

23. OR, vol. 21, 87.

24. Marvel, *Burnside*, 169–72; Whan, *Fiasco at Fredericksburg*, 31–34; OR, vol. 21, 63–64, 87–88, 180–82.

25. OR, vol. 21, 88, 106–7.

26. Robert Underwood Johnson and Clarence Clough Buel, eds., *Battles and Leaders of the Civil War*, 4 vols. (New York: Century, 1887–88), 3:107–8, 126 (hereafter cited as *B&L*); Malles, ed., *Bridge Building in Wartime*, 107–8; Robertson, ed., *Civil War Letters of McAllister*, 233, 239; Carter, *Four Brothers in Blue*, 184.

27. William H. Tatum to John Tatum, December 10, 1862, Tatum Letters; Adams, ed., *Post of Honor*, 289.

28. Brian Jenkins, *Britain and the War for the Union*, 2 vols. (Montreal: McGill-Queen's University Press, 1974–80), 2:170–82; Howard Jones, *Union in Peril: The Crisis over British Intervention in the Civil War* (Chapel Hill: University of North Carolina Press, 1992), 181–218, 220–23; Kohl and Richard, eds., *Irish Green and Union Blue*, 62.

29. Malles, ed., *Bridge Building in Wartime*, 112. For events of December 11, see Whan, *Fiasco at Fredericksburg*, 37–44; Steve C. Hawley, "Barksdale's Mississippi Brigade at Fredericksburg," CWH 40 (March 1994): 5–24; Richard F. Miller and Robert F. Mooney, "Across the River and into the Streets: The 20th Massachusetts Infantry and the Fight for Fredericksburg," CWR 4 (1995): 101–26.

30. Robert S. Robertson to father and sister, December 12, 1862, Robert S. Rob-

ertson Letters, vol. 219, FSNMP; Herb S. Crumb and Katherine Dhalle, eds., *No Middle Ground: Thomas Ward Osborn's Letters from the Field (1862–1864)* (Hamilton NY: Edmonston Publishing, 1993), 91; George T. Stevens, *Three Years in the Sixth Corps* (Albany NY: S. R. Gray, 1866), 167.

31. Crary, ed., *Dear Belle*, 173; Mary Thom to Marianne Claiborne, December 29, 1862, Claiborne Family Papers, VHS; Willis et al., eds., *Journal of Jane Beale*, 71; William H. Runge, ed., *Four Years in the Confederate Artillery: The Diary of Private Henry Robinson Berkeley* (Chapel Hill: University of North Carolina Press, 1961), 35–36.

32. Jedediah Hotchkiss, *Make Me a Map of the Valley: The Civil War Journal of Stonewall Jackson's Topographer*, ed. Archie P. McDonald (Dallas: Southern Methodist University Press, 1973), 99; Hawley, "Barksdale's Mississippi Brigade," 19.

33. Crary, ed., *Dear Belle*, 174; OR, vol. 21, 283–84.

34. OR, vol. 21, 283–84; Miller and Mooney, "Across the River," 116, 118.

35. Gallagher, ed., *Fredericksburg Campaign*, 154–55; Willis et al., eds., *Journal of Jane Beale*, 72–74; Goolrick, *Historic Fredericksburg*, 44–45.

36. *Charleston Mercury*, December 10, 15, 1862; *New York Herald*, December 14, 1862.

37. John S. Weiser to parents, December 1862, John S. Weiser Letters, USAMHI (CWMC); "Personal Recollections of the First Battle of Fredericksburg," p. 4, typescript by unknown author, Center for American History, Austin TX.

## 3. TERRIBLE UPROAR AND DESTRUCTION

1. Gary W. Gallagher, ed., *Fighting for the Confederacy: The Personal Recollections of General Edward Porter Alexander* (Chapel Hill: University of North Carolina Press, 1989), 172.

2. Samuel S. Partridge to Edward Partridge, December 17, 1862, Partridge Letters; *B&L*, 3:108.

3. Sparks, ed., *Inside Lincoln's Army*, 188–89; William H. Peacock to Sarah, December 30, 1862, William H. Peacock Letters, USAMHI (CWMC); Charles W. Bardeen, *A Little Fifer's War Diary* (Syracuse NY: C. W. Bardeen, 1910), 103–5.

4. Gallagher, ed., *Fredericksburg Campaign*, 155–58; Sears, ed., *For Country, Cause and Leader*, 288–89.

5. Grimsley, *Hard Hand of War*, 105–10; Bardeen, *Little Fifer's Diary*, 105; Robert S. Robertson to father and sister, December 12, 1862, Robertson Letters.

6. *New York Herald*, December 14, 1862; *Charleston Mercury*, December 15, 1862.

7. OR, vol. 21, 89–90.

8. Whan, *Fiasco at Fredericksburg*, 51–55.

9. Robert S. Robertson to father and sister, December 12, 1862, Robertson Letters; Runge, ed., *Four Years in the Confederate Artillery*, 36.

10. Burnside, *Marvel*, 180–86; Whan, *Fiasco at Fredericksburg*, 55–56.

11. Charles A. Malloy Diary, December 13, 1862, USAMHI (CWMC). Frank A.

O'Reilly, *"Stonewall" Jackson at Fredericksburg: The Battle of Prospect Hill, December 13, 1862* (Lynchburg VA: H. E. Howard, 1993), provides the best description of the fighting on the Confederate right wing, but for a capsule of this portion of the battle, see A. Wilson Greene, "Opportunity to the South: Meade Versus Jackson at Fredericksburg," *CWH* 33 (December 1987): 295–314.

12. William H. Andrews, *Footprints of a Regiment: A Recollection of the 1st Georgia Regulars, 1861–1865* (Atlanta: Longstreet Press, 1992), 97–98; "Personal Recollections of the First Battle of Fredericksburg," 13.

13. Edward J. Stackpole, *Drama on the Rappahannock: The Fredericksburg Campaign* (New York: Bonanza Books, 1957), 110–11.

14. There is speculation that Jackson purposely left the gap in his line in hopes of luring in the Yankees and crushing them. See Clay Ouzts, "Maxcy Gregg and His Brigade of South Carolinians at the Battle of Fredericksburg," *South Carolina Historical Magazine* 95 (January 1994): 13–17.

15. Jennings C. Wise, *The Long Arm of Lee, or The History of the Artillery of the Army of Northern Virginia*, 2 vols. (Lynchburg VA: J. P. Bell, 1915), 1:381–82; Gregory A. Mertz, "'A Severe Day on the Artillery': Stonewall Jackson's Artillerists and the Defense of the Confederate Right," *CWR* 4 (1995): 70, 75, 94.

16. Stephen Z. Starr, *The Union Cavalry in the Civil War*, 3 vols. (Baton Rouge: Louisiana State University Press, 1979–85), 1:324–28.

17. Henry B. McClellan, *The Life and Campaigns of Major General J. E. B. Stuart* (Boston: Houghton Mifflin, 1885), 192–93; OR, vol. 21, 547.

18. O'Reilly, *Jackson at Fredericksburg*, 51–52.

19. William Tatum to father, December 17, 1862, Tatum Papers.

20. O'Reilly, *Jackson at Fredericksburg*, 54–65.

21. O'Reilly, *Jackson at Fredericksburg*, 63–64, 76–82.

22. O'Reilly, *Jackson at Fredericksburg*, 80–87.

23. Judy Yandoh, "Brief Breach at Fredericksburg," *ACW* 8 (March 1995): 42–48.

24. Jubal A. Early, *Narrative of the War Between the States*, ed. Gary W. Gallagher (1912; rpt. New York: Da Capo, 1989), 172–74; Robert Emory Dunn to William M. S. Dunn, February 21, 1863, Dunn Family Papers, VHS.

25. O'Reilly, *Jackson at Fredericksburg*, 155.

26. Sears, ed., *For Country, Cause and Leader*, 298.

27. Marvel, *Burnside*, 191–92; OR, vol. 21, 93–94, 128.

28. OR, vol. 21, 92–94, 219.

29. Gallagher, ed., *Fighting for the Confederacy*, 175.

30. Whan, *Fiasco at Fredericksburg*, 77–84; *Supplement*, 3:764–65; Gallagher, ed., *Fighting for the Confederacy*, 176.

31. George F. Hopper to brother, December 21, 1862, George F. Hopper Letter, vol. 123, FSNMP. For Hooper's official report, see OR, vol. 21, 308.

32. David M. Jordan, *Winfield Scott Hancock: A Soldier's Life* (Bloomington: Indiana University Press, 1988), 63.

33. Whan, *Fiasco at Fredericksburg*, 86–87; OR, vol. 21, 625–27.

34. Kevin E. O'Brien, ed., "'The Breath of Hell's Door': Private William McCarter and the Attack of the Irish Brigade on Marye's Heights, an Unpublished Memoir," CWR 4 (1995): 67–68.

35. O'Brien, "'Breath of Hell's Door,'" 63, 68; John McDonald to Fannie King, January 24, 1863, John McDonald Letters, vol. 80, FSNMP; Bardeen, *Little Fifer's Diary*, 108. For a fictional account of the Irish confrontation, see Kirk Mitchell, *Fredericksburg: A Novel of the Irish at Marye's Heights* (New York: St. Martin's Press, 1996).

36. Whan, *Fiasco at Fredericksburg*, 89–93; Johnson and Buel, eds., B&L, 3, 113.

37. Carter, *Four Brothers in Blue*, 196; Samuel S. Partridge to Edward Partridge, December 17, 1862, Partridge Letters.

38. Nathaniel W. Brown to Albert M. Given, December 23, 1862, Nathaniel Weede Brown Letter, vol. 74, FSNMP; OR, vol. 21, 432. Carol Reardon gives an excellent account of the charge by Humphreys's division in Gallagher, ed., *Fredericksburg Campaign*, 80–112.

39. Hebert, *Fighting Joe Hooker*, 159; Timothy J. Reese, *Sykes' Regular Infantry Division, 1861–1864: A History of Regular United States Infantry Operations in the Civil War's Eastern Theater* (Jefferson NC: McFarland, 1990), 175–79; Thomas H. Evans, "'The Cries of the Wounded Were Piercing and Horrible,'" *Civil War Times Illustrated* 7 (July 1968): 31.

40. Aaron K. Blake to sister, December 18, 1862, Aaron K. Blake Letters, USAMHI (CWMC); Gallagher, ed., *Fighting for the Confederacy*, 179; OR, vol. 21, 626.

41. Evans, "'Cries of the Wounded,'" 32; Reuben Kelly to sister, January 8, 1863, Reuben Kelly Letters, vol. 123, FSNMP; U.S. War Department, *Medical and Surgical History*, 2:133–34; Isaac Morrow to brother, December 21, 1862, Isaac and Joseph Morrow Letters, USAMHI (H); Carter, *Four Brothers in Blue*, 198.

42. Maury Diary, December 28, 1862; U.S. War Department, *Medical and Surgical History*, 2:130, 133; Abraham Welch to Mary Ann, December 27, 1862, Abraham Welch Letter, HC; Stephen B. Oates, *A Woman of Valor: Clara Barton and the Civil War* (New York: Free Press, 1994), 111–15.

43. Carter, *Four Brothers in Blue*, 201–4.

44. Johnson and Buel, eds., B&L, 3:116; Evans, "'Cries of the Wounded,'" 32–33.

45. O'Reilly, *Jackson at Fredericksburg*, 165–66; U.S. War Department, *Medical and Surgical History*, 2:131–32.

46. George H. Legate to sister, December 27, 1862, George H. Legate Letter, USAMHI (HC); O'Reilly, *Jackson at Fredericksburg*, 178.

47. Robert S. Robertson to father and sister, December 13, 1862, Robertson Letters; John Buchanan to wife, December 16, [1862], John Buchanan Family Papers, UMB.

## 4. NOT A PLEASANT TOPIC

1. O'Reilly, *Jackson at Fredericksburg*, 168; Whan, *Fiasco at Fredericksburg*, 100.

2. O'Reilly, *Jackson at Fredericksburg*, 181–82.

3. Gallagher, ed., *Fredericksburg Campaign*, vii, xiii.

4. Robert T. Scott to Fanny Scott, December 14, 1862, Keith Family Papers, VHS.

5. Reese, *Sykes' Regular Infantry Division*, 179–80; Evans, "'Cries of the Wounded,'" 33.

6. William W. Teall, "Ringside Seat at Fredericksburg," *Civil War Times Illustrated* 4 (May 1965): 29; Carter, *Four Brothers in Blue*, 200–201.

7. U.S. Congress, *Report of the Joint Committee on the Conduct of the War*, Senate Report No. 71, 37th Cong., 3d sess., 4 vols. (Washington DC: Government Printing Office, 1863), 1:6–7.

8. Hodnett Diary, December 14, 1862, Letters from Confederate Soldiers, 4:247.

9. "Personal Recollections of the First Battle of Fredericksburg," 18–19.

10. Scott, ed., *Fallen Leaves*, 155; Freeman, *R. E. Lee*, 2:470–71.

11. Francis M. Coker to wife, December 18, 1862, Hodgson Heidler Collection, Special Collections, University of Georgia.

12. Charles T. Bowen to wife, December 18, 1862, Charles Thomas Bowen Letters, vol. 209, FSNMP; John M. Priest, ed., *One Surgeon's Private War: Doctor William H. Potter of the 57th New York* (1888; rpt. Shippensburg PA: White Mane, 1996), 54; O'Reilly, *Jackson at Fredericksburg*, 189; Carter, *Four Brothers in Blue*, 205.

13. Sears, ed., *For Country, Cause and Leader*, 298–99; Lucius B. Shattuck to Gill and Mary, December 16, 1862, Lucius B. Shattuck Papers, UMB; Augustus Buell, *"The Cannoneer": Recollections of Service in the Army of the Potomac* (Washington DC: National Tribune, 1890), 44.

14. Charles T. Bowen to wife, December 18, 1862, Bowen Letters.

15. Scott, ed., *Fallen Leaves*, 155–56; William H. Peacock to Sarah, December 30, 1862, Peacock Letters.

16. Gallagher, ed., *Fighting for the Confederacy*, 184.

17. Jay Luvaas, ed., *The Civil War: A Soldier's View* (Chicago: University of Chicago Press, 1958), 94–100, offers a good summation of the pros and cons of a Confederate counterattack from the writings of George F. R. Henderson.

18. Thomas C. Elder to wife, December 21, 1862, Elder Papers; *Richmond Enquirer*, December 23, 1862; Osmun Latrobe Diary, December 16, 1862, VHS.

19. John L. G. Wood to father, December 18, 1862, Letters from Confederate Soldiers, 4:129–30; Edward Samuel Duffey Diary, December 17, 1862, VHS; Runge, ed., *Four Years in the Confederate Artillery*, 38–39.

20. Runge, ed., *Four Years in the Confederate Artillery*, 39.

21. Francis M. Coker to wife, December 18, 1862, Heidler Collection; Louis P. Masur, ed., *"The Real War Will Never Get in the Books": Selections from Writers During the Civil War* (New York: Oxford University Press, 1993), 255–56; U.S. War Department, *Medical and Surgical History*, 2:130–34.

22. Gallagher, ed., *Fredericksburg Campaign*, 98–99; Kohl and Richard, eds., *Irish Green and Union Blue*, 43; James R. Coye to wife, December 19, 1862, James R. Coye Letters, vol. 147, FSNMP; George F. Hopper to brother, December 21, 1862, Hopper Letter; Crumb and Dhalle, eds., *No Middle Ground*, 94; Isaac Hillyer to wife and children, December 18, 1862, Isaac Hillyer Letters, vol. 33, FSNMP.

23. John L. G. Wood to father, December 18, 1862, Letters from Confederate Soldiers, 4:129–30; Henry T. Owen to Harriet Owen, December 14, 1862, Henry Thweatt Owen Papers, VHS; James W. Lineberger to Elizabeth Lineberger, December 17, 1862, Lineberger Family Papers, VHS; W. H. Burges to David McKnight, December 20, 1862, Burges and Jefferson Family Papers, Center for American History, Austin TX; Robert B. Jones to wife, December 27, 1862, Robert B. Jones Family Papers, VHS.

24. Daniel I. Underhill to sister, December 21, 1862, Daniel Isaac Underhill Letters, vol. 71, FSNMP; Fitzpatrick, *Letters to Amanda*, 37; P. E. Fouts to parents, February 11, 1863, P. E. Fouts Collection, North Carolina State Archives, Raleigh.

25. William Speed to Charlotte Speed, December 29, 1862, William Speed Letters, Clements Library, University of Michigan, Ann Arbor; Scott, ed., *Fallen Leaves*, 152; W. H. Burges to David McKnight, December 20, 1862, Burges and Jefferson Family Papers; George G. Meade, *Life and Letters of George Gordon Meade*, 2 vols. (New York: Charles Scribner's Sons, 1913), 1:337–38.

26. Beale, ed., *Diary of Gideon Welles*, 1:191–92.

27. Donald, *Lincoln*, 399; *New York Herald*, December 19, 1862.

28. Allan G. Bogue, ed., "William Parker Cutler's Congressional Diary of 1862–63," *CWH* 33 (December 1987): 322; William Alan Blair, ed., *A Politician Goes to War: The Civil War Letters of John White Geary* (University Park: Pennsylvania State University Press, 1995), 73; Donald, *Lincoln*, 399–401; *Supplement*, 3:672.

29. Nevins, *War for the Union*, 2:352–65; Donald, *Lincoln*, 401–3; John M. Taylor, *William Henry Seward: Lincoln's Right Hand* (New York: HarperCollins, 1991), 207–9; John Niven, *Salmon P. Chase: A Biography* (New York: Oxford University Press, 1995), 309–12; Francis Fessenden, *Life and Public Services of William Pitt Fessenden*, 2 vols. (Boston: Houghton Mifflin, 1907), 1:231–48, Theodore C. Pease and James G. Randall, eds., *The Diary of Orville Hickman Browning*, 2 vols. (Springfield: Illinois State Historical Library, 1925–26), 1:596–601.

30. Beale, ed., *Diary of Gideon Welles*, 1:194.

31. U.S. Congress, *Report of the Joint Committee on the Conduct of the War*, Senate Report No. 71, 1.

32. Bogue, ed., "Cutler's Congressional Diary," 322; Meade, *Life and Letters*, 1:340; U.S. Congress, *Report of the Joint Committee on the Conduct of the War*, Senate Report No. 71, 8.

33. Williams, *Lincoln Finds a General*, 2:502–6; OR, vol. 21, 794.

34. U.S. Congress, *Report of the Joint Committee on the Conduct of the War*, Senate Report No. 71, 40.

35. Marvel, *Burnside*, 207–8.

36. *New York Herald*, December 23, 1862; Nevins and Thomas, eds., *Diary of Strong*, 3:282; Masur, ed., *"The Real War,"* 67–68.

37. Niven, ed., *Chase Papers*, 3:345; Ford, ed., *War Letters*, 71. The New Englander later admitted that Burnside was probably guilty of "culpable carelessness" in the matter of the pontoons.

38. Basler, ed., *Works of Lincoln*, 6:13; Nevins, ed., *Diary of Battle*, 149.

39. Kent, ed., *Three Years with Company K*, 149; Robert S. Robertson to parents, December 24, 1862, Robertson Letters; Nevins and Thomas, eds., *Diary of Strong*, 3:281–82; Virginia J. Laas, ed., *Wartime Washington: The Civil War Letters of Elizabeth Blair Lee* (Urbana: University of Illinois Press, 1991), 219.

40. Gallagher, ed., *Fredericksburg Campaign*, 3–4, 10–17, 20–22; Nevins, ed., *Diary of Battle*, 147–48; Kent, ed., *Three Years with Company K*, 149–50; *Supplement*, 3:695. The best tactical analysis of the battle is George F. R. Henderson, *The Campaign of Fredericksburg, Nov.–Dec., 1862: A Tactical Study for Officers* (London: Kegan Paul, Trench and Company, 1886), and reprinted with annotations in Luvaas, *Civil War*.

41. The most balanced criticism of Burnside is Williams, *Lincoln Finds a General*, 2:525–26, 536–39; for Burnside's defense see Marvel, *Burnside*, and his essay in Gallagher, ed., *Fredericksburg Campaign*, 1–25.

42. John D. McQuaide to W. D. McQuaide, December 26, 1862, John D. McQuaide Letters, USAMHI Civil War Times Illustrated Collection; "On Historic Spots," *SHSP* 36 (1908): 197–99.

43. Laas, ed., *Wartime Washington*, 216, 217n; William H. Cocke to family, December 25, 1862, Cocke Family Papers, VHS; Crumb and Dhalle, eds., *No Middle Ground*, 95; Daniel I. Underhill to brother, December 15, 1862, Underhill Letters.

44. Teall, "Ringside Seat at Fredericksburg," 32–33; Zachariah Chandler to wife, December 24, 1862, Zachariah Chandler Papers, LC.

## 5. MIRED HOPES AND MUD MARCHES

1. Nevins and Thomas, eds., *Diary of Strong*, 3:282–84.

2. Kohl and Richard, eds., *Irish Green and Union Blue*, 41–42; Thomas F. Darby to Mary Ann Connolly, January 4, 1863, Thomas F. Darby Letters, VHS; Timothy C. Emerton to sister, December 21, 1862, Timothy C. Emerton Letters, USAMHI (CWMC).

3. Kermit M. Bird, ed., *Quill of the Wild Goose: Civil War Letters and Diaries of Private Joel Molyneux, 141st P.V.* (Shippensburg PA: Burd Street Press, 1996), 54–55; Samuel S. Partridge to Edward Partridge, December 17, 1862, Partridge Letters.

4. Walter Lowenfels, ed., *Walt Whitman's Civil War* (New York: Knopf, 1961), 35–39.

5. Hodnett Diary, December 24, 25, 1862, Letters from Confederate Soldiers, 4:247; Curtis G. Pollack to mother, January 26, 1863, Pollack Letters; Halsey Wig-

fall to mother, December 28, 1862, Wigfall Family Papers; Andrews, *Footprints of a Regiment*, 100.

6. Adams, ed., *Post of Honor*, 297; Samuel Angus Firebaugh Diary, December 25, 1862, USAMHI (CWMC); John Simmons Shipp Diary, December 25, 1862, Shipp Family Papers, VHS; Joseph W. Griggs to father, December 19, 1862, Joseph W. Griggs Letter, VHS.

7. Gallagher, ed., *Fredericksburg Campaign*, 113–41; Dowdey and Manarin, eds., *Wartime Papers of Lee*, 365; Runge, ed., *Four Years in the Confederate Artillery*, 37–38. Almost three years after the war, Longstreet claimed that had Hood attacked Franklin's right flank sooner and more forcefully, as Longstreet's orders implied that he should, the Confederates could have "destroyed Burnside's Army," but given the limited number of men Franklin had committed to his own attack, this seems doubtful. OR, vol. 21, 570; *Supplement*, 3:804–5.

8. Gallagher, ed., *Fredericksburg Campaign*, 127–29; Spencer G. Welch, *A Confederate Surgeon's Letters to His Wife* (New York: Neale, 1911), 39; Dowdey and Manarin, eds., *Wartime Papers of Lee*, 380.

9. Isaac Hillyer to brother, January 14, 1863, Hillyer Letters.

10. Kent, ed., *Three Years with Company K*, 148; Alfred E. Doby to wife, January 8, 1863, Alfred E. Doby Letters, Museum of the Confederacy, Richmond VA; John H. Bevan to sister, December 21, 1862, John H. Bevan Letters, USAMHI (CWMC); John R. Coye to wife, January 7, 1863, Coye Letters; Lucius B. Shattuck to Gill and Mary, December 16, 1862, Shattuck Papers.

11. Hodnett Diary, December 20, 21, 1862, Letters from Confederate Soldiers, 4:247; E. P. Miller Diary, January 2, 1863, vol. 63, FSNMP; Alfred E. Doby to wife, January 8, 15, 1863, Doby Letters; Adams, ed., *Post of Honor*, 296.

12. Hodnett Diary, January 1–4, 1863, Letters from Confederate Soldiers, 4:248; Adams, ed., *Post of Honor*, 297.

13. *New York Herald*, December 25, 1862; Francis M. Coker to wife, December 18, 1862, Heidler Collection; Mary Thom to Marianne Claiborne, December 31, 1862, Claiborne Family Papers, VHS; Thomas C. Elder to wife, December 21, 1862, Elder Papers; William H. Cocke to family, December 25, 1862, Cocke Family Papers; Latrobe Diary, December 12, 1862.

14. Drawer 491, and Mary Layton to M. Slaughter, January 17, 1863, Damage Inventories, Office of Clerk of Circuit Court, Fredericksburg VA; Frances Bernard Goolrick, "Suffering in Fredericksburg," SHSP 37 (1909): 357–59; Catherine Thom to Marianne Claiborne, December 31, 1862, January 4 [1863], Claiborne Family Papers; Elizabeth (Alsop) Wynne Diary, December 29, 1862, January 1, 1863, VHS; Abraham Welch to Mary Ann, December 27, 1862, Welch Letter; Fredericksburg, Virginia, Death Records, November–December 1862, VHS.

15. Thomas C. Elder to wife, December 21, 1862, Elder Papers.

16. Gallagher, ed., *Fredericksburg Campaign*, 156–59; Abner Crump Hopkins Diary, January 16, 1863, VHS; Damage Inventories.

17. OR, vol. 21, 549–50; Gallagher, ed., *Fredericksburg Campaign*, 179–89; *Supplement*, 3:679–80.

18. Williams, *Lincoln Finds a General*, 2:539–43; Basler, ed., *Works of Lincoln*, 6:46–48.

19. William R. Williams to wife, December 26, 1862, William R. Williams Letters, USAMHI (CWMC); Robertson, ed., *Civil War Letters of McAllister*, 249; Scott, ed., *Fallen Leaves*, 152, 155.

20. John Bigelow Jr., *The Campaign of Chancellorsville: A Strategic and Tactical Study* (New Haven: Yale University Press, 1910), 36; Gallagher, ed., *Fredericksburg Campaign*, 175; OR, vol. 21, 96.

21. James M. McPherson, *For Cause and Comrades: Why Men Fought in the Civil War* (New York: Oxford University Press, 1997), 117–30; Alan D. Gaff, *On Many a Bloody Field: Four Years in the Iron Brigade* (Bloomington: Indiana University Press, 1996), 214–16; Anson B. Shuey to wife, January 11, 1863, Anson B. Shuey Letters, USAMHI (CWMC); Edward W. Peck to mother, January 3, 1863, Edward W. Peck Letters, USAMHI (CWMC); Jacob W. Haas to brother, January 1, 1863, Jacob W. Haas Letters, USAMHI (H).

22. McPherson, *For Cause and Comrades*, 126–27; Kohl and Richard, eds., *Irish Green and Union Blue*, 62; Charles R. Johnson to Nellie, February 1863, Charles R. Johnson Letters, USAMHI (HC).

23. Anthony G. Graves to father, December 19, 1862, Anthony G. Graves Letters, vol. 123, FSNMP; Edward W. Peck to mother, January 3, 1863, Peck Letters; Aaron K. Blake to sister, December 26, 1862, Aaron K. Blake to Aunt Adda, January 16, 1863, Blake Letters; Curtis C. Pollack to mother, December 18, 1862, Pollack Letters.

24. Miles Peabody to parents, December 1, 1862, Miles Peabody Letters, USAMHI (CWMC); James R. Coye to wife, December 17, 1862, Coye Letters.

25. Gary W. Gallagher, ed., *Chancellorsville: The Battle and Its Aftermath* (Chapel Hill: University of North Carolina Press, 1996), 2–4; Abel G. Peck to Lina, January 16, 1863, Abel G. Peck Letter, vol. 212, FSNMP; James Laird to wife, January 28, 1863, James Laird Letters, vol. 33, FSNMP; John H. Bevan to sister, January 1, 1863, Bevan Letters.

26. John H. Bevan to sister, January 16, 1863, Bevan Letters; John Morton to mother, January 13, 1863, John Morton Letters, USAMHI (CWMC).

27. Alexander Way to wife, December 17, 1862, Alexander Way Letters, vol. 33, FSNMP; Robert S. Robertson to James S. Coon, January 9, 1863, Robert S. Robertson to mother, January 14, 1863, Robertson Letters; Charles T. Bowen to wife, December 18, 1862, Bowen Letters; Edward H. C. Taylor to Bill, January 25, 1863, Taylor Papers; Edward W. Peck to mother, January 3, 1863, Peck Letters; George H. Legate to sister, December 27, 1862, Legate Letter.

28. James A. Carman to father, December 17, 1862, James and Francis Carman

Papers, USAMHI; Curtis G. Pollack to mother, December 9, 1862, Pollack Letters; Jacob W. Haas to brother, December 18, 1862, January 1, 1863, Haas Letters.

29. William Speed to Charlotte Speed, December 29, 1862, Speed Letters; Charles T. Bowen to wife, December 18, 1862, Bowen Letters; Nathaniel W. Brown to Albert M. Given, December 23, 1862, Brown Letter.

30. Robert E. Lee to Charlotte Lee, December 25, 1862, George Bolling Lee Papers, VHS; OR, vol. 21, 1091–92.

31. OR, vol. 21, 954; Gallagher, ed., *Fredericksburg Campaign*, 193–98.

32. Sparks, ed., *Inside Lincoln's Army*, 204; Nevins, ed., *Diary of Battle*, 157–58; Gallagher, ed., *Fredericksburg Campaign*, 192.

33. Sears, ed., *For Country, Cause and Leader*, 299, 305; John H. Pardington to wife, January 18, 1863, John H. Pardington Letters, vol. 153, FSNMP.

34. Robert E. Lee to Mary Custis Lee, January 21, 1863, Robert Edward Lee Papers, VHS; John McDonald to Fannie King, January 24, 1863, McDonald Letters.

35. Nevins, ed., *Diary of Battle*, 158; Dayton E. Flint to father, January 27, 1863, Dayton E. Flint Letters, USAMHI (CWMC); Charles H. Littlefield to wife, January 24, 1863, Charles H. Littlefield Letters, USAMHI (CWMC); Gallagher, ed., *Fredericksburg Campaign*, 199–202.

36. Edward H. C. Taylor to Bill, January 25, 1863, Taylor Papers.

37. Bird, ed., *Quill of the Wild Goose*, 66; Joseph H. Law to Mary E. Law, January 26, 1863, Joseph Harrison Law Letters, Civil War Miscellaneous Collection, USAMHI (CWMC); Dayton E. Flint to father, January 27, 1863, Flint Letters; Crumb and Dhalle, eds., *No Middle Ground*, 105.

## 6. HURRAH FOR HOOKER

1. Edward H. C. Taylor to Bill, January 25, 1863, Taylor Papers; Robert H. Rhodes, ed., *All for the Union: A History of the 2nd Rhode Island in the War of the Great Rebellion* (Lincoln RI: Andrew Mowbray, 1985), 98; Joseph H. Law to Mary E. Law, January 26, 1863, Law Letters.

2. Stephen W. Sears, *Chancellorsville* (New York: Houghton Mifflin, 1996), 54–56. The best biography of Hooker is Hebert, *Fighting Joe Hooker*.

3. Hebert, *Fighting Joe Hooker*, 165–66; Williams, *Lincoln Finds a General*, 2:547–61.

4. OR, vol. 25, pt. 2, 4; Hebert, *Fighting Joe Hooker*, 169–70.

5. OR, vol. 25, pt. 2, 12–13; Sears, ed., *For Country, Cause and Leader*, 308.

6. Henry A. Morrow, "To Chancellorsville with the Iron Brigade: The Diary of Colonel Henry A. Morrow: Part I," *Civil War Times Illustrated* 14 (January 1986): 14; Emory Upton to sister, December 23, 1862, Emory Upton Letter, USAMHI (H); Paul Fatout, ed., *Letters from a Civil War Surgeon* (West Lafayette IN: Purdue University Press, 1961), 78; John S. Willey to wife, December 19, 1862, John S. Willey Letters, USAMHI Harrisburg Civil War Round Table Collection—Norman Daniels Collection.

7. Buell, *"Cannoneer,"* 48–49; Clement Hoffman to mother, February 12, 1863, Clement Hoffman Letters, USAMHI (H); Henry W. Grubbs to Cornelia, February 1, 1863, Henry W. Grubbs Letter, vol. 210, FSNMP; Nevins, ed., *Diary of Battle*, 161–62; Scott, ed., *Fallen Leaves*, 165.

8. Worthington C. Ford, ed., *A Cycle of Adams Letters, 1861–1865*, 2 vols. (Boston: Houghton Mifflin, 1920), 1:250; Nevins, ed., *Diary of Battle*, 162.

9. Sparks, ed., *Inside Lincoln's Army*, 209. Hooker's reforms are described in the following paragraphs, but for general discussions see Hebert, *Fighting Joe Hooker*, 172–84; Gallagher, ed., *Chancellorsville*, 9–27; Sears, *Chancellorsville*, 62–75; Ernest B. Furgurson, *Chancellorsville 1863: The Souls of the Brave* (New York: Knopf, 1992), 29–35.

10. Sparks, ed., *Inside Lincoln's Army*, 209; Nevins, ed., *Diary of Battle*, 162–63.

11. Williams, *Lincoln Finds a General*, 2:553, 830–31; OR, vol. 25, pt. 2, 10–12; Nevins, ed., *Diary of Battle*, 163.

12. David W. Blight, ed., *When This Cruel War Is Over: The Civil War Letters of Charles Harvey Brewster* (Amherst: University of Massachusetts Press, 1992), 212.

13. Ruth Silliker, ed., *The Rebel Yell and the Yankee Hurrah: The Civil War Journal of a Maine Volunteer, Private John W. Haley, 17th Maine Regiment* (Camden ME: Down East Books, 1985), 71.

14. Sears, ed., *For Country, Cause and Leader*, 308–9.

15. OR, vol. 25, pt. 2, 38, 152; Sears, *Chancellorsville*, 72.

16. Gallagher, ed., *Chancellorsville*, 13.

17. OR, vol. 25, pt. 2, 56, 87, 120.

18. John Gourlee to brother, January 29, 1863, John Gourlee Letters, USAMHI (CWMC); OR, vol. 25, pt. 2, 55, 58, 89, 138.

19. Edwin C. Fishel, *The Secret War for the Union: The Untold Story of Military Intelligence in the Civil War* (Boston: Houghton Mifflin, 1996), 286, 322–25; Luther C. Furst Diary, December 17–December 31, 1862, USAMHI (H); Blight, ed., *When This Cruel War Is Over*, 216.

20. Fishel, *Secret War for the Union*, 287–300; Nevins, *War for the Union*, 2:436–37.

21. William H. Walling to sisters, January 11, 1863, Walling Letters; Nevins, ed., *Diary of Battle*, 163, 165, 169; Kent, ed., *Three Years in Company K*, 155–56; Dawes, *Service with the Sixth Wisconsin*, 115, 125–26.

22. Morrow, "To Chancellorsville," 16; Crumb and Dhalle, eds., *No Middle Ground*, 107; A. Caldwell to brother, March 7, 1863, Caldwell Family Letters, USAMHI (CWMC); Scott, ed., *Fallen Leaves*, 170; John H. Pardington to wife, February 13, 1863, Pardington Letters; Furst Diary, January 1–March 14, 1863; Edward W. Peck to mother, March 19, 1863, Peck Letters; Bird, ed., *Quill of the Wild Goose*, 89.

23. Robertson, ed., *Civil War Letters of McAllister*, 267; John H. Pardington to wife, February 21, 1863, Pardington Letters.

24. U.S. War Department, *Medical and Surgical History*, 1:174–79; Kohl and Richard, eds., *Irish Green and Union Blue*, 81.

25. U.S. War Department, *Medical and Surgical History*, 1:174–75; James M. Richmond to wife, March 22, 1863, James M. Richmond Letters, vol. 38, FSNMP.

26. Rhodes, ed., *All for the Union*, 100; William H. Peacock to Sarah, March 3, 1863, Peacock Letters.

27. Miles Peabody to parents, April 1, 1863, Peabody Letters; Noel G. Harrison, *Fredericksburg Civil War Sites*, 2 vols. (Lynchburg VA: H. E. Howard, 1995), 1:70; Bird, ed., *Quill of the Wild Goose*, 80; Robertson, ed., *Civil War Letters of McAllister*, 275–76, 281, 286–88.

28. William H. Peacock to Sarah, February 5, 1863, Peacock Letters; Bird, ed., *Quill of the Wild Goose*, 85–86; William H. Myers to parents, February 15, 1863, William H. Myers Letters, USAMHI (CWMC).

29. Joseph E. Law to Mary E. Law, February 12, 1863, Law Letters; James I. Robertson Jr., ed., "An Indiana Soldier in Love and War: The Civil War Letters of John V. Hadley," *Indiana Magazine of History* 59 (September 1963): 228–29.

30. Buell, "*Cannoneer*," 49; Alexander Seiders to wife, February 24, 1863, Alexander Seiders Letters, vol. 210, FSNMP; Hiram S. Wilton to wife, February 6, 1863, Hiram S. Wilton Letters, USAMHI (CWMC).

31. John H. Pardington to father, March 11, 1863, Pardington Letters; William H. Patterson to mother, March 13, 1863, William H. Patterson Papers, USAMHI (H); David Nichol to father, March 28, 1863, David Nichol Papers, USAMHI (H); Kohl and Richard, eds., *Irish Green and Union Blue*, 78.

32. McPherson, *For Cause and Comrades*, 124–27; Hiram S. Wilton to wife, February 6, 1863, Wilton Letters; Miles Peabody to brother and sister, February 14, 1863, Peabody Letters; William A. Guest to brother, March 11, 1863, William A. Guest Letters, USAMHI (CWMC).

33. Anson B. Shuey to wife, February 14, 1863, Shuey Letters; Fatout, ed., *Letters of a Civil War Surgeon*, 80.

34. Frank L. Clement, *The Limits of Dissent: Clement L. Vallandigham and the Civil War* (Lexington: University Press of Kentucky, 1970), 123–25; Bogue, ed., "Cutler's Congressional Diary," 321.

35. Isaac Plumb Diary, January 31, 1863, vol. 147, FSNMP; A. Caldwell to brother, March 7, 1863, Caldwell Family Letters; John H. Pardington to father, March 11, 1863, Pardington Letters; Bird, ed., *Quill of the Wild Goose*, 89.

36. Robertson, ed., "An Indiana Soldier," 230–31; John H. Pardington to father, March 11, 1863, Pardington Letters; Robertson, ed., *Civil War Letters of McAllister*, 272–73.

37. James Magill to mother, February 1, 1863, James Magill Letters, USAMHI (CWMC); Robertson, ed., "An Indiana Soldier," 230; J. Henry Blakeman to Friend, March 5, 1863, J. Henry Blakeman Letters, USAMHI (CWMC).

38. Robertson, ed., "An Indiana Soldier," 232; Meshach P. Larry to sister, March 25, 1863, Meshach P. Larry Letters, USAMHI (CWMC).

39. U.S. Congress, *Report of the Joint Committee on the Conduct of the War*, Senate Report No. 108, 37th Cong., 3d sess, 4 vols. (Washington DC: Government Printing Office, 1863), 2:687–754; Meade, *Life and Letters*, 1:357–60; Nevins, ed., *Diary of Battle*, 173–74.

40. Meade, *Life and Letters*, 1:362; Hiram H. Chubbuck to sister, March 30, 1863, Hiram H. Chubbuck Letter, USAMHI (HC).

## 7. THE CHINESE GAME

1. Freeman, *R. E. Lee*, 2:479; Dowdey and Manarin, eds., *Wartime Papers of Lee*, 387, 389.

2. Dowdey and Manarin, eds., *Wartime Papers of Lee*, 389.

3. John B. Jones, *A Rebel War Clerk's Diary at the Confederate States Capital*, 2 vols. (Philadelphia: J. B. Lippincott, 1866), 1:243, 279.

4. Dowdey and Manarin, eds., *Wartime Papers of Lee*, 389, 411; Woodworth, *Davis and Lee at War*, 213–17; OR, vol. 25, pt. 2, 638–39.

5. Freeman, *R. E. Lee*, 2:478–84; Jeffry D. Wert, *General James Longstreet: The Confederacy's Most Controversial Soldier, a Biography* (New York: Simon & Schuster, 1993), 228–31; Adams, ed., *Post of Honor*, 312, 316; John E. Burwell to sister, March 1, 1863, Burwell Family Papers, VHS.

6. OR, vol. 25, pt. 2, 597; Meriwether Stuart, "Samuel Ruth and General R. E. Lee: Disloyalty and the Line of Supply to Fredericksburg, 1862–1863," VMHB 71 (January 1963): 35–109.

7. Emory M. Thomas, *The Confederate Nation, 1861–1865* (New York: Harper & Row, 1979), 199–201; Edmund Cody Burnett, ed., "Letters of a Confederate Surgeon: Dr. Abner Embrey McGarity, 1862–1865, Pt. 1," *Georgia Historical Quarterly* 29 (June 1945): 97; William M. Dame to mother, March 19, 1863, William Meade Dame Letters, vol. 138, FSNMP.

8. Dowdey and Manarin, eds., *Wartime Papers of Lee*, 418; Sears, *Chancellorsville*, 36–37.

9. Hattaway and Jones, *How the North Won*, 352–53; Sears, *Chancellorsville*, 33–36; Freeman, *R. E. Lee*, 2:480–84, 491–93; OR, vol. 25, pt. 2, 604, 606, 622, 627, 646, 686–87; Dowdey and Manarin, eds., *Wartime Papers of Lee*, 404, 417–18.

10. Dowdey and Manarin, eds., *Wartime Papers of Lee*, 400, 408; Welch, *Confederate Surgeon's Letters*, 45.

11. Wise, *Long Arm of Lee*, 1:412–25; Halsey Wigfall to mother, January 22, 1863, Wigfall Family Papers.

12. Charles C. Osborne, *Jubal: The Life and Times of General Jubal A. Early, C.S.A., Defender of the Lost Cause* (Chapel Hill: Algonquin Books, 1992), 141–42; Mary Thom to Marianne Claiborne [January 1863], Claiborne Family Papers; Doug-

las H. Gordon to Ann Eliza Gordon, January 27, 30, February 1, 2, 4, 1863, Douglas H. Gordon Letters, vol. 19, FSNMP.

13. Harrison, *Fredericksburg Civil War Sites*, 2:77–78.

14. A. M. Randolph to Sallie Randolph, February 26, 28, 1863, Randolph Family Papers, VHS.

15. Jeffry D. Wert, *Mosby's Rangers* (New York: Simon & Schuster, 1990), 17–21, 39–49, 54.

16. Starr, *Union Cavalry in the Civil War*, 1:345–47.

17. Sutherland, *Seasons of War*, 217–21.

18. Martin D. Coiner to Katherine M. Palmer, March 22, 1863, Coiner Family Papers, VHS.

19. Adams, ed., *Post of Honor*, 315; Joseph F. Shaner to sister, March 9, 1863, Joseph F. Shaner Letter, vol. 19, FSNMP; William R. Stillwell to Molly, March 7, 1863, Letters from Confederate Soldiers, 14:157.

20. John McDonald to Susan H. McDonald, February 28, 1863, March 9, 29, 1863, April 11, 1863, John McDonald Letters, vol. 80, FSNMP; William H. Davidson, ed., *War Was the Place: A Centennial Collection of Confederate Soldier Letters* (Alexandria City AL: Outlook Publishing, 1961), 85–86.

21. James W. Silver, ed., *A Life for the Confederacy as Recorded in the Pocket Diaries of Pvt. Robert A. Moore* (Jackson TN: McCowst-Mercer Press, 1959), 129; John McDonald to Susan H. McDonald, April 11, 1863, McDonald Letters. Drew Gilpin Faust, "Christian Soldiers: The Meaning of Revivalism in the Confederate Army," *Journal of Southern History* 53 (February 1987): 63–90, gives several reasons for the Confederate revival movement, which she believes started in the autumn of 1862. Samuel J. Watson, "Religion and Combat Motivation in the Confederate Armies," *Journal of Military History* 58 (January 1994): 29–55, confirms this timing and provides an excellent review of the subject.

22. Dowdey and Manarin, eds., *Wartime Papers of Lee*, 411.

23. Mike to pa, March 22, 1863, Flinn Collection in possession of Thomas H. Flinn, Austin, Texas; John E. Burwell to sister, March 22, 1863, Burwell Family Papers; Richard H. Watkins to Mary Watkins, February 19, 1863, Richard Henry Watkins Papers, VHS.

24. Nevins, *War for the Union*, 2:439; Leroy S. Edwards to father, February 15, 1863, Leroy Summerfield Edwards Correspondence, VHS.

25. Sears, *Chancellorsville*, 112–14, 168; Mike to pa, February 16, 22, March 22, 1863, Flinn Collection.

26. Mike to pa, February 18, 1863, Flinn Collection; Hassler, ed., *General to His Lady*, 226; Robert J. Trout, ed., *With Pen and Saber: The Letters and Diaries of J. E. B. Stuart's Staff Officer* (Harrisburg PA: Stackpole, 1995), 172.

27. Alexander C. Haskell to father, March 19, 1863, Alexander Cheves Haskell Papers, Southern Historical Collection, University of North Carolina, Chapel Hill; John McDonald to Susan H. McDonald, February 21, 1863, McDonald Letters;

Hassler, ed., *General to His Lady*, 224, 226. James A. Kegel, *North with Lee and Jackson: The Lost Story of Gettysburg* (Harrisburg PA: Stackpole, 1996), insists that Stonewall Jackson had urged an invasion of Pennsylvania early in the war.

28. H. J. David to parents, April 13, 1863, Letters from Confederate Soldiers, 2:124; Thomas, *Confederate Nation*, 190–99; Rable, *Confederate Republic*, 176–77, 192–94.

29. Jones, *Rebel War Clerk's Diary*, 1:250, 274, 278; Ernest B. Furgurson, *Ashes of Glory: Richmond at War* (New York: Knopf, 1996), 182, 188, 191; E. Merton Coulter, *The Confederate States of America, 1861–1865* (Baton Rouge: Louisiana State University Press, 1950), 229–35.

30. Hassler, ed., *General to His Lady*, 205.

31. Hassler, ed., *General to His Lady*, 212, 217–18.

32. Ford, ed., *Cycle of Adams Letters*, 1:251.

33. Thomas, *Confederate Nation*, 183–88; Jenkins, *Britain and the War for the Union*, 2:235–48, 260–65; Thomas W. Greer to Sophronia Marable, March 25, 1863, Thomas W. Greer Letters, USAMHI (CWMC); Silver, *A Life for the Confederacy*, 135.

34. Woodworth, *Davis and Lee at War*, 218–19.

35. Robertson, *Stonewall Jackson*, 667–68, 681, 688–89; Mary Anne Jackson, *Memoirs of Stonewall Jackson* (Dayton OH: Morningside, 1993), 404.

36. Emory M. Thomas, *Robert E. Lee: A Biography* (New York: Norton, 1995), 277–78; Dowdey and Manarin, eds., *Wartime Papers of Lee*, 419; OR, vol. 25, pt. 2, 683.

37. Woodworth, *Davis and Lee at War*, 219–20; Jones, *Rebel War Clerk's Diary*, 1:281–82.

## 8. PRACTICING STRATEGY

1. OR, vol. 25, pt. 2, 700–701.

2. Furgurson, *Ashes of Glory*, 193–96; Michael B. Chesson, "Harlots or Heroines? A New Look at the Richmond Bread Riot," *VMHB* 99 (1984): 131–75.

3. Woodworth, *Lee and Davis at War*, 219–20; Dowdey and Manarin, eds., *Wartime Papers of Lee*, 427–28; Jack D. Welsh, *Medical Histories of Confederate Generals* (Kent OH: Kent State University Press, 1995), 134; Samuel M. Bemiss to children, April 10, 1863, Bemiss Family Papers, VHS.

4. Nevins, ed., *Diary of Battle*, 177; Sears, *Chancellorsville*, 114–16; Donald, *Lincoln*, 433–34; Miles M. Quaife, ed., *From the Cannon's Mouth: The Civil War Letters of General Alpheus S. Williams* (Detroit: Wayne State University Press, 1959), 176; Robert S. Robertson to mother, April 5, 1863, Robertson Letters; James M. Richmond to wife, April 8, 1863, Richmond Letters.

5. Basler, ed., *Collected Works of Lincoln*, 6:164–65.

6. Donald, *Lincoln*, 433–34; Nevins, *War for the Union*, 2:430, 432.

7. OR, vol. 25, pt. 2, 199–200.

8. OR, vol. 25, pt. 2, 200–202; Sears, *Chancellorsville*, 120.

9. Dowdey and Manarin, eds., *Wartime Papers of Lee*, 431–32; OR, vol. 25, pt. 2, 713; Sears, *Chancellorsville*, 111–12.

10. Sears, *Chancellorsville*, 121–22, 134.

11. Burnett, ed., "Letters of a Confederate Surgeon," 101.

12. Meade, *Life and Letters*, 1:366–67, 369; OR, vol. 25, pt. 2, 238.

13. Williams, *Lincoln Finds a General*, 2:566–69; Gallagher, ed., *Chancellorsville*, 69–70; Sears, *Chancellorsville*, 129–32.

14. OR, vol. 25, pt. 2, 724–25, 737.

15. OR, vol. 25, pt. 2, 724–26, 740–41; Gary W. Gallagher, ed., *Lee the Soldier* (Lincoln: University of Nebraska Press, 1996), 358–60; Dowdey and Manarin, eds., *Wartime Papers of Lee*, 438.

16. Richard C. Price to Virginia E. Price, April 24, 1863, Richard Channing Price Papers, VHS; Freland N. Holman to sister, April 23, 1863, Freland N. Holman Letters, USAMHI (CWMC).

17. Nevins, ed., *Diary of Battle*, 179, 181–82; Meade, *Life and Letters*, 1:364–67.

18. Williams, *Lincoln Finds a General*, 2:569–72; Sears, *Chancellorsville*, 132–33, 136–44, 150; Basler, ed., *Collected Works of Lincoln*, 6:190.

19. William R. Williams to wife, May 2, 1863, Williams Letters; Jacob W. Haas to brother, May 12, 1863, Haas Letters; John H. Varney to Charles H. Nichols, April 8, 1863, Charles H. Nichols Papers, LC; Crumb and Dhalle, eds., *No Middle Ground*, 110–11; Meade, *Life and Letters*, 1:366.

20. Freland N. Holman to sister, April 23, 1863, Holman Letters; Nevins, ed., *Diary of Battle*, 182–83.

21. Sears, *Chancellorsville*, 145–59; Dawes, *Service with the Sixth Wisconsin*, 135–37.

22. Furgurson, *Chancellorsville*, 101–4; Freeman, *R. E. Lee*, 2:508–12; OR, vol. 25, pt. 2, 756.

23. OR, vol. 25, pt. 2, 759–60.

24. Sears, *Chancellorsville*, 161–65, 168–69, 175–84; Ralph Happell, "The Chancellors of Chancellorsville," *VMHB* 71 (July 1963): 262, 267–69; Cary D. Batte to Abbie Chancellor, April 21, 1863, Cary D. Batte Letter, VHS; Bigelow, *Campaign of Chancellorsville*, 213–22.

25. Sue M. Chancellor, "Personal Recollections of the Battle of Chancellorsville," *Register of the Kentucky Historical Society* 66 (April 1968): 139–41. For an interesting perspective on Sue Chancellor's adventures during the campaign, see James Marten's essay in Gallagher, ed., *Chancellorsville*, 219–43.

26. Noel G. Harrison, *Chancellorsville Battlefield Sites*, (Lynchburg VA: H. E. Howard, 1990), 62–63, 83–84, 99.

27. Gallagher, ed., *Chancellorsville*, 73–74; McClellan, *Life and Campaigns of Stuart*, 225–29.

28. Bigelow, *Campaign of Chancellorsville*, 19, 229–30; Richard E. Winslow III,

*General John Sedgwick: The Story of a Union Corps Commander* (Novato CA: Presidio Press, 1982), 66–67; OR, vol. 25, pt. 1, 384, 558.

29. Michael Barton, ed., "The End of Oden's War: A Confederate Captain's Diary," *Alabama Historical Quarterly* 43 (summer 1981): 80; Fitzpatrick, *Letters to Amanda*, 61.

30. OR, vol. 25, pt. 2, 761.

31. OR, vol. 25, pt. 2, 762.

32. Freeman, *R. E. Lee*, 2:512–16; Gallagher, ed., *Lee the Soldier*, 9, 362; Dowdey and Manarin, eds., *Wartime Papers of Lee*, 449.

33. OR, vol. 25, pt. 1, 1098.

34. Sears, *Chancellorsville*, 184, 191, 195–96; Quaife, ed., *Cannon's Mouth*, 185.

35. Sears, *Chancellorsville*, 191–92; OR, vol. 25, pt. 1, 171.

36. Sears, *Chancellorsville*, 181–82, 186–87, 191–92; Williams, *Lincoln Finds a General*, 2:576–77; OR, vol. 25, pt. 2, 311–12; U.S. Congress, *Report of the Joint Committee on the Conduct of the War*, Senate Report No. 142, 38th Cong., 2d sess., 3 vols. (Washington DC: Government Printing Office, 1865), 1:140.

## 9. DAYS OF HARD MARCHING AND DERRING-DO

1. Meade, *Life and Letters*, 1:370; Edward J. Stackpole, *Chancellorsville: Lee's Greatest Battle* (Harrisburg PA: Stackpole, 1958), 101–2; Reuben Kelly to sister, May 15, 1863, Kelly Letters; Sears, *Chancellorsville*, 193–94, 200–201.

2. Williams, *Lincoln Finds a General*, 2:578–81; Sears, *Chancellorsville*, 199–202; Quaife, *Cannon's Mouth*, 186.

3. Sears, *Chancellorsville*, 197–99, 204–8, 213; Cyrus Bacon, "A Michigan Surgeon at Chancellorsville One Hundred Years Ago," *University of Michigan Medical Bulletin*, No. 29 (November–December 1963): 319; Reese, *Sykes' Regular Infantry*, 210–13; Warren B. Persons to uncle, May 30, 1863, Warren B. Persons Letter, vol. 147, FSNMP.

4. Sears, *Chancellorsville*, 208; John C. Ellis to nephew, May 23, 1863, Ellis-Marshall Families Papers, USAMHI (H).

5. Williams, *Lincoln Finds a General*, 2:580–82; Sears, *Chancellorsville*, 207, 210–13; OR, vol. 25, pt. 2, 323–24.

6. Micajah D. Martin, "Chancellorsville: A Soldier's Letter," *VMHB* 37 (July 1929): 223; John L. G. Wood to Aunt, May 10, 1863, Letters from Confederate Soldiers, 4:134; William M. Dame to mother, May 2, 1863, Dame Letters.

7. Gallagher, ed., *Chancellorsville*, 147–49; Quaife, ed., *Cannon's Mouth*, 186–87.

8. K. Jack Bauer, ed., *Soldiering: The Civil War Diary of Rice C. Bull, 123rd New York Volunteer Infantry* (San Rafael CA: Presidio Press, 1977), 47–48; OR, vol. 25, pt. 2, 328.

9. Bacon, "A Michigan Surgeon," 319–20; U.S. War Department, *Medical and Surgical History*, 2:135.

10. Sears, *Chancellorsville*, 194–96, 213–17; OR, vol. 25, pt. 2, 330, 338, 340–42.

11. Barton, ed., "End of Oden's War," 80.

12. Gallagher, ed., *Chancellorsville*, 74, 76–80; McClellan, *Life and Campaigns of Stuart*, 227–32.

13. Fitzhugh Lee, "Chancellorsville," *SHSP* 7 (December 1879): 566; Freeman, *R. E. Lee*, 2:518–20.

14. Gallagher, ed., *Lee the Soldier*, 9, 365–66; Robertson, *Stonewall Jackson*, 709–15; *Confederate Veteran* 5 (June 1897): 287; Gallagher, ed., *Fighting for the Confederacy*, 201–2.

15. George H. Nichols to mother, May 2, 1863, George H. Nichols Letters, Clements Library, University of Michigan, Ann Arbor.

16. Sears, *Chancellorsville*, 237–38, 243–45, 248, 252; OR, vol. 25, pt. 2, 765.

17. Chancellor, "Personal Recollections," 141; Bacon, "A Michigan Surgeon," 320.

18. Sears, *Chancellorsville*, 243–47.

19. Sears, *Chancellorsville*, 228–30, 249–50; Freeman, *R. E. Lee*, 2:529–30.

20. OR, vol. 25, pt. 1, 386–87.

21. Robert C. Cheeks, "Fire and Fury at Catherine's Furnace," *ACW* 8 (May 1995): 34–37.

22. Freeman, *Lee's Lieutenants*, 2:552–55; Bigelow, *Campaign of Chancellorsville*, 289–90.

23. Bigelow, *Campaign of Chancellorsville*, 285–95; Freeman, *Lee's Lieutenants*, 2:555–58.

24. OR, vol. 25, pt. 1, 558.

25. D. G. Brinton Thompson, ed., "From Chancellorsville to Gettysburg: A Doctor's Diary," *Pennsylvania Magazine of History and Biography* 39 (July 1965): 299–300; Carl M. Becker and Ritchie Thomas, eds., *Hearth and Knapsack: The Ladley Letters, 1857–80* (Athens OH: Ohio University Press, 1988), 128; Oliver O. Howard, *Autobiography of Oliver Otis Howard*, 2 vols. (New York: Baker & Taylor, 1907), 1:365–69; *B&L*, 3:196.

26. Thompson, ed., "From Chancellorsville to Gettysburg," 299–300; Sears, *Chancellorsville*, 272–75.

27. Sears, *Chancellorsville*, 275–78, 280; Becker and Thomas, eds., *Hearth and Knapsack*, 121.

28. To Dear Father, May 17, 1863, Hamilton Papers, North Carolina State Archives, Raleigh.

29. Gallagher, ed., *Lee the Soldier*, 369–70.

30. Warren B. Persons to uncle, May 30, 1863, Persons Letter; Chancellor, "Personal Recollections," 141–42; Sears, *Chancellorsville*, 284.

31. Robertson, *Stonewall Jackson*, 723–27; Donald W. Olson, "A Fatal Moon: Stonewall Jackson at Chancellorsville," *Blue and Gray Magazine* 8 (spring 1996): 24–29.

32. Gallagher, ed., *Chancellorsville*, 107–13.

33. Crumb and Dhalle, eds., *No Middle Ground*, 127–28.
34. Gallagher, ed., *Chancellorsville*, 119–31.
35. OR, vol. 25, pt. 2, 359, 365–66.
36. Winslow, *General John Sedgwick*, 68–70; Osborne, *Jubal*, 148–51.
37. Sears, *Chancellorsville*, 300–302; Philip N. Racine, ed., *"Unspoiled Heart":
The Journal of Charles Mattocks of the 17th Maine* (Knoxville: University of Tennessee Press, 1994), 13.
38. Gallagher, ed., *Chancellorsville*, 75–80.
39. OR, vol. 25, pt. 2, 385.


## 10. THE HARDEST BATTLE EVER FOUGHT

1. OR, vol. 25, pt. 2, 385.
2. OR, vol. 25, pt. 1, 558–59; Bigelow, *Campaign of Chancellorsville*, 383–86.
3. Sears, *Chancellorsville*, 312–16; Furgurson, *Chancellorsville*, 215–22; Freeman, *R. E. Lee*, 2:534–37.
4. McClellan, *Campaigns of Stuart*, 255.
5. Peter S. Carmichael, *Lee's Young Artillerist: William R. J. Pegram* (Charlottesville: University Press of Virginia, 1995), 87–89; Gallagher, ed., *Fighting for the Confederacy*, 206–10.
6. S. B. David to parents, May 9, 1863, S. B. David Letters, vol. 27, FSNMP; Luther A. Granger to wife, May 7, 1863, Luther A. Granger Letters, USAMHI (CWMC); Joseph H. Law to Mary E. Law, May 7, 1863, Law Letters; Crumb and Dhalle, eds., *No Middle Ground*, 133; James Laird to wife, May 8, 1863, Laird Letters.
7. John L. G. Wood to father, May 10, 1863, Letters from Confederate Soldiers, 4:135; Luther A. Granger to wife, May 7, 1863, Granger Letters; Fatout, ed., *Letters of a Civil War Surgeon*, 94; Morrow, "To Chancellorsville," 19; Dawes, *Service with Sixth Wisconsin*, 137–38; Martin, "Chancellorsville," 225; Cullen Andrew Battle, "The Third Alabama Regiment," 171, typescript in VHS.
8. Freeman, *R. E. Lee*, 2:537–40; Furgurson, *Chancellorsville*, 240–42, 246–47; Chancellor, "Personal Recollections," 142–43.
9. OR, vol. 25, pt. 2, 383.
10. Winslow, *General John Sedgwick*, 72–73.
11. Sears, *Chancellorsville*, 347–55.
12. Furgurson, *Chancellorsville*, 257–65; Bigelow, *Campaign of Chancellorsville*, 385–93; Duffey Diary, May 3, 1863; Wetheds Ardron to Lister, May 12, 1863, Wetheds Ardron Letter, vol. 75, FSNMP.
13. Danny Davis, "Return to Fredericksburg," ACW 5 (September 1992): 30–37; Osborne, *Jubal*, 156–57.
14. OR, vol. 25, pt. 1, 856–57; Sears, *Chancellorsville*, 374–77.
15. Furgurson, *Chancellorsville*, 274–76; Sears, *Chancellorsville*, 377–80.
16. John L. G. Wood to aunt, May 10, 1863, Letters from Confederate Soldiers, 4:135.

17. Furgurson, *Chancellorsville*, 276–79; Sears, *Chancellorsville*, 380–84; *Supplement*, 4:675.

18. OR, vol. 25, pt. 1, 559; Winslow, *General John Sedgwick*, 78–79.

19. Sears, *Chancellorsville*, 364–66; Reuben Kelly to sister, May 15, 1863, Kelly Letters; Burnett, ed., "Letters of a Confederate Surgeon," 104.

20. Furgurson, *Chancellorsville*, 283–84.

21. OR, vol. 25, pt. 1, 201, pt. 2, 379.

22. Sears, *Chancellorsville*, 387–89; OR, vol. 25, vol. 1, 203, pt. 2, 396.

23. Gallagher, ed., *Chancellorsville*, 81–90.

24. Sears, *Chancellorsville*, 393–96.

25. Henry G. McGinnis to sister, May 4, 1863, Henry G. McGinnis Letter, vol. 210, FSNMP; Sparks, ed., *Inside Lincoln's Army*, 241–42; Nevins, ed., *Diary of Battle*, 198–200.

26. OR, vol. 25, pt. 2, 405–10.

27. OR, vol. 25, pt. 2, 407–10.

28. George T. Stevens, *Three Years in Sixth Corps* (Albany NY: S. R. Gray, 1866), 204; Sears, *Chancellorsville*, 400–403, 410–17; Furgurson, *Chancellorsville*, 294–99.

29. Furgurson, *Chancellorsville*, 299–300.

30. OR, vol. 25, pt. 2, 421–22, 432.

31. Blight, ed., *When This Cruel War Is Over*, 229; Mary Thom to Marianne Claiborne, May 24, 1863, Claiborne Family Papers.

32. Hotchkiss, *Make Me a Map of the Valley*, 145; Davis Tinsley to mother, May 20, 1863, Letters from Confederate Soldiers, 10:141–42.

33. Racine, ed., *"Unspoiled Heart,"* 23–24; Sparks, ed., *Inside Lincoln's Army*, 242; Edward W. Steffan to Fred, May 3, 1863, Edward W. Steffan Letters, vol. 115, FSNMP; William J. Evans to parents, May 5, 1863, William J. Evans Papers, New Jersey Historical Society, Newark; Sears, *Chancellorsville*, 405–6; Furgurson, *Chancellorsville*, 313–17; Nevins, ed., *Diary of Battle*, 201.

34. Sears, *Chancellorsville*, 428–29; Malles, ed., *Bridge Building in Wartime*, 144–45.

35. Dawes, *Service with Sixth Wisconsin*, 139.

36. Hotchkiss, *Make Me a Map of the Valley*, 141; Furgurson, *Chancellorsville*, 317–18; Freeman, *R. E. Lee*, 2:557–58; Dowdey and Manarin, eds., *Wartime Papers of Lee*, 456–57.

37. Barton, ed., "End of Oden's War," 82–84; Priest, ed., *One Surgeon's Private War*, 66–67; Bacon, "A Michigan Surgeon," 324; U.S. War Department, *Medical and Surgical History*, 2:137; Burnett, ed., "Letters of a Confederate Surgeon," 108.

38. Shipp Diary, May 6, 1863; Adams, ed., *Post of Honor*, 353; Henry C. Carter to John W. Carter, May 16, 1863, Carter Family Papers, VHS; Furgurson, *Chancellorsville*, 322.

39. U.S. War Department, *Medical and Surgical History*, 2:137; Bacon, "A Michigan Surgeon," 323; Furgurson, *Chancellorsville*, 330, 364–65; Sears, *Chancel-*

*lorsville*, 440–42, 492, 501. Sears's casualty figures are higher than Furgurson's for the Army of Northern Virginia but slightly lower for the Army of the Potomac.

40. Gallagher, ed., *Chancellorsville*, 87–91, 96.

## EPILOGUE: LUCK FAVORED PLUCK AND SKILL

1. Sears, *Chancellorsville*, 432; William H. Peacock to Sarah, May 6, 1863, Peacock Letters.

2. Samuel P. Hand to uncle, May 9, 1863, Mary A. Bludworth Papers, Perkins Library, Duke University, Durham, NC; Thomas C. Elder to wife, May 8, 1863, Elder Papers; Carmichael, *Lee's Young Artillerist*, 91–92.

3. OR, vol. 25, pt. 1, 805; Woodworth, *Davis and Lee at War*, 220–21, 228–32.

4. *Charleston Mercury*, May 11, 1863; Beth Gilbert Crabtree and James W. Patton, eds., *"Journal of a Secesh Lady": The Diary of Catherine Ann Devereux Edmondston* (Raleigh: North Carolina Division of Archives and History, 1979), 391; Gary W. Gallagher, *The Confederate War* (Cambridge MA: Harvard University Press, 1997), 138–40.

5. W. S. Trimble to Nancy Bowden, May 9, 1863, Nancy Bowden Ellis Letters, USAMHI (CWMC); Fatout, ed., *Letters of a Civil War Surgeon*, 94; Alexander Seiders to wife, May 8, 1863, Seiders Letters; Crumb and Dhalle, eds., *No Middle Ground*, 138.

6. John H. Pardington to wife, May 8, 13, 1863, Pardington to sister, May 9, 1863, Pardington Letters; Edward H. C. Taylor to sister, May 12, 1863, Taylor Papers; Robertson, ed., "An Indiana Soldier," 244; Carter, *Four Brothers in Blue*, 264.

7. Quaife, ed., *Cannon's Mouth*, 204; OR, vol. 25, pt. 1, 171; Nevins, ed., *Diary of Battle*, 202.

8. Nevins, ed., *Diary of Battle*, 203; Kohl and Richard, eds., *Irish Green and Union Blue*, 93; Robert E. Lee to Mary Custis Lee, May 14, 1863, R. E. Lee Papers, VHS.

9. Furgurson, *Chancellorsville*, 318–19, 330–31; Sears, *Chancellorsville*, 433–36.

10. Donald, *Lincoln*, 419–21, 437–38.

11. OR, vol. 25, pt. 2, 435, 438, 479.

12. Sears, *Chancellorsville*, 434–38, 560 n. 8; *Supplement*, 4:475; Freeman Cleaves, *Meade of Gettysburg* (Norman: University of Oklahoma Press, 1960), 115–19.

13. Hebert, *Fighting Joe Hooker*, 223, 228.

14. Carmichael, *Lee's Young Artillerist*, 91–92.

15. Sears, *Chancellorsville*, 436–38; U.S. Congress, *Report of the Joint Committee on the Conduct of the War*, Senate Report No. 142, 1:xlix.

16. Becker and Thomas, eds., *Hearth and Knapsack*, 121–22, 127–29.

17. OR, vol. 25, pt. 1, 1066.

18. Sears, *Chancellorsville*, 266, 271; Starr, *Union Cavalry in the Civil War*, 1:360–61, 364–65; Gallagher, ed., *Chancellorsville*, 96–99.

19. Joshua G. Wilbur to wife, May 8, 1863, Joshua G. Wilbur Letters, vol. 70, FSNMP; James A. Carman to uncle, May 17, 1863, Carman Papers; William Stowe to parents, May 10, 1863, William Stowe Letters, vol. 47, FSNMP.

20. Nevins, ed., *Diary of Battle*, 203; Clement Hoffman to mother, May 17, 1863, Hoffman Letters.

21. *B&L*, 3:161.

22. Carmichael, *Lee's Young Artillerist*, 91; Nevins, ed., *Diary of Battle*, 193–94.

23. Hebert, *Fighting Joe Hooker*, 224–26; Sears, *Chancellorsville*, 339, 358–59, 388–89, 505–6.

24. Crumb and Dhalle, eds., *No Middle Ground*, 139; Gallagher, ed., *Fighting for the Confederacy*, 217.

25. Edward H. C. Taylor to Lottie, May 7, 12, 1863, Taylor Letters.

26. Gallagher, ed., *Fighting for the Confederacy*, 195; *B&L*, 3:171.

27. C. G. Chamberlayne, ed., *Ham Chamberlayne—Virginian: Letters and Papers of an Artillery Officer in the War for Southern Independence* (Richmond: Dietz, 1932), 176, 181.

28. J. G. C. to George Peter, May 23, 1863, J. G. C. Letter, USAMHI (HC); Roberson, *Weep Not for Me*, 103; Fred H. West to Maggie, May 18, 1863, Fred West Letter, vol. 4, FSNMP.

29. Williams, *Lincoln Finds a General*, 2:613.

30. Meade, *Life and Letters*, 1:374; Williams, *Lincoln Finds a General*, 2:618–23; Basler, ed., *Works of Lincoln*, 6:257.

31. Hebert, *Fighting Joe Hooker*, 232–38.

32. Sutherland, *Seasons of War*, 277–304.

# Index

In the Great Campaigns of the Civil War series

*Fredericksburg and Chancellorsville*
*The Dare Mark Campaign*
By Daniel E. Sutherland

*Six Armies in Tennessee*
*The Chickamauga and Chattanooga Campaigns*
By Steven E. Woodworth